PIOUS FLAMES

PIOUS FLAMES
European Encounters with Sati 1500–1830

by
Andrea Major

OXFORD
UNIVERSITY PRESS

OXFORD

UNIVERSITY PRESS

YMCA Library Building, Jai Singh Road, New Delhi 110001

Oxford University Press is a department of the University of Oxford. It
furthers the University's objective of excellence in research, scholarship, and
education by publishing worldwide in

Oxford New York
Auckland Cape Town Dar es Salaam Hong Kong Karachi
Kuala Lumpur Madrid Melbourne Mexico City Nairobi
New Delhi Shanghai Taipei Toronto

With offices in
Argentina Austria Brazil Chile Czech Republic France Greece
Guatemala Hungary Italy Japan Poland Portugal Singapore
South Korea Switzerland Thailand Turkey Ukraine Vietnam

Oxford is a registered trade mark of Oxford University Press
in the UK and in certain other countries

Published in India
by Oxford University Press, New Delhi

ISBN-13: 978-0-19-567818-5
ISBN-10:0-19-567818-4

Typeset in 10/12 Aldine 401 BT
by InoSoft Systems, Noida
Printed in India at Rakmo Press Private Limited,
C-59, Okhla Industrial Area, Phase-I, New Delhi-110 020.
Published by Manzar Khan, Oxford University Press
YMCA Library Building, Jai Singh Road, New Delhi 110 001

CONTENTS

ॐ

ILLUSTRATIONS

CR&D

PREFACE

CREO

This book is based on doctoral and postdoctoral research carried out at the University of Edinburgh between 1999 and 2004. Numerous, people in Edinburgh have helped and supported me during this period. I would like to thank the staff and students who have made my time there so enjoyable and productive, especially the various members of the Centre for South Asian Studies who provided such a stimulating and mutually supportive environment in which to pursue the study of the Subcontinent. I would particularly like to thank Ian Duffield, Roger Jeffery, and Patricia Jeffery for their support and advice. Also Markus Daechsel, Jim Mills, and Clare Anderson for demonstrating that there is life after the viva voce and for all the other, more tangible, assistance they have offered. Special thanks, however, must be reserved for Crispin Bates, whose belief in my ability and potential frequently exceeded my own and without whose encouragement, support and friendship over the last ten years none of this would have happened.

Research for this book was carried out at a number of institutions in the UK and India. I would like to express my gratitude to the staff of the Oriental and India Office (British Library) for all their assistance during my numerous visits. Also those at the National Library of Scotland, Bodlean Library Oxford, Council for World Mission Archive (SOAS), and Baptist Missionary Archive (Regent's Park College, Oxford). In India I was greatly helped by the staff and archivists at the National Archives of India (New Delhi), National Library of India (Kolkata), Nehru Memorial Museum and Library (New Delhi), x *Preface*

and Royal Asiatic Society Library (Kolkata). I also thank Suranjan Das, Nandini Sunder, and Sudhir Chandra for their support and advice during my stay in India. Mention must also be made of the financial support received from various institutes, including full MSc and PhD studentships funded by the Arts and Humanities Research Board and a postdoctoral fellowship funded by the Economic and Social Research Council. In addition, various travel expenses have been offset in part by grants from the Society for South Asian Studies, Carnegie Foundation, British Academy, and the University of Edinburgh George Scott Travelling Fellowship.

I would also like to thank everybody at Oxford University Press, New Delhi, who have worked on this book. In particular I would like to thank Shashank Sinha and Sutapa Ghosh, who have both had the patience of saints as I juggled the demands of new motherhood with the preparation of this volume.

Last, but certainly not the least, I would like to thank my wonderful family. My parents have supported me in so many ways over the years, but I particularly thank my mum, Verena, for the seemingly endless proofreading and for managing to keep her worries about her only daughter travelling alone in India to a low hum of maternal concern. I also thank my husband Garry, for his unshakable faith in me, for believing me unquestioningly when I tell him my research is important, and for not complaining even when I jetted off to India, again, within days of coming back from our heneymoon. Finally, I would like to dedicate this, my metaphorical baby, to my real one, Alex, who was born the same week as the manuscript was accepted for publication and who will always be my most precious endeavour.

1

RE-ORIENTING SATI

CRSD

An interesting exchange took place in the *Guardian* in the wake of 11 September 2001. In an article attacking 'the fuzzy idea on the soft Left of an Islamic cultural otherness that supersedes basic human rights',[1] Polly Toynbee began by using an example that originated from parliamentary papers published by the British in the years prior to their prohibition of widow-burning in India in 1829:

A nineteenth century general in India was confronted with an angry delegation complaining that the suppression of suttee was an attack on their national culture and customs. He replied: 'It is your custom to burn widows. Very well. We also have a custom: when men burn women alive we tie a rope around their necks and hang them. Build your funeral pyre and beside it my carpenters will build a gallows. You may follow your national custom—then we shall follow ours.' No moral or cultural relativism here: a burning widow feels the same pain whatever her culture.[2]

She used this example to uphold the position of what she refers to as 'hard liberals' who

...hold basic human rights to be non-negotiable and worth fighting for. They do not turn the other cheek, understand the other guy's point of view or respect his culture when it comes to universal rights. Promoting liberal values everywhere...is not neo-colonialism, but respect for a universal right to freedom from oppression.[3]

A few days later a reply to this article appeared in the same newspaper. The respondent sought to defend the middle ground, claiming:

There are universal values, but they are open to different interpretations in different contexts. Only a handful (the right to life, freedom from torture and degrading treatment) can be asserted without qualification. Suttee and the Taliban's treatment of women are in this category and are indefensible. But few issues are so clear, especially when it comes to women; why is wearing a veil degrading, when living in a culture where pornography is not tolerated. Human rights conflict all the time and cultures resolve them differently.[4]

The ideological problems raised in these two articles are innumerable, but for the present I wish to concentrate on one specific assumption, common to both—that suttee (or sati[5], as it is now more correctly designated) is an unproblematic example of an 'indefensible' cultural custom.

Let us move back in time some eighteen years. On 4 September 1987, in the village of Deorala in Rajasthan, an eighteen year old woman burnt on the funeral pyre of her husband. Roop Kanwar had been married for eight months when her husband Mal Singh died suddenly. Within hours she too was dead and thousands of onlookers were celebrating her deification as a *satimata*. The political and intellectual debate that followed continues today. For those who celebrated her immolation, Roop Kanwar was following in a long and glorious tradition of devoted Hindu women, whose conjugal fidelity and devotion to their husbands led them to prefer fiery deaths on the funeral pyre to lives of obloquy as widows. The sati's sacrifice, it is believed, draws her husband's soul out of hell; brings glory to the families of her mother, father, and husband; and ensures for the widow both deification on earth and felicity in heaven for 'as many years as there are hairs on the human body'.[6] For those who opposed the immolation, on the other hand, Roop Kanwar was just one in a line of female victims murdered either by the machinations of self-interested relatives or by the indoctrination in a pseudo-religious tradition that set women's lives at nought.

The polarization between these two interpretations of sati is at the heart of an ongoing controversy. In the wake of the Deorala sati, hundreds of feminists from eleven different organizations took to the streets of Jaipur to protest the oppression of women inherent in the rite. In response to this and to government legislation which made the glorification of sati a criminal act, the Sati Dharma Raksha Samhiti, an organization of orthodox Rajputs, was created and held a 70,000-

strong rally in Jaipur in mid-October 1987. Debate raged in newspapers and journals, with feminists and liberals pitted against orthodox Hindu groups. Despite the government ban on glorification, somewhere in the region of 250,000–300,000 people descended on Deorala to pay their respects to the satimata in the days following her immolation. Clearly there was a widespread feeling both among certain intellectuals and among members of the general public that sati was far from a reprehensible act. In December 1991 *The Times* carried an interview with the only female high priestess in India, Maa Oma Kumari, in which she was asked her views on sati. *The Times* reported:

She has strong feelings on women's rights. She regards suttee, the former Hindu custom whereby a widow burnt herself to death on her husband's funeral pyre, as a fundamental right, though it has been outlawed since British times. 'But it still goes on in the villages of Rajasthan. When suttee ends the sky and the earth will meet and the world will end', she said.[7]

For Maa Oma Kumari it is not sati that is an infringement of human rights, but the state intervention against it. She is not alone; feminist investigations after the Deorala sati found many, both men and women, who supported the practice.[8] Even among Indian women academics sati remains a controversial issue—as Lata Mani points out, 'Sati functions both as the act confirming the stoicism of women and the practice that epitomises their weakness.'[9]

Under these circumstances, though I would in no way condone sati, I would argue that to suggest that it is a clearcut issue represents a moral judgement that fails to understand both the contentiousness of the debate about sati in India and the complexity of the West's[10] own relationship with the rite. In a debate about the nature of cultural relativism, the fact that proponents on both sides of the liberal argument can dismiss sati unproblematically as 'wrong' suggests that sati is understood as something constantly and diametrically opposed to a coherent Western morality. As perhaps the most prominent and widely recognized symbol of Hindu women's oppression,[11] sati has been viewed as one of many cultural indices against which the comparative social progress of 'civilization' can be measured. Even in our self-consciously postcolonial world, *The Times* can talk of the 'enlightened' governor general who outlawed the custom in 1829, and comment with surprise that 'Mrs Kanwar was not an illiterate peasant, but had been to secondary school.'[12] The assumption is that sati and its proponents

are uncivilized and its support by a faction of the country's intelligen-
tsia is reflective of India's overall backwardness in matters of human
rights. Concomitant to this view is the assumption that repugnance at
sati is the normative moral reaction of a progressive and advanced
society—the natural and absolute response of a civilized man.

This book sets out to show that this is very far from the case. It is
my contention that the ease with which the two protagonists in the
Guardian reject sati as culturally indefensible is a manifestation of a
specific, if unconscious, set of assumptions about the meaning and
nature of the rite. These assumptions do not represent a universal
Western morality, but rather are based on a peculiarly British interpretation of the rite that came to prominence in the early nineteenth
century, as a result of the convergence of a variety of contemporary
ideas and concerns. When taken over a wider period, far from being
monolithic in their condemnation, the response of British and European observers (who I take to represent the so-called West) have in
fact been characterized by heterogeneity, ambivalence, and fluidity;
both over time and between different nationalities, genders, and religious denominations. The following chapters will attempt to place
the early nineteenth-century British response to sati, which has come
to so predominate in the contemporary Western understanding of the
rite, in the context of a decidedly multifaceted, sometimes contradictory, often ambivalent, and constantly changing series of Western
interpretations of and reactions to sati. In doing so, I will demonstrate
that while sati was at times used to emphasize Hindu cultural otherness and thus to support the political agenda of colonialism, at others
it was understood primarily through the location of similarities, analogies, and resonances with the Western society and ideas.

The assumptions so clearly expressed in the popular press do not
exist in a vacuum. As Vasudha Dalmia-Luderitz points out, the key
terms of the contemporary discussion on sati, both in India and the
West, have their history in the debate about the rite that occurred in
the years prior to its 'abolition' in 1829.[13] Over a course of three
decades, the British tried to reconcile the possible prohibition of sati
with their conception of it as a sacred act and their professed neutrality
in religious issues. In doing so they privileged the question of a
widow's volition in legal terms, while at the same time undermining
her agency and casting her as a passive victim of a barbaric pagan
practice. Ambivalence in official circles about the feasibility of abolishing sati was not reflected in the popular response to the rite,

however, which in the early nineteenth century was characterized by collective condemnation, as the British attempted to assert their moral superiority through their denigration of Hindu practices and customs. The British prohibition of sati (Regulation XVII of 1829) enshrined this moral position in history and on the statute books, and the prominence that this legislation achieved as the *piece-de-resistance* of colonial social reform has meant that Western attitudes towards sati have often been defined by the ideas of this period. In reality, however, far from being an absolute position dictated by some hegemonic Western morality or rationality, this rejection of and opposition to sati as a legitimate cultural practice was the result of the emergence of a particular range of thoughts, ideas, and concerns about issues such as suicide, religion, gender, and the treatment of the human body that coalesced at the beginning of the nineteenth century to create a reaction that was historically specific. Changing attitudes to related issues such as these, both over time and between observers from different backgrounds, were as instrumental in informing reactions to sati as any dichotomy between East and West. Thus, rather than being the natural and unchanging reaction of a civilized West to a barbaric oriental custom, the nineteenth-century British construction of sati, which is still so influential today, was part of an ongoing process of understanding that was dependent not only on the changing relationships of power between colonizer and colonized, but also on a multifaceted dialectic in which ideological, sociological, and cultural trends in the metropole both informed and were informed by the encounter with India.

Sati, Said, and Subjectivity: Colonial Discourses

As with so much postcolonial scholarship, the underlying principles that inform my treatment of Western discourses on sati begin, though they do not end, with Edward Said's *Orientalism*. In this seminal work published in 1978, Edward Said redefined our understanding of the framework through which colonial knowledge was created.[14] His thesis rests upon the assumption that Occident and Orient, East and West are labels that represent certain conceptions and misconceptions, and do not exist as innate entities in themselves. Rather, they are the products of a historical discourse that underlies the imperial project and seeks to define the colonial 'self' in reference to the colonized 'other'.

By using Foucauldian discourse theory—the idea that the articula-
tion of knowledge is indefatigably linked to the expression of power—
and combining this with Gramscian theories of cultural hegemony,
Said asserts that it is the imperatives of control and subjugation that
inform all Western attempts to 'know' the so-called East. As a result,
all expressions of Western 'understanding' of the East are implicitly,
if not explicitly, political, even when articulated through seemingly
apolitical media such as: art, literature, and academia. He argues that
'...ideas, cultures and histories cannot be seriously studied without
their force, or more precisely their configurations of power, also
being studied.'[15] Because the actuality, or at least the potentiality, of
colonial control was an inescapable element of the Occidental presence in the east, the possibility of a Western observer uncovering the
reality of the Orient was undermined by the consciously or subconsciously imbibed preconceptions and assumptions. The pursuit of
knowledge in the colonial context could not be disinterested due to
the unequal relationship between colonizer and the object of study,
and because the knowledge that was created was repeatedly put at the
service of the colonial administration.[16] Thus for Said, the Orientalists
of the late eighteenth and nineteenth centuries created an India that
was based primarily upon their perceptions of it, rather than upon its
actuality. The image of the Orient constructed by Western scholars
and observers was to become so deeply imbedded in the collective
psyche of hegemonic culture in the West that it was to take on the value
of truth for those who used it to understand and control the East.
Words such as Orient, East, India, Hindu, Arab, etc. were to take on
a variety of connotations and come to represent a collection of stereotypes and caricatures that were indistinguishable from reality for many
in the West. The truth of the Orient, as it was displayed in the West,
is for Said, an illusion created by a West whose political and technological dominance gives it pretensions to omniscience. In this way he
undermines the veracity of the huge body of knowledge about the
Orient acquired during the colonial period and beyond.

The body of knowledge referred to by Said, incorporated not only
images of the Orient as a homogenous entity, but also to the multifari-
ous collection of languages, customs, and institutions that constituted
it. In the context of the study of sati, the whole body of colonial
knowledge on the subject is thrown into doubt by Said's theory. What
is represented when, for example, the British discuss sati is not the
reality of the institution, rather a construction of it that is informed

by the imperatives of dominance over the society in which it occurs. This is certainly true to some extent as the terms in which the British, particularly in the early nineteenth century, sought to understand sati were closely tied both to an essentialist image of the nature of Indian society and to the imperatives of a political debate on sati. This idea is taken up with vigour in what is perhaps the most influential study of the British encounter with sati yet written, that by Lata Mani. In articles published in Francis Barker's *Europe and its Others* (1985), and *Economic and Political Weekly* (1986), and later in her much-vaunted monograph *Contentious Traditions: The Debate on Sati in Colonial India, 1780–1833*,[17] Mani argued that British preoccupation with sati was less about burning women than it was about defining the parameters of colonial control. For Mani the debate on sati was entirely political and was concerned with testing the boundaries of legitimate interference in what had previously been the uncolonized space of religion.

Mani's ideas have been extremely influential in deconstructing the traditional image of Bentinck's regulation on sati as one of the crowning glories of the so-called 'era of reform'. That said, both her adherence to a Saidian paradigm that sees the colonial discourse as a unidirectional process and her tendency to isolate the 'official' discourse of the early nineteenth century from both the contemporaneous popular debate on the subject and from earlier and later interpretations of the rite, both in Britain and Europe, mean that she does not always recognize the complexity of the Western encounter with sati in its broadest sense. It is my contention that it is insufficient to understand the changing British reactions to sati solely in the context of changing political relationships, or indeed any relationship with India, since—as I will demonstrate—the encounter with sati in the early nineteenth century was as much about British identity as it was about constructing an image of India. British ideas about sati were deeply entwined with a variety of social, ideological, and moral issues that shaped interpretations of the rite in different ways at different historical junctures.

An understanding of attitudes to sati, as reflecting not only ideas about India but also concerns about the self, is to some extent rooted in Said's idea of 'negative definition'. For Said, the primary imperative in the discourse on the Orient lay in the process of constructing it as an inferior 'other' and thus creating a diametrically opposed entity whose very existence defines and secures the limits of the occidental self. This othering process is achieved through the codification of racial/cultural characteristics by the assignation of immutable 'essences' that are assumed to be an inherent part of its nature. The essentialization of the East simplifies the process of understanding by creating an unchanging frame of reference for events and phenomena, many of which can be written off as a result of the essential qualities of the Orient without the need for sustained analyses or damaging revelations. More importantly, however, it also acted as a means of producing an identity for the West. By ascribing to the 'other' certain undesirable qualities, the self can silently claim its implied opposites. Thus, the Occident defines itself by projecting onto other cultures all that it is not, or does not wish to be. For example, the depiction of the East as spiritual, passive, and weak—characteristics also found in the Western depiction of women—lead to a characterization of the East as essentially feminine. In his book *The Intimate Enemy*, Ashis Nandy discusses the possibility that it was the West's desire to be perceived as masculine, rather than any particular qualities possessed by the East, that led to its feminization. He suggests that during the post-Enlightenment period the development of Western military and technological prowess and growth of expansionist nationalism were accompanied by an emerging sense of European masculinity.[18] With the West associating itself with such palpably masculine traits as progress, rationality, technological-scientific superiority, and military dominance: it was a natural progression to transmute feminine characteristics onto the passive and subdued Orient, reinforcing the West's virility and normalizing colonial relations in terms of the 'natural' domination of male over female.

Although some academics have dismissed Said's reworking of the relationship between knowledge and colonial power—Ernest Gellner, for example, claimed that *Orientalism* was entertaining, but intellectually insignificant—[19] for most, Said's ideas have become crucial to any reinterpretation of the processes of Western understanding and representation of oriental societies and cultures. Many, including Gayatri Spivak and Homi Bhabha, view it as the foundation stone of postcolonial theory. As with other such breakthrough texts, *Orientalism* contains several ideological and theoretical flaws, inconsistencies, and paradoxes that have formed the basis for a wealth of literature criticizing, critiquing, and reworking Said's ideas. A comprehensive survey of these is beyond the scope of this introduction, but in order to delineate my own theoretical position in approaching a study of British and European interpretations of sati, certain salient issues must be discussed.

Perhaps the most important problem posed by *Orientalism* in the present context is that in his portrayal of a unified colonial hegemony, Said fails to take sufficient account of counter-hegemonic trends and dissenting voices from within the dominant culture itself. Dennis Porter overstates the point and misunderstands Said when he accuses him of ascribing to the West a monolithic discourse spanning the millennia, yet he and many critics after him are justified in viewing the emphasis on the West as a cohesive entity informed by imperatives of domination and control as verging on occidentalism.[20] Bart Moore-Gilbert suggests that Said himself vacillates between recognition of the heterogeneity of colonial discourse and the conviction of its essential consistency. At same time, however, he recognizes that Said's creation of a homogenized orientalist discourse suppresses important cultural, geographical, and historical differences within the colonial discourse.[21]

Both Said's critique of labels such as East and West and the resulting attack on his assumption of a unified occidental discourse have led many scholars to question the utility of discussing 'western' ideas and attitudes when the West itself does not exist as a unified entity. Lisa Lowe, for example, develops this idea of the heterogeneity of the European colonial discourse in her study of French and British orientalisms.[22] While acceding to the existence of unequal power relations between colonizer and colonized, she resists the idea of orientalism as a totalizing monolithic discourse that uniformly constructs orient as the other. Instead, she views orientalism (or rather various orientalisms) as heterogeneous and contradictory, consisting of an uneven matrix of situations across different cultural and historical sites. She stresses the fluidity both of discourse, which she views as a 'complex and uneven terrain composed of heterogeneous textual, social and cultural practices',[23] and of hegemony, which she views as a process of negotiation, consent, and compromise between dominant and subaltern groups. In doing so she opens up the possibility of an unstable orientalist terrain that is intersected by other discourses such as nationality, race, gender, and class. Building on Lowe's ideas, it is the intention of this study to show that the Western discourses that emerged about sati depended almost entirely on the specific historical and cultural subjectivities in the observer. These subjectivities were the result not only of a racial/cultural divide between East and West, but also of ideological, cultural, and social trends within Europe that informed the changing understanding of the rite. Thus, in the case of sati, Said's dichotomy between Orient and Occident is crosscut by both shared assumptions such as those of gender and class, and by a myriad of historically specific concerns and issues.

This is not to suggest, of course, that practices such as sati were not sometimes used to reinforce the 'otherness' of India. Certainly there is an element of such negative definition in the West's encounter with sati, especially in the early nineteenth century, as explicit and vitriolic condemnation acted to distance the 'civilized' Western observer from the 'barbaric' Hindu practitioner. The treatment of women was commonly used as an index of civilization. Assertions about the degraded status of Indian women (epitomized by customs such as purdah, child marriage, and sati) were used to denigrate Indian society as backward and barbaric, while at the same time implying the comparative freedom and autonomy of Western women, even at a time when a gender ideology based on their inherent frailty, incapacity, and inequality kept many socially, if not spatially, confined. However, when we look more closely, it appears that these were aspects of specific discourses (e.g., British missionary writing) that referred not to a monolithic West, but to specific groups within Britain and Europe (e.g. British Evangelical Christians) at specific times. At other times and in other contexts, both British and European understandings of sati were constructed in terms of areas of similarity, as the representative of various patriarchal European societies recognized underlying themes in the Indian tradition that resonated with their own. More than this, not only was the European image of sati shaped by the immediate concerns and subjectivities of the observer, but sati itself could often play a significant role in the development of discourses that were not ostensibly about it. The image of sati was thus not only an object of interest in itself but an icon that could be used within debates about issues such as gender, suicide, religion, and treatment of the human body, which was changed by and helped to change these debates.

Shifting Dialogues: Contextualizing Sati

In order to represent the heterogeneity of Western responses to sati and to contextualize early nineteenth-century British ideas within a broader framework, this study draws on an eclectic mixture of material from a variety of British and European sources across a period of some 500 years. While the main focus of the study remains British interpretations of the rite in the early nineteenth century, it is one of the author's key contentions that the events and ideas of this period cannot be understood in isolation, they rather have to be viewed as part of an ongoing process of understanding that builds both on previous British experiences and on an awareness of a longer tradition of European encounters with sati. Ideas that became prominent in the early nineteenth century did not arise in a vacuum, but were informed by the permutations of a discourse, or discourses, on sati, which had their modern roots in the travel literature of the sixteenth and seventeenth centuries. The English incarnation of this genre incorporated works in translation, by men from a variety of European backgrounds and the accounts of these travellers form the backdrop to changing ideas in the eighteenth and nineteenth centuries.

The first two chapters of this book, then, look at responses to sati in the early modern and Enlightenment periods, drawing on both British and continental European travel accounts and works of synthesis. This is not intended to imply a homogenized Western discourse on sati, but to emphasize the lack of one by highlighting the disparities both within these accounts and between these and later nineteenth-century ideas. In my choice of European sources, which include the writings of men from France, Germany, Spain, Portugal, Italy, Holland, Scotland, and England, I have confined myself to those which appeared in an English translation and would have been available to at least a section of the reading public in Britain. Many of the assumptions and ideas that appeared in these earlier texts were vital in shaping the course of nineteenth-century British discourse on sati, while areas of divergence are particularly informative in the context of this study, showing as they do how attitudes changed over time. By tracing this development I am able to illustrate the ambivalence, mutability, and heterogeneity of Western discourse on sati which was riddled with variations, contradictions, and counter-hegemonic voices.[24]

The final three chapters of the book deal with the debate on sati in British India. In some ways this is well-worn ground, but it is the intention of this volume to challenge previous historical accounts that see the ideas of this period as normative, by showing them to be based on a historically specific set of ideas and concerns. By linking the debate on sati to other debates that were going on in the metropole at the time, I hope to add a new dimension to Lata Mani's interpretation of the sati debate as predominantly political, by emphasizing its interconnectedness with ideological changes and concerns within the British society. Moreover, by treating the subject thematically rather than dealing with different types of sources (official, missionary, press, etc.) separately, I will counter the impression put forward by Mani—of an isolated political debate. Indeed, I consider Mani's segregation of official and popular debates to be one of its main flaws.[25] As I show in these chapters, the official and popular debates on sati, far from being isolated from each other, were very much intertwined. Colonial officials would have been very much aware of, and indeed were sometimes directly involved in, the popular debate as it appeared in newspapers, journals, and missionary tracts. Similarly, official debate on sati was placed very much in the public domain with the publication of the parliamentary papers on sati from 1821 onwards. It seems unhelpful and arbitrary, therefore, to discuss these two discourses in isolation, when in reality they were mutually reinforcing.

Not only does a thematic approach allow me to highlight the importance of the changing ideas in Britain, in shaping both official and popular reactions to sati, but it also provides a context for a discussion of the impact that sati itself had on these ideas. The impact of colonialism, though unequal, was far from unidirectional and the encounter with India had definite consequences for ideological, social, political, and economic realities in Britain. A recurrent criticism of Edward Said is that his depiction of the intellectual traffic of the orientalist discourse is too unidirectional and does not take account of a counter-flow. As Dennis Trotter points out, a discourse such as Orientalism must also implicate the dominant imperial subject as well as the subjugated indigenous one.[26] If we accept that 'the white man's subjectivity is equally worthy of study,'[27] we lay open all manner of questions as to the forces and ideologies that shaped this subjectivity. Why did he create the specific images of sati which he did at specific historical junctures, and how did these images act to reinforce or to alter his own self-perception and cultural outlook? What impact did the experience of sati have on the formation of ideas about issues such as suicide and gender in Britain itself? Far from being something that was simply constructed, images of sati in their various forms helped redefine and reshape a variety of British assumptions and ideas, both about India and about Britain, and so played a role in the multidirectional and dialectic process which characterized the colonial encounter.

The 'creation of colonial knowledge' was, then, a multi-dimensional and shifting process that cannot be understood in isolation of any of its elements. David Cannadine says of his recent work *Ornamentalism:*

...there can be no satisfactory history of Britain without empire, and no satisfactory history of empire without Britain. By stressing the interconnections between social visions of the metropolis and the periphery, and the structures and systems that unified and undergirded them, it seeks to put the history of Britain back into the history of the empire and the history of the empire back into the history of Britain.[28]

To fully appreciate the processes by which the West sought to understand the East, it is not enough to reduce them to a political dynamic of power and control, although this certainly played a part. Rather, we must look at a wider picture that incorporates colonizers and colonized, periphery and metropolis, ideology and practice, and knowledge and experience in a series of dialectic and multifaceted processes that change over time and space, and which are as much about the recognition of similarities as about the assertion of differences.

Notes

1. Polly Toynbee, 'Limp Liberals Fail to Protect Their Most Profound Values', in the *Guardian*, 10 October 2001.
2. Ibid.
3. Ibid.
4. Madeleine Bunting, 'Defending the Middle', in the *Guardian*, 15 October 2001.
5. 'Sati' literally translates as 'virtuous woman' and is most properly used to refer to the woman who burns on her husband's funeral pyre. In the colonial period the word also came to designate the rite by which the widow burned (in Hindi known as *sahagamana*—going with, or *anugamana*—going after). I use it in both contexts in the course of this book.
6. Cited in A. Sharma, *Sati: Historical and Phenomenological Essays* (Delhi: Motilal Banarsidass, 1988), p. 32. This passage also appears in the *Parasara*, *Brahmapurana* (Gautamimahatmya), *Mitaksara*, and *Suddhitattva*.
7. Christopher Thomas, 'Priestess Praises Merit of Suttee', in *The Times*, 16 December 1991.
8. For an account of rural women's reactions to the sati, see Kavita *et al.*, 'Rural Women Speak', in *Seminar*, vol. 342, 1988 pp. 40-4.
9. Cited in Chilla Bulbeck, *Re-orienting Western Feminisms* (Cambridge: Cambridge University Press, 1998), p. 92.
10. I use 'West' here, and throughout, to denote the predominantly Christian countries of Britain and Europe. In using this term it is not my

intention to suggest that there is a coherent 'western' discourse on
sati—indeed it is one of the key contentions of this book that there is
not. Neither is it my intention to suggest the existence of a monolithic
'western' culture of the type Said critiques. Indeed, I use the term in
order to deconstruct it by arguing that what has come to be termed
'western' attitudes to human rights issues such as sati have historically
been very far from unified.

11. A report in *The Times* on the Deorala sati, for example, began with the
following assertion: 'Of all the signs of how women are regarded in
Indian society, perhaps the clearest is the reverence given to the suttee—the "true wife"—who cradles her husband's head on her lap as his
funeral pyre is lit and thus joins him in death.' 'Thousands Flock to
Village Suttee Site', in *The Times*, 21 September 1987.
12. Ibid.,
13. Vasudha Dalmia-Luderitz, 'Sati as a Religious Rite, Parliamentary Papers
on Widow Immolation, 1821–1830', in *Economic and Political Weekly,*
vol. 27: 4, 26 April 1986, p. 58.
14. Edward Said, *Orientalism* (London: Penguin, 1995).
15. Ibid., p. 5.
16. Bart Moore-Gilbert, *Post-Colonial Theory: Contexts, Practices, Politics*
(London: Verso, 1997), p. 38.
17. Lata Mani, *Contentious Traditions: The Debate on Sati in Colonial India,
1780–1833* (Berkeley: University of California Press, 1998); 'Production of an Official Discourse on Sati in Early 19th Century Bengal',
in *Economic and Political Weekly*, vol. 21:17, 1986, pp. 32–40; *Europe and
its Others: Proceedings of the Essex Conference on the Sociology of Literature,
July 1984* (Colchester: University of Essex, 1985).
18. A. Nandy, *The Intimate Enemy: Loss and Recovery of Self Under Colonialism* (New Delhi: Oxford University Press, 1983).
19. Cited in John MacKenzie, *Orientalism: History, Theory and the Arts*
(Manchester: Manchester University Press, 1995), p. 10.
20. Denis Porter, 'Orientalism and its Problems', in Patrick Williams and
Laura Chrisman, *Colonial Discourse and Post-Colonial Theory* (Hemel
Hempstead: Harvester Wheatsheaf, 1993), p. 152.
21. Moore-Gilbert, *Post-Colonial Theory*, op. cit., p. 45.
22. Lisa Lowe, *Critical Terrains: French and British Orientalisms* (Ithaca:
Cornell University Press, 1991).
23. Ibid., p. 11.
24. In the process of discussing sources from a variety of European backgrounds, it is sometimes necessary to refer to 'Western' or 'European'
ideas and attitudes. This is not intended to suggest a homogenous
Western understanding of sati—indeed this study seeks to demonstrate
the opposite—but to highlight areas of overlap in a heterogeneous
collection of sources. While there was certainly no monolithic Euro-

pean discourse on sati, at times certain shared cultural assumptions among Europeans allowed for similar interpretations between men of different backgrounds and it is in this limited context that I refer to Western ideas.

25. It is not necessarily my intention to undermine the internal logic of Mani's reading of each of these debates, but rather to argue that a more complete picture can be drawn by understanding them as interlocking and mutually reinforcing.

26. Cited in MacKenzie, *Orientalism*, p. 12.

27. Ibid.

28. David Cannadine, *Ornamentalism: How the British Saw Their Empire* (London: Penguin, 2002), p. iv.

2

STRANGE AND BEASTLY DEEDS
Early European Encounters with Sati

CRØSO

The elder wife went away lamenting, with the band around her head rent, and tearing her hair, as if tidings of some great disaster had been brought her; and the other departed, exalting at her victory, to the pyre, crowned with fillets by the women who belonged to her, and decked out splendidly as for a wedding. She was escorted by her kinsfolk who chanted songs in praise of her virtue. When she came near the pyre she took off her adornments and distributed them to her familiars and friends, leaving a memorial for herself, as it were, to those who had loved her....In conclusion, she said farewell to her familiars and was helped by her brother onto the pyre, and there, to the admiration of the crowd that had gathered together for the spectacle, she ended her life in heroic fashion. Before the pyre was kindled, the whole army in battle array marched round it thrice. She meanwhile lay down beside her husband and as the fire seized her no sound of weakness escaped her lips. The spectators were moved, some to pity, and some to exuberant praise. But some of the Greeks present found fault with such customs as savage and inhumane.[1]

In 316 BC the youngest wife of Keteus, a Hindu general who died in the battle between Antigonos and Eumenes, immolated herself on her husband's funeral pyre. The event was witnessed and recorded by Greek observers and is the oldest-known historical instance of sati. It is also the first recorded encounter of the West with a rite that would capture its imagination and achieve an unprecedented prominence in its vision of Indian society and culture. Appropriately, this first Western account of sati incorporates many of the characteristics that were to underpin later European representations of it. Perceptions of Hellenic civilization are juxtaposed against those of Hindu barbarism, as some of the Greek observers denigrate the rite and its supporters for savagery and inhumanity. This condemnation is by no means absolute, however. Though explicit disapprobation is finally asserted, the tenor of the account precludes us from assuming homogenous Greek disapproval. The description of the event is couched in heroic terms and the widow is represented as a voluntary and autonomous agent in her own death. Actively seeking the opportunity for honour, she mounts the pyre of her own free will and does not flinch at the flames. She is the epitome of the romantic sati, her death a spectacle of courage and devotion. The reaction of the crowd is divided between pity and praise, emotions that we meet repeatedly among western observers of sati in more modern times. Indeed, two millennia later the seventeenth-century English traveller William Methold would echo this sentiment almost exactly, commenting that he was 'yet unresolved whether their love to their dead husbands be more to be admired or pitied.'[2] We do not know what proportion of this crowd was Greek— the Hellenistic setting suggests that many might have been—or how many of the Greeks disapproved, but the implication is that not all of the Western observers found fault and the explicit condemnation of some is undermined by the laudatory language of the account.

The juxtaposition between the claims of heroism and barbarism is a recurrent feature in the Western discourse on sati; the interwoven aspects of glorious martyrdom and cruel execution solicit a dual response in the observer. Even in the early nineteenth century, when any suggestion of admiration was consciously suppressed, it still found subconscious expression through the tendency to romanticize sati in literature. This duality of response suggests that Western reactions to sati were about more than just the othering of Hindu society. They were the product of an ambivalent male conception of the position and status of women. Patriarchal European society may have found sati incompatible with chivalric notions about the protection of the weaker sex, but it did find resonance with its ideals of feminine virtue, leading to a more complex and ambivalent reaction to sati than has often been assumed. Emerging ideas of Western superiority necessitated the outward condemnation of the rite, but tensions remained as ideas about sati coalesced not just with a changing colonial relationship but also with shifting ideological and social trends in Europe itself. Thus the Greek conflation of praise and condemnation reoccurred repeatedly in the complex and sometimes contradictory currents that informed reactions to sati throughout the period of Western interaction with India.

Of Miracles and Monsters: Classical and Medieval Heritage

Although some Europeans had known of sati since classical times, the first substantial body of writing on the custom in Europe appeared in the sixteenth and seventeenth centuries, when travellers of a variety of backgrounds and nationalities[3] arrived in India as traders, missionaries, adventurers, and ambassadors. Many of the narratives, letters, and journals that they left behind were published for public perusal, both individually and in compendiums, at home and abroad. These texts provide an invaluable source of information both about India in the early modern period and about the cultural ideas and preconceptions of the authors themselves. The images that these travellers formed did not exist in a vacuum, but were influenced by ideas belonging to a long tradition of European interest in India. Thus, although these men were in many ways pioneers, they were not free from preconceptions about 'the Indies' and any discussion of their ideas must be set in the context of this influential classical and medieval heritage.

The history of interaction between Europe and India stretches back into antiquity.[4] The existence of India was an established fact in ancient Greek society, even before its invasion by Alexander the Great in 326 BC. Many later perceptions of India were based on the works of early Greek writers such as Herodotus and Ctasias. In these fantastic ethnographic accounts, some fact was merged with much fiction to present a land that was at once rich and tropical, strange and barbarous. With Alexander's invasion, and the accounts that were written of it, some real empirical data emerged, though many myths continued to hold currency well into the early modern period. The stories of men like Nearchus and Onesicritus, who accompanied Alexander, were collected by the historian Arrian and used in his narrative of the campaign. The work of Megasthenes, who went as an ambassador to the court of Chandragupta Maurya in 302 BC, was another important source of information from a firsthand observer. Later, the geographer Strabo produced an encyclopaedic, if sometimes misguided, account of the people and customs of various countries, including India.

The custom of sati, observed (as we have seen) by members of Alexander's expedition, found mention in these classical accounts alongside various other horrors and wonders, both factual and fictional. The discovery of the monsoon winds by Hippalus in AD 45 considerably shortened the sea voyage and, for a time, contributed to an increasing flow of both literature and trade between Europe and India. However, the decline of the Roman Empire and the accompanying regression in European cohesion and stability, combined with the spread of Muslim power in what is now the Middle East, meant that over the following centuries connections between Europe and India became sporadic and sources of new information severely limited. Knowledge of India became vague and distorted, based primarily on what survived of classical accounts.

The lack of new material and information led, in the Middle Ages, to the construction of a world view which was far more Eurocentric than that of antiquity. Areas that had been incorporated into the 'known world' by the Greeks and Romans were pushed onto the peripheries of medieval European geography, which centred round Christendom. Indeed, so vague was the medieval conception of the location of India that its name was applied indiscriminately, in its plural form, to the whole of Asia. The cosmology of the pre-Renaissance world was constructed within a Christian religious framework, with Jerusalem at the centre of this divine plan. India was a distant land of mythical proportion, as Thomas Metcalf puts it, 'A land of miracles and monsters'.[5] For some it was the location of paradise, a living Garden of Eden, for others the abode of demons and perhaps of Lucifer himself.[6] The accounts that survived from classical sources and those that filtered back from individual traders and explorers tended to reinforce these ideas, both good and bad, with fantastic details and near-magical occurrences. The east was both a source of wealth and trade and the abode of monstrous creatures and heathen idolaters, but in general it was distant enough to feature only on the peripheries of European consciousness—an obscure other to the unified centre of Christendom.

The Tartar peace of the thirteenth century reopened the route to India, for those who dared to try it. Of those traders, mainly Italians, who made the journey, no account of note survives until that of Marco Polo in the late thirteenth century. By this time the mythical image of India was so firmly entrenched in the European mind that even his well-observed and relatively objective account[7] could do little to dislodge it. Polo visited India on his return from China, and though he deals with it in far less detail than he does the Far East, his account represented the first new empirical data of note to be received in Europe for many centuries. His reference to sati is short and factual, mentioning the existence of the custom and telling his reader that, '…such women as do this have great praise from all'.[8]

The existence of sati was also reported by the Franciscan Friar Odorico da Pordenone, who visited India in 1321 and left behind a narrative of his journey that detailed both the ecology of the country and the customs of its people. He commented:

When any man die they burn his dead corpse to ashes: and if his wife survive him, her they burn quick, because (say they) she shall accompany her husband in his tithe and husbandry, when he is come into a new world. Howbeit, the said wife having children by her husband, may, if she will, remain alive with them, without shame or reproach: not withstanding for the most part they all of them make choice to be burnt with their husbands. Now albeit the wife die before her husband, that law bindeth not the husband to such inconvenience, but he may marry another wife also.[9]

Where Polo merely notes the existence of the custom, and that its performance was considered praiseworthy, Odorico attempts to give some explanation, attributing it to the prehistoric belief that a man needs possessions from this life in the next.[10] With a glancing irony he also notes that sati is inflicted on women but not on men. It is interesting that he feels the need to make this point explicit. Patriarchal Europe would certainly not have been shocked by the operation of such a double standard, so perhaps his caveat suggests rather that India was at this time so strange and remote that men sacrificing themselves on the death of their wives might even be conceivable there.

Despite the emergence of these valuable and more or less objective accounts, the European conception of India until the sixteenth century remained mired in fantasy. The average reader in Europe had very little hope of verifying personally what he read, and under these circumstances fact and fiction could easily become intertwined. Even as late as 1494, a pamphlet on the Subcontinent could 'exhibit an extraordinary conception of India: there are one-eyed, dog-headed and headless men, pygmies, men and women with large feet used as parasol, a winged snake, a flying panther and other strange beasts, birds and insects.'[11] The continued popularity of such images only four years before Vasco da Gama's voyage suggests just how tenacious a hold the fabulous myths of the Orient had on the European imagination.

The extent to which the new empirical information was submerged into older medieval fictions of the east is highlighted by the remarkable career of Sir John Mandeville, whose supposed travels became something of a national *cause celebre*, and whose fictional narrative was accepted as fact even as late as the eighteenth century. Scholars now believe that Mandeville never left Europe—some doubt whether he even existed—but the narrative he left, a plagiarism of existing sources in which the fabulous and the factual appear side by side, was hugely influential. His account of sati is clearly taken from Odorico:

And if any men die in that country, they burn them...and if his wife has no children, then they burn her with him, and they say that it is good reason, that she keep him company in the other world as she did in this. But if she has children with him, they let her live with them, to bring them up if she will. And if that she love more to live with her children than to die with her husband, men hold her for false and cursed; nay she shall never be loved and trusted of the people. And if the woman dies before the husband, men burn him with her, if that he will; and if he will not, no man constraineth him thereto, but he may wed another time without blame or reproof.[12]

Mandeville here elaborates on his source; Odorico's tacit recognition of the double standard is turned into a joke for the perceptive, another wonder for the credulous. Despite the mendacity of his project and the fantastic nature of much of the rest of his material, Mandeville here gives a reasonably accurate outline of sati, showing how fact and fiction could become easy bedfellows in an environment where both could be equally hard to believe.

Sati was known, then, in the medieval period, but it reached European consciousness as just one facet of a much larger imagined East, some of which was real, but most of which was not. Factual accounts like those of Odorico and Polo gave little detail beyond the existence of the custom, and even this was often subsumed into the fictional mythology of India characterized by Mandeville's account. One important exception to this rule is the account of an actual sati given by the early fifteenth-century traveller Nicolo de Conte, whose travel narrative was collected by the humanist scholar Poggio Bracciolini and published as part of his great work *On the Vicissitude of Fortune* in 1448. De Conte's description of sati is worth quoting here in full, as it foreshadows many of the ideas found in the later accounts. De Conte states:

In Central India the dead are burnt, and the living wives, for the most part, are consumed in the same funeral pyre as their husband, one or more, according to the agreement at the time the marriage was contracted. The first wife is compelled by law to be burnt, even though she should be the only wife, but others are married under the express agreement that they should add to the splendour of the funeral ceremonies by their death, and this is considered a great honour for them. The deceased husband is laid on a couch, dressed in his best garments. A vast funeral pyre is erected over him in the form of a pyramid, constructed of odiferous woods. When the pile is lighted, the wife, richly dressed, walks gaily round it, singing, accompanied by a great concourse of people, amid the sounds of trumpets, flutes and songs. In the meantime one of the priests, standing on some elevated spot, exhorts her to a contempt for life and praises death, promising her all kinds of enjoyment with her husband, much wealth and abundance of ornaments. When she has walked round the pyre several times, she stands near the elevation on which the priest is standing, and, taking off her dress, puts on a white linen garment, her body having first been washed according to custom. In obedience to the exhortation of the priest, she then springs into the fire. If some show fear (for it frequently happens that they become stupefied by terror at the sight of the struggles of the others suffering in the fire), they are thrown into the fire by bystanders, whether willing or not. Their ashes are afterwards collected and placed in urns, which form an ornament for the sepulchres.[13]

Here the splendour of the spectacle is juxtaposed with the struggles of the suffering woman in the fire. The autonomous agency that the Greeks perceived, which many early modern travellers would so admire and pity, is subsumed by the insidious influence of the priests; a theme that would re-emerge at the end of the seventeenth century and which was taken up with a vengeance by British anti-sati campaigners in the nineteenth century. In de Conte's account, the free will of the widow is subjugated to the dictates of law (whether religious or civil is not specified) and, should she choose not to exercise it correctly, to the overt use of force. In this rendition, her life, from the time of the marriage contract, is dedicated to the act of glorifying her husband's funeral; even her earthly remains are used to add splendour to his memorial. In many ways this account was ahead of its time; it would take a further 300 years for European observers of sati to organize their mixed reactions to the rite into the dark acceptance of the widow's helplessness implicit in this account.

Early Modern Travellers in India

During the sixteenth and seventeenth centuries there was a significant increase in the number of travel accounts dealing with the Indian subcontinent, its people, and its customs. Vasco da Gama's discovery of the sea route round the Cape of Good Hope in 1498, and subsequent establishment of the Portuguese enclave at Goa, paved the way for an influx of foreign visitors from various European nations. The granting of a royal charter to the English East India Company in 1600 and the creation of the Dutch East India Company in 1602 legitimized trade from these nations in defiance of the Portuguese monopoly and helped to bring Europe and India into closer contact. The burgeoning number of European travellers, traders, missionaries, and envoys heading east was representative of the growing interest that Europe had in India, in both commercial and intellectual terms. The travel narratives that these visitors left behind form a substantial body of literature, and were to be hugely influential in an ongoing reconceptualization, both of the 'Orient' and of Europe's own identity in relation to it.

The great religious schism of the Reformation and the intellectual ferment of the Renaissance exploded the medieval construction of the world. The Christian centre was no longer unified; religious dogma had lost its certainty and with it the clear sense of what represented a Christian identity. This, together with scientific advances that cast doubt on the preconceived Christian world order, undermined the foundations of the medieval cosmology. Moreover, these cataclysmic ideological shifts took place at a time when the known world was changing geographically, as in 1492 Christopher Columbus discovered the Americas. The New World was a source of both gold and souls,[14] but its discovery also necessitated a reassessment of Europe's role in a wider world to both east and west. Thus the traders, ambassadors, and adventurers who wrote about India and the east in this period did not have a neat context into which to fit their observations. Rather, their reports themselves played an important role in redefining Europe's sense of its identity and its relationship to other countries.

Perhaps the most striking aspect of the European encounter with sati in the sixteenth and seventeenth centuries was the heterogeneity of response that the act evoked among its observers, both in terms of the literary manner in which the subject was treated and the emotional reaction it induced. Far from eliciting a consistent moral response based on racial or cultural difference, the reactions of early modern observers to sati varied widely and depended to a great extent on the myriad forces that shaped their own personal subjectivity. During this period our accounts of sati are derived not from official documents or even from a homogenous group of sources sharing a common set of imperatives, but from a diverse selection of individual journals, narratives, and travelogues. The very nature of these sources predisposes them to individual interpretation. As Barbara Korte points out, travel writing 'provides us not only with an impression of the travelled word, but the travelling subject is always also laid bare: accounts of travel are never objective; they invariably reveal the culture specific and individual patterns of perception and knowledge which every traveller brings to the travelled world'.[15] The diversity of backgrounds from which the authors of these accounts came, their different religions, nationalities, and occupations played an important part in determining the way in which they individually sought to understand or represent sati.

The media through which many of these travellers reported their findings, or experiences, in itself influenced the way in which they dealt with their subject matter. Some, like the Englishman Ralph Fitch, who travelled India in the late sixteenth century, restricted themselves to merely mentioning the existence of sati. Fitch simply comments that 'when the husbande dieth, his wife is burned with him, if shee be alive; if shee will not her head is shaven, and then is never any account made of her after.'[16] Part of the reason for this brevity may be that many accounts, particularly those by traders, were not originally written for publication. They were intended as a source of information about a country which could be used to further commercial interests, not as a platform for the author to expound his moral interpretations to the reading public. Many of the travellers whose accounts were later published were not literary, or even very well educated and, as Arnold Wright points out, it was often the 'utilitarian rather than the romantic side of the tour'[17] that they aimed at presenting. They tended to stick to bare facts and 'refused to treat a subject imaginatively even where they could conveniently do so.'[18] There were, of course, numerous exceptions to this rule; men who presented their narrative in a literary manner and who entered into more detailed consideration of local customs and their causes, effects, and meanings as well as their personal responses to what they had witnessed, or heard of from others. It is within this corpus of more detailed accounts that we find emerging the varying strands of a discourse, or discourses, on sati which were at once both strikingly divergent and subliminally unified. The intrinsic interest that arises from the study of reactions to sati in this period is found in the 'culture specific and individual patterns of perception'[19] that informed this diversity and, perhaps more importantly, in the location of areas of agreement as the travellers sought to use their own cultural experiences to create an understanding of sati that utilized analogy as much as it asserted difference.

Eyewitness to the Incredible: Observing Sati

For those who sought to present more detailed accounts of sati, the first expedient was to assert their credentials as sources of accurate information. As Jenny Mecziems points out, the major appeal of early travel literature lay in its scope for the imagination, but this scope lay in the re-ordering of the world not by fictions, but by new facts.[20] The difficulty for the travel writer was establishing his credibility. In medieval and Renaissance literary tradition the travel narrative was associated with romance and fantasy. The new, mostly factual, accounts of the wider world had somehow to be repositioned to assert their veracity, but

> The new material, however factual, was strange and therefore romantically exciting; the readers themselves would give the narrative the status of literature... and accommodate it within the existing literary tradition. But in this tradition travellers from Odysseus onwards were conventionally liars or poetic inventions, and their accounts real only as myth is real....[21]

This problem was exacerbated for India because a large number of the marvels and wonders that constituted the medieval European image of the peripheries of its world were located there, making people at once both credulous and suspicious of reports of strange customs in that area. The early modern narrator needed to separate the reality of sati, however unbelievable, from the other fictions of the Orient. For the reader, however, deciding what to believe was not an easy task, especially when seasoned travellers could be found attesting to miracles and monsters that they had not themselves encountered. One of Mandeville's more fantastic extravagances, the anthropophagi, for example, were defended by no less a traveller than Sir Walter Raleigh, who commented:

Such a nation was written of by Mandeville, whose reports were holden for fables many yeeres, and since the East Indies were discovered, we find his relations true of things that heretofore were held incredible... for mine owne part I saw them not, but I am resolved that so many people did not all combine, or forthinke to make such a report.[22]

The result of such credulity, and its disillusionment, was that travel writers of the period worked hard to establish their veracity. Writers who had actually been witness to a sati take pains to emphasize their presence and the accuracy of their account. The French adventurer Charles Dellon, writing in 1698, for example, stated: 'The first time I was an eyewitness of this tragical ceremony, I took most particular notice of all the passages and circumstances that attended it.'[23] The German ambassador, Albert de Mandelslo went one step further and took a keepsake as proof of his presence at the event.

I was something near her on horseback, with the two English merchants, and I think that she perceived in my countenance that I pitied her, whence it came that she cast me one of her bracelets, which I had the good hap to catch and still keep in remembrance of so extraordinary an action.[24]

Those who had not witnessed the event themselves stressed the reliability of their sources. The famous French traveller and physician Francois Bernier, who was himself present at many satis, chose to relate the tale of one which he did not see himself, justifying this decision as follows.

But let us proceed to another of these dreadful scenes, not witnessed indeed by myself, but selected in preference to those at which I happened to be present on account of the remarkable incident by which it was distinguished. I have seen so many things that I should have pronounced incredible, that neither you nor I ought to reject the narrative in question merely because it contains something extraordinary. The story is in every person's mouth in the Indies, and is universally credited. Perhaps it has already reached you in Europe.[25]

The sati referred to is also related by the Italian traveller Niccolao Manucci in his famous *Storio do Mogor*.[26] Manucci claims to have been present at the immolation in question and specifically places the event with the chronology of his journey, saying, 'I reached the Qasim Bazaar, at three days journey from Hugli.... From the Qasim Bazaar

I took the road to Rajmahal, and there waited to see a Hindu woman burnt, although I had already seen many.'[27] Bernier's use of this story is significant not because he borrows it from Manucci, but because he feels the need to emphasize its veracity. In doing so he echoes Raleigh's caution about not disregarding the incredible. That the two men display such a similar concern over their audience's acceptance, one in defence of a fiction and one of a fact, shows the extent to which the two were intertwined in the European vision of India. Sati was a fact that the travel writers feared might be taken for fiction, at a time when many fictions were being taken for facts. Only as the number of reports coming back grew did the writers begin to feel that their tales would be given credence. As Bernier comments at the outset of his discussion of sati, 'What has been said about women burning themselves will be confirmed by so many travellers that I suppose people will cease to be sceptical upon this melancholy fact.'[28]

The need to establish the veracity of one's account is reflected in the primacy given to the eyewitness narrative. Sati had become one of a stock of 'wonders' that were almost indispensable to an account of India. Plagiarism in this period was not an unusual or unacceptable means of assisting a flagging memory or supplementing a stolid tale, and those who had not witnessed a sati would draw upon the experiences of others, either openly or covertly. This tendency to 'borrow' descriptions of sati makes it difficult for us to gain an accurate picture of the rite's prevalence and of the regional variations in its practice, as several ostensibly different accounts of satis in several different parts of India might in fact all draw their inspiration from the same event. That said, the interest in the custom at home, as well as the voyeurism of a period in which executions were a form of public entertainment, meant that those who had the opportunity to witness a sati, usually took it. Manucci, as we have already seen, delayed his journey to witness one, despite having already been present at many others. The result was that the rite took on the dimensions of a tourist attraction for travelling Europeans. Albert De Mandelslo tells us that he was invited to witness a burning almost as an act of hospitality.

I was soon joined by two of the English Merchants at Cambay who obligingly reproached me with the slur I put on their nation in preferring the house of a Mahometan to their lodge.... They proffered me their company to walk and promised to carry me the next morning to a place where an Indian woman was to be burnt of her own consent. The next day the English merchants came to my lodgings, whence we went together to the riverside, outside the city, where this voluntary execution was to be done.[29]

It is hardly surprising that men who went to witness the rite as an entertainment or as a means of satisfying curiosity should report it as a spectacle—a production at which the European observer is both audience and reviewer. The cast, setting, costume, and sound are vividly reported. The early sixteenth century Portuguese traveller Duarte Barbosa tells us:

And in this manner all collect together, and entertain and pay court to her, and she spends what she possesses among her relations in feasting and singing, in dances and playing on musical instruments, and amusements of jugglers. And when the term fixed has ended, she dresses herself in her richest stuffs, and adorns herself with many precious jewels, and the rest of her property she divides among her children, relations, and friends, and then mounts a horse, with a great sound of music and a large following. The horse must be grey, or very white if possible, for her to be seen better. And so they conduct her through the whole city, paying court to her as far as the place where the body of her husband was burned; and in the same grave they place much wood, with which they light a very great fire, and all around it they make a gallery with three or four steps, whither she ascends with all her jewels and robes; and when she is on top she takes three turns around it, and raises her hands to heaven, and worships towards the east three times.[30]

Likewise Manucci gives the following account.

...no sooner has the news of a Rajah's death arrived in his country, and the wife is satisfied that he no longer lives, than she is accorded three days of grace. During those days she is permitted to adorn herself as magnificently as she can; and thus arrayed she goes about the streets with lemons tied to her head like a crown; her body is uncovered from the waist upward and rubbed with saffron, as also is her face. In this state she takes leave of all those she meets in the streets with a smiling face and free manners, and speeches repugnant to her sex and her claim to nobility. When three days have passed they prepare in an open field a circular pit, deep and wide, which is filled with wood and cowdung. Fire is then applied. On beholding this pyre, she who is to be the victim of her honour, issues, clad in new attire, covered with diverse flowers, some arranged like crowns, others like necklaces.[31]

The aspects of carnival in these accounts cannot be missed, and contemporary readers would surely have recognized the parallels between these descriptions and the medieval festivals of the Lord of

Misrule, in which social norms were temporarily inverted and sub-
verted to socially sanctioned chaos. The alien nature of the widow's
sacrifice is located in the arena of spectacle and show, in a context
where normal expectations for behaviour are suppressed.

This air of unreality was maintained in these accounts by the fact
that the fatal denouement of this tragedy was often passed over with
theatrical skill. Barbosa concludes his account:

> ... she springs into it [the fire]... with as much good will as though she were
> jumping into a pool of water. And the relatives have ready for this occasion
> many pitchers and pots full of oil and butter, and dry wood, which they
> immediately throw in, so that a great flame is at once kindled, that she is
> suddenly reduced to ashes.[32]

The apparent insouciance of the sati to the prospect of bodily pain,
combined with the unfeasible speed with which the fire does its
work, allows the curtain to fall on the climax of the spectacle without
troubling the reader with a vision of physical suffering. Similarly,
Mandelslo concludes his description by denying the widow the opportunity to vocally register her pain:

> ... the rest of the assembly filled the air with their cries and shouts, such as
> must needless have hindered those of the widow to be heard, if she had the
> time to make any in the fire, which had made a sudden dispatch of her as
> if it had been lightening.[33]

Not all observers could so easily conceal the tortuous culmination
of the rite, but it seems to have been common practice to avoid
graphic descriptions of the widow's pain. When her suffering is recognized, it is usually done implicitly. French jeweller and traveller
Jean Baptiste Tavernier, writing in 1676, makes a dark joke about
abortive satis, saying, 'I have observed, because there is a scarcity of
wood in Bengala, that when these poor creatures are half griddled,
they cast their bodies into the Ganges, where the remains are de-
voured by the crocodiles.'[34] The widow's suffering is not usually
made explicit, but is rather implied by the reactions of the observers.
In the account from which the following extract is taken, Bernier fails
to mention the dying moments of the sati at all, but the whole se-
quence is given a nightmarish quality—an interesting inversion of the
carnival theme—by his assertion of his inability to accurately represent it within the confines of reality.

Well indeed I may despair of representing this whole scene with proper and genuine feeling, such as I experienced at the spectacle itself, or of painting it in colours sufficiently vivid. My recollection of it is indeed so distinct that it seems only a few days since the horrid reality passed before my eyes, and with pain I persuade myself that it was anything but a frightful dream.[35]

European observers seem to have been at once compelled and repelled by the witnessing of a sati. For some it takes on a cathartic quality, for others it causes only pain. Englishman Nicholas Witherington, who was in India between 1612 and 1618, relates: '... our Agent was soe greeved, and amazed at the undaunted Resolution of the younge Woman, that hee said hee would never see more burnte in that Fashion while hee lived.'[36]

Ambivalent Attitudes: Positioning the Sati

Perhaps the most striking aspect of the accounts of sati from this period, and the area in which the complexity of the European reaction to it is most clearly visible, is the extent to which they focused on the figure of the widow herself as an actor in the events that surrounded her death. This is not to suggest that the widow was viewed unproblematically as an autonomous agent in her own destruction; the possibility and reality of various forms of coercion, both overt and insidious, were often either implicitly or explicitly acknowledged. What is important, however, is that the forces acting on the widow were understood primarily in human terms, rather than as the imper- sonal, theoretical considerations of later centuries. Lata Mani has argued that in the nineteenth century the widow was marginalized, and the debate on sati used as the site on which the authority of tradition and the parameters of colonial power could be contested.[37] In this earlier period, however, the widow herself was still central to European attempts to understand sati. The issues that arise out of their encounter with sati are primarily ones that concern the widow her- self; her motives, status (as a widow and as a sati), and inherent nature. This focus on the figure of the sati, rather than on an abstract construc- tion of the rite, created a space in which a variety of subjective images could emerge. Few observers would defend the custom of burning widows alive in itself: even the Italian humanist and traveller Pietro Della Valle, who was most forthright in expressing his admiration for the sati, called it 'a custom indeed cruel and barbarous'.[38] Unlike the eighteenth and nineteenth centuries, however, when the nature and status of the rite became the central theme of discussion, in the early modern period it was the sati herself who was the centre of attention and evoked a wide variety of emotional responses.

European reactions to the sati ranged from explicit admiration to outright condemnation and could often incorporate a measure of both in the same account. Ideologically this ambivalence in the collective response is perhaps best understood by placing the sati within the framework of preconceived ideas about women, that the Europeans brought with them and through which their perceptions were invariably filtered. Their responses to her actions were complicated by the lack of a unified European construction of femininity during this period. Within the medieval framework of Christian morality, the position and nature of women was determined by the culpability of Eve in the fall from Eden and by Pauline assertions of women's inherent sinfulness, frailty, and inferiority. Men and women might benefit alike from God's grace, but in the temporal world the flawed nature of woman provided the basis for her subjugation. The dual impact of Reformation and Renaissance on received wisdom, both in terms of religion and of nature, opened the way to a reassessment of this fundamentally misogynistic view of femininity. This is not to suggest that the status of women or notions about their nature changed drastically during this period, but rather that ideological space was created for a variety of ideas and opinions and a range of different constructions of femininity. The late sixteenth and early seventeenth centuries witnessed the production of numerous pamphlets, sermons, and tracts on the status and duties of women, with both favourable and unfavourable constructions being posited. Under these circumstances, the reactions that the image of the sati engendered could be as diverse and ambivalent as the prevailing attitude to women generally. Moreover, her example, either as heroic paragon of wifely fidelity or as hell-bound devotee of demonic superstition could be integrated into the debate on either side.[39]

Although, as we shall see, patriarchal attitudes to women played a central role in determining European attitudes to the sati, responses were also conditioned by more basic factors. The first and most important variable in determining the nature of a European observer's response to sati was the series of events surrounding the actual immolation in question. Obviously the observer who saw a helpless child dragged against her will to the pyre would have a very different experience than one who watched a composed woman resist all attempts to dissuade her and mount the pyre of her own free will. This is not to subscribe to the early nineteenth century idea of 'good' and 'bad' satis, in which the agency of the widow can be neatly compartmentalized as voluntary or coerced. Indeed, the body of writing on sati from this period, when taken as a whole, shows a remarkably perceptive (if only partially developed) appreciation of the complicated forces acting on the widow as she made the decision to commit sati, and of the many shades of grey which existed between the extremes of volition and coercion. For the sake of clarity I shall here separate this spectrum of response into three broad areas. First I shall look at reactions to sati when perceived as an act of pure volition, then at the attempts to understand the varying degrees of covert or insidious coercion acting on the widow, such as societal pressure and religious indoctrination, and finally at reactions to overt coercion, the use of drugs or that of physical force in compelling a widow to the pyre.

Eternal Fires: Sati and Suicide

If the observer acknowledged, as East India Company Chaplain Edward Terry did, that the widow acted in a manner 'voluntary, not compelled'[40] in committing sati, he was faced with an ethical dilemma. In the strictest sense the sati had committed suicide, an act with inescapable moral implications in the Christian context. The outcome of such an act should be clear, for, as St Augustine forcefully asserted in *City of God Against the Pagans*, 'certainly a suicide is also a homicide',[41] a sin that would lead to eternal damnation. He warned '... that no man inflict upon himself a voluntary death thinking to escape temporary ills, lest he find himself among ills that are unending.'[42] Under these circumstances, it seems logical that sati as a voluntary action should have been universally condemned by its Christian observers. The hell-bound perpetrator of self-murder does in fact appear in some accounts, most often, though not exclusively, in those of missionaries or others from a religious background. Moreover, much of the imagery of sati, as it was presented to the reading public in Europe, suggested the sati's self-propelled descent into Hell. As Kate Teltscher points out in *India Inscribed,* the frontispiece of Abraham Roger's *La Porte Ouverte* (*The Open Door to Hidden Heathendom*) (Fig. 3) shows a half-naked sati leaping into the fire amid a crowd of revellers, while a demon overhead proclaims the title of the book. Similarly engravings in Dutchman Jan Huygen van Linschoten's *Voyages* (Fig. 1) and Franscois Bernier's *Histoire de la dernier revolution des Etats du Gran Mogol* (*The History of the late revolution of the Empire of the Great Mogol*) (See Fig. 4) both show the half-naked sati jumping into a pit of fire.[43] While the implications of Roger's demon are inescapable and the connotations of the fiery pit would certainly have not been lost on European audiences of the time, it is important to remember that one of the methods employed for committing sati actually was that of jumping into a flaming pit, and that these images, while implying a Christian moral judgement, were also literal renditions of travellers' accounts.[44] More explicit in their condemnation were the predictions made for the fate of the sati's soul. The French Abbe Le Carre, for example, tells us of the sati that occurred on the death of the Hindu general Mandala Naik: '...they burnt the corpse of this Hindu Prince, with four of his wives who had the courage to throw themselves alive on the flames: the

Fig. 1. 'Bramenes cum mortus est' from Jan Huygen van Linschoten, *His discours of Voyages into ye Easte and West Indies*, translated from Dutch to English by William Phillip (London: J. Wolfe. 1598), foll. P. 58. By permission of the British Library, C. 55g. 7.

latter consumed their bodies, but sent their souls to other eternal fires much hotter than those terrestrial ones',[45] while Althanasius Kircher, in his *China d'Athanase Kircher* of 1667, speaks of the '…infernal troop of sacrificers…who rather than conducting her to the Elysian Fields, as they believe, lead her into eternal flames to continue a never ending torture there.'[46]

The image of the sati mistakenly committing herself to eternal damnation was one that fitted neatly with existing ideas both about the nature of suicide,[47] which in medieval and early modern Europe was widely believed to be the work of the Devil, and about the susceptibility of women to diabolical suggestion.[48] Even as late as 1716, pamphlet writer John Cockburn could warn of:

> …the Devil's watching men, and entering them readily, when not upon their guard, and neither mindful or careful to resist him. For without the instigation and influence of that evil, envious and malicious spirit, it cannot be supposed that men of themselves, even left to themselves, could be transported to such detestable things, and to act so contrary to nature, to reason, to duty and to self interest, and to all both divine and humane obligations, as we see they sometimes do.[49]

The Devil was the author of deception and of despair in the human heart, which might lead men to diabolical acts such as witchcraft or suicide. The inherent nature of a woman made her particularly susceptible to his wiles; James I of England (VI of Scotland), for example, could comment: '…for as that sex is frailer than men is, so it is easier to be entrapped in these grosse snares of the Devill, as was well proved to be true by the Serpent's deceiving of Eve at the beginning, which makes him homelier with that sex ever since.'[50]

The image of the sati as acting under the inspiration of Beelzebub was reinforced ideologically by her perceived position as an idolater or pagan. Partha Mitter tells us that in the Middle Ages the Church fathers gave the so-called pagan gods a real existence in the Christian mind by designating them as demons and minions of Satan. That these assumptions were carried forward into the early modern period is illustrated graphically by early travellers' representations of Hindu gods as devils and demons.[51] When Edward Terry, the chaplain to Sir Thomas Roe, wrote that though there are many sects of Hindus, '…I know Satan (the father of division) to be the seducer of them all…',[52] he was expressing a widely held belief in the diabolical origins of the pagan religions. The sati, therefore, was doubly implicated; as a woman she was particularly susceptible to Satanic beguilement, as a pagan she was already under its sway. In her darkest form the sati is a physical representation of the metaphysical idea of Satan as the author of suicide. Some observers made this connection explicit by representing the sati less as a suicide than as a sacrifice to the Devil. Ludovico de Varthema described the priests at a sati as '...men clothed like devils, who carry fire in their mouths...'[53] and reported that:

They also offer a sacrifice to Deumo. And the wife goes many times up and down that place, dancing with the other women. She goes many time to the men clothed like Devils, to entreat them and tell them to pray the Deumo that he will be pleased to accept her as his own.... Do not imagine however that she is unwilling to do this; she even imagines that she will be carried forthwith into heaven....'[54]

Earlier in his narrative De Varthema had explicitly associated the idol Deumo with the Devil[55] and his depiction of the sati's action is closer in tone to a satanic ritual than anything else, with the sati being represented as the ultimate dupe of the Devil.

It is hardly surprising, then, that the image of a sati going voluntarily to her death was sometimes attributed to diabolical influence. Francois Bernier, whose accounts of devilish Brahmins were to so influence later depictions of sati, attributes a sati's determination to die to infernal intervention, saying:

...fixing a determined look on me, she said, 'Well, if I am prevented from burning myself, I will dash my brains out upon a wall.' What a diabolical spirit has taken possession of you, thought I. 'Let it be so then', I rejoined, with undissembled anger, 'but first take your children, wretched and unnatural mother! Cut their throats, and consume them on the same pile; otherwise you will leave them to die of famine....[56]

For Bernier the manifestation of her demonic possession may not be limited to self-destruction, but might feasibly extend to other praetor-natural acts such as infanticide. The infernal quality of the scene has already been made explicit as Bernier represents it in terms that would have carried unmistakable associations for his European audience:

[I] found on entering the apartment a regular witches sabat of seven or eight old hags, and another four or five excited, wild and aged Brahmens standing round the body, all of whom gave by turns a horrid yell, and beat their hands with violence. The widow was seated at the feet of her dead husband; her hair was dishevelled and her visage pale, but her eyes were tearless and sparkling with animation while she cried and screamed aloud with the rest of the company, and beat time with her hands to this horrible concert. The hurly-burly having subsided, I approached the hellish group....[57]

The reference to a 'witches sabat' is particularly suggestive here, as witchcraft was considered to result from a pact with the Devil, and to be another channel through which he encouraged the weak or unwary to their eternal destruction. With this in mind, the image of the demon that appears in Roger's frontispiece (Fig. 3) can be compared to that which appears in a wood carving of a witch burning in Derneburg in Germany in 1555 (Fig. 2). In both pictures, diabolical creatures preside over the women's fiery ends, suggesting a link between the European understanding of the causes of witchcraft, suicide, and sati.

Perhaps at this juncture it may be appropriate to consider further the extent to which the European experience of burning witches may have influenced their perceptions of sati. In her recent book *Burning*

Fig. 2. Woodcut of a witch-burning in Derneburg 1555. By permission of the Dover Pictorial Archive.

Women, Poompa Bannerjee contends that the lack of overt reference to witch burning in early modern accounts of sati indicates a European desire to maintain the impression of Indian otherness by ignoring the obvious similarities between the two practices.[58] While Bannerjee makes many important and perceptive observations during the course of her argument, especially with relation to early modern perceptions of women, her central contention appears to be premised on a too-literal reading of the texts—which fails to give sufficient weight to the implicit connections that appear in some of them, as outlined above. By concentrating on the absence of explicit comparisons between scenes of witch burning and widow burning, she fails to take into account the complexities of European attitudes to both and bases her

Fig. 3. Frontispiece from Abraham Roger, *Le Theatre de l'Idolatrie, ou la Porte Ouverte* (Amsterdam: J. Schipper, 1670). By permission of the British Library, C. 188. b. 42.

argument on the flawed assumption that direct similarities would be immediately apparent to the majority of observers. As I have already pointed out, European responses in this period were marked by vivid heterogeneity. Some, as we have seen, did make correlations, if not with witchcraft itself then with the diabolical associations that under-pinned it. If other Europeans failed to comment on the outward resemblance between the two acts, it was primarily because they saw them as having very different meanings.

It is easy with hindsight to draw broad sociological correlations between the witch craze in Europe and the popularity of sati in India. Recent historians have rejected the stereotypical image of the accused witch as an elderly widow, dependent on community charity for her support and isolated on the margins of society, and replaced it with a reading of witchcraft allegations as an idiom of conflict between more closely matched individuals. Despite this, it is clear that the majority of the accused were women (86 per cent in Scotland, for example) and a significant number of these (20 per cent) were widows.[59] Witchcraft was thus a gendered phenomenon '...arising from women struggling for prominence within patriarchally bounded female spheres.'[60] More-over, the common contemporary stereotype of a witch was of an elderly widow and the conventional allegation one where misfortune followed the rebuff of this dependent old lady.[61] The emphasis placed by contemporaries on the figure of the dissatisfied beggar as the source of witchcraft in the community, despite the fact that statistically this was a relatively rare version of events, suggests concern over the nature of charity at a time when responsibility for support of the disempowered was shifting from the community to the authority. What is clear is that though the specific form allegations took varied depending on local context, allegations in general tended to be aimed at individuals who were deemed troublesome or dangerous, either to the community or to an individual accuser. The figure of the Hindu widow can be fitted neatly into this context, whether because she represented an eco-nomic burden, or because her new status had to be accommodated within the existing family or social structures.

As we will see, early modern observers were often distinctly aware of the social threat posed by the widow, particularly in regards to her sexuality, and the potential conflict that might arise as the family tried to assimilate or eliminate her new situation. This does not mean, however, that they were attuned to the sociological similarities be-tween the sati and witch burning. Witchcraft in the early modern period was considered a very real phenomenon and those who were executed for it were deemed guilty of the most heinous of crimes. For the Protestant Church, witchcraft was apostasy, or even idolatry, and was prominent as a religious error as well as for its antisocial and destructive elements, while in the Roman Catholic tradition it was directly associated with heresy. Burning witches represented the infliction of a righteous punishment on those who had already alienated themselves from God and the Christian society. The sati on the other hand was usually viewed as an innocent, at least until the point where her wilful immolation made her guilty of self-murder.[62] For those who viewed her sacrifice as suicide, her ultimate act of religious error could be conflated with the witch, whose own religious error brought her, by different means, to the same fiery end—a connection made apparent in the references to and imagery of devils, demons, and fiery pits as seen above.[63] Certainly diabolical undercurrents in some accounts of sati appear to indicate a tendency to understand her actions in the context of characteristics such as women's frailty and susceptibility, which are by some observers seen to be constant, regardless of race. For others, however, the sati's action was best understood as analogous with another European practice of burning women, that of martyrdom.[64]

Out of Sheer Love: Redeeming the Sati

The Christian construction of suicide appears to leave little available scope for the redemption of a self-willed sati. It seems somewhat surprising, therefore, that it is this very image of the purely voluntary sati that also evokes the strongest expressions of admiration. Kate Teltscher has suggested that the context for the sati's reclamation lay in positioning her as a tragic heroine, within a literary tradition that allowed classical or pagan suicide to be represented outside the framework of Christian morality.[65] While there is certainly a great deal of merit in this argument, I would suggest that the basis for the sati's redemption lies primarily in the ideological space created when patriarchal ideas about femininity intersect with Christian morality about suicide. What redeems a sati is the perception that her suicide is motivated by love for her dead husband and the desire to preserve her chastity. Even within the Christian tradition, women who killed themselves to avoid dishonour were admired for their virtue rather than condemned for suicide. The fifteen-year-old St Pelagia was canonized despite throwing herself from a building to escape rape by her captors. Even the intractable St Augustine could not wholly denounce women who preserved their chastity in this way, saying, 'Who so lacks human sympathy as to refuse to pardon them?'[66] The Christian abhorrence of suicide as a mortal sin was thus juxtaposed against the patriarchal imperative for ensuring female chastity, providing a framework for a more sympathetic understanding of sati.

To fully understand the importance of this ideal of feminine chastity, or fidelity, in informing European responses to the voluntary sati, it will be useful to consider the contemporary European view of widowhood, which was in essence not so very different to Hindu ideas on the subject. Although the concept of burning widows on the death of their husbands was certainly alien to European culture—they preferred to burn women for being witches, or for professing a different faith—some of the assumptions and ideas about women, and about widows in particular, that formed the rationale for sati were common to both cultures. While the European widow did not undergo the physical deprivations and indignities inflicted on her Hindu counterpart, the idea that after her husband's death she should retire to live a chaste and quiet life, dedicated to the welfare of her children and the contemplation of God, was held up as the ideal. In *The English Gentlewoman* of 1631, Richard Braithwaite writes:

Are you widows? You deserve much honour if you be so indeed.... Great difference is there between those widows who live alone and retire themselves from public concourse and those who frequent the company of men. For a widow to love society...gives speedy wings to spreading infamy...for in such meetings she exposes her honour to danger, which above all things she ought to incomparably tender.... In popular Concourse and Court-resorts there is no place for widows.[67]

The reality of course was somewhat different, especially in London where a widow was automatically entitled to one-third of her deceased husband's estate. Under these circumstances, the wealthy widow often enjoyed a lifestyle and independence that few other circumstances would have afforded her. The issue of widow remarriage was also characterized by this divergence between ideal and reality. While high mortality rates and a low life expectancy for both men and women made remarriage for both sexes a far from uncommon occurrence,[68] the remarriage of widows was generally socially stigmatized. Referring to the remarriage of the Countess of Sunderland in 1652, her friend Dorothy Osborne commented, 'She lost by it much of the repute she had gained by keeping herself a widow.'[69] The differences between ideal and reality notwithstanding, the desirability of chastity and fidelity to the deceased husband would certainly have been a familiar concept to the European observer. It is because of her fulfilment of this ideal, in the most ultimate sense, that the sati acquires the most praise. Pietro Della Valle, for example, on seeing a potential sati parading through the streets in a prelude to being burnt, declared: 'If I can find out when it will be I will not fail to go and see her, and by my presence honour her funeral with that compassionate affection which so great conjugal fidelity and love seem to me to deserve.'[70]

The elevation of the ideal of female chastity underlies the positive representations of the voluntary sati as a form of martyrdom. The distinction between suicide and martyrdom had always been somewhat blurred in Christian ideology. Tertullian, writing in AD 200 encouraged Christian martyrs with the example of famous suicides and, although this line of thought was soon rejected, there remained ambivalence in distinguishing between suicide for honour and martyrdom for religion. In these circumstances it was possible for some observers, with their patriarchal preconceptions, to conflate martyrdom for the love of God with martyrdom for the love of the husband. Henry Lord writing in 1630, for example, tells us that the sati 'maketh herself a martyr to approve her love',[71] while Kate Teltscher points to the similarity between the account of a sati by Nicholas Witherington and the account of the martyrdom of Mistress Lewis in John Foxe's *Acts and Monuments*.[72] Similarly, the following account by English adventurer Robert Coverte makes use of imagery that would have been familiar to those living in the times of religious persecution.

...and so she was brought to the place of execution, where there was a stake, and a hole to set her feet in; and so being tied to the stake, her kindred kneeling round about her, and praying to the sun and their other idols, the fire was set to her, and she having under each arm a bag of gunpowder, and a bag betwixt her legs, and so burnt to death, the fire being made of benjamin, storax, lignomalloes and other sweet woods.[73]

The sati was not a true martyr in the Christian sense, of course, but it is not surprising that men living in or just after an era that saw the wholesale burning of heretics, both in Britain and on the Continent, could see the analogy. As late as the second half of the eighteenth century, John MacDonald could write of a sati: 'why should I think this woman has done wrong? She has done this to obtain heaven and God's favour; and have not the greatest and most learned men in England and other Christian countries done the same, who had the Bible to direct them?'[74] For MacDonald the force that motivates the sati is the same as that which motivated the martyrs, and is worthy of praise, albeit that the sati is misguided by her ignorance of the Bible. Edward Terry is more scathing in his assertion of the sati's mistake.

...many young women are ambitious to die with honor (as they esteeme it), when their fiery love brings them to the flames (as they think) of martyrdom most willingly; following their dead husbands into the fire, and there imbracing are burnt with them; but this they doe voluntary, not compelled. The parents and friends of those women will most joyfully accompanie them, and when the wood is fitted for this hellish sacrifice and begins to burne, all the people assembled shoute and make a noyse, that the screeches of this tortured creature may not bee heard. Not much unlike the custome of the Ammonites, who, when they made their children passe through the fire to Moloch, caused certain tabret or drums to sound, that their cry might not be heard (2. *Kings*. 23.10).[75]

For Terry, the pretence to martyrdom is an illusion, which he quickly reduces to the level of pagan barbarity again with his reference to the fires of Moloch. His conflation of the sati's supposed martyrdom with the more diabolical aspects of her actions is particularly informative, illustrating as it does the tension created by this key dichotomy of the early modern understanding of sati. By using the rhetoric of witchcraft and martyrdom, early modern observers subconsciously contextualized their encounter with sati within their own experience of burning women. Whether that picture be flattering or otherwise, depended on the point of view of the observer but underlying this essential dichotomy between sinner and saint is a shared assumption that sati could be understood with reference to European customs and practices, and as such was not wholly alien.

The idea of the voluntary sati as the ultimate expression of conjugal love and fidelity was also at the root of many of the more romantic interpretations of sati and was the element that most captured the imagination of many of its observers. The fact that Hindu marriages were arranged, often in early childhood, made this love all the more noteworthy as it was a situation that the European observer could well relate to. Marriages in Europe in that period, especially among the upper classes, were more often a matter of expediency than of personal choice; the Roman Catholic Church even discouraged love as a motive for marriage as it was seen to detract from the love of God. However, the Reformation and the emergence of a religious ideal that stressed the importance of the inner voice in forging relationships, both with God and with man, encouraged a trend towards romantic affection and undermined the idea that priestly celibacy was superior to married love.[76] The distant ideal of courtly love, and the prescriptions for female virtue that were embodied in the purity and self-sacrifice of Griselda and Lucretia, were by this point being tempered by more emotional and romantic representations of devotion.[77] This tendency towards the romantic can be seen in some of the more positive European responses to sati. English traveller John Ovington, for example, writing in 1689, puts forward the following quixotic explanation for sati.

...some of the Gentile Sects, before they feel any great Warmth of this amorous Passion are by their Parents joined together in their very infancy, at three or four Years of Age. From which time they endeavour mutually to kindle this tender Passion, till the growing Years blow it up into a lively Flame. And by a thousand little Tricks and Arts of Love they endeavour to stamp their Affections on their Infant Souls, which like melted wax are pliant and easy to receive the Impression, and so they are insensibly captivated by each other's Snares. The young Lover wins upon his Mistress's Passions by frequent Visits, large Presents and munificent Gifts, whilst her soft Looks and Innocent Air form his mind into kind and amorous Inclinations towards her. And thus being happily prepossessed with a mutual good liking, even as it were from the Womb, as if they had been born Lovers, they are taken off from all Objects, and freed from the disappointments of fickle Mistresses, and from being wearied with the whining Addresses of coy Damsels. Which beside other may be some of the Reason why *Indian* Wives committed themselves with so much cheerfulness into the Funeral Flames with their Dead Husbands; because their Sympathetic Minds, linked together since their Infancy, were then fed with such early Tastes of Love as became the Seminary of those strong and forcible Inclinations in their riper Years and made the Pains of Death become preferable to a life abandoned by the Society of those who they so entirely loved.[78]

This love, were it as mutual and well founded as Ovington suggests, would surely extend to the husband as well. In fact, Ovington does suggest the possibility of men performing sati, referring to the Hindu belief that suicide could be advantageous to the soul and saying that

'for this reason the loving Husband enamoured of his kind and beautiful Wife would sometimes burn himself with her in the Funeral Pile,
in expectation of a happy future Enjoyment of her.'[79] He is unusual in
suggesting that the love that supposedly motivated the sati could
extend to the husband, however. Most European observers, informed
by a cultural framework in which the ideal woman subsumes her own
existence into that of her husband, found no difficulty in conceiving
sati as a gendered response to the death of a beloved spouse.

If interest in the romantic aspects of sati could be seen as representative of changing attitudes to love and marriage in Europe, it could
also be utilized as a forum for discussing the nature of these changes
and of European women more generally. Ovington's description of
the purity of Indian love, which seemingly is nurtured until the
commission of sati, is seen as a natural outcome, and can perhaps be
read as much as a criticism of European structures (and coy damsels)
as a tribute to the Hindu system. The Dutch factor Francisco Pelsaert
also compares the sati's actions to those of European women, saying,
'Surely this is as great a love as the women of our country bear their
husbands, for the deed was done not under compulsion, but out of
sheer love.'[80] This glorification of love as a motive for sati is in striking
contrast to the popular images of the Indian women as licentious and
sexually fickle. The devotion of a sati to her husband is made all the
more noteworthy by the implicit comparison that both Pelsaert and
Ovington make between this degree of conjugal love and that which
can be expected of European women. That the Indian wife can be
capable of such an extreme display of devotion is presented as a
romanticized image that counters prevalent views of her debased
nature, but in this context it is also possible to read it as a criticism
of Western women's values: if such devotion is observable in the
degenerate Indian, how much greater is the failing of the European
woman who, in her perceived superiority of race, does not display it?
In the preface to the first printed edition of his play *Aureng-Zebe*, John
Dryden makes this comparison explicit, saying that while he 'dares
not vindicate' sati 'so neither can…[he] wholly condemn it' and commenting that:

I have made my Melesinda…a woman passionately loving of her husband,
patient of injuries and contempt, and constant in her kindness to the last;
and in this, perhaps, I may have erred, because it is not a virtue much in use.
Those Indian wives are loving fools, and may do well to keep themselves in

their own country, or at least to keep company with the Arrias and Portias of old Rome; some of our ladies know better things.[81]

Here, with piercing irony, he praises the virtues of the sati and condemns the vices of her contemporaries in Europe. At the same time, however, he also implies the context within which the sati should be viewed. Her sacrifice is noble in the setting of her own—pagan—country, or when grouped with sacrifices of the women of antiquity: whose world was also free from the constraints of Christian morality as regards this ultimate sacrifice.[82]

A Woman of Honour: Agency and Coercion in Sati

For those who did not ascribe the motive of pure love to the actions of a sati, the next variation was that of honour. Pietro Della Valle commented:

But this burning of Women upon the death of their Husbands, is at their own choice to do it or not, and indeed, very few practice it; but she who does it acquires in the Nation a glorious name of Honour and Holiness. Tis most usual among great persons, who prize Reputation at a higher rate than others do; and in the death of Personages of great quality, to whom their Wives desire to do Honour by burning themselves quick.[83]

Della Valle here continues to view sati as a purely voluntary action—it is an exceptional deed done solely to attain benefit rather than to escape misfortune. Similarly, the early seventeenth-century sailor William Hawkins states:

The custome of the Indians is to burne their dead, as you have read in other authors, and at their burning many of their wives will burne with them, because they will bee registred in their bookes for famous and most modest and loving wives, who, leaving all worldly affaires, content themselves to live no longer then their husbands.[84]

Significant here is the humanization of a sati's motives. The emphasis on conjugal devotion and the analogy with martyrdom resulted in a portrayal of the sati as almost saintly. Hawkins, while appreciating the motivating force of honour, puts a different angle on things by suggesting not that a sati is the 'most modest and loving' wife, but merely that she wishes to be remembered as such. For some the sati's actions were proof positive of her conjugal fidelity, for others a pre-meditated action performed to create a specific impression, or to achieve a specific goal, which might or might not be consistent with her behaviour during life.

Several writers of the period recognize the promises of eternal honour and bliss held out to the widow as a motivating force for sati, although they differ in how they interpret the implications of this. French jeweller and traveller Jean Baptiste Tavernier mentions:

Besides that, the Bramins make them believe that in dying after that manner, they shall revive again with him in another world, with more honour and more advantages than they enjoyed before. These are the motives that persuade women to burn with their husbands; besides that the priests flatter them with hope that while they are in the midst of the flames, before they expire, Ram will appear and reveal wonderful visions to them; and that after their souls have transmigrated into various bodies, they shall at length obtain a high degree of honour to eternity.[85]

Tavernier clearly implies that this belief is false, but also recognizes its power of attraction. For him, posthumous benefit in another world and honour in this one are bribes held out to encourage the wavering soul. His contemporary, Francois Bernier, on the other hand inverts this view—for him the sati is blackmailed by the threat of honour withheld:

Many persons who I then consulted on the subject would fain have persuaded me that an excess of affection was the cause why these women burn themselves with their deceased husbands; but I soon found that this abominable practice is the effect of early and deeply rooted prejudices. Every girl is taught by her mother that it is virtuous and laudable in a wife to mingle her ashes with those of her husband, and that no woman of honour will refuse compliance with the established custom.[86]

For Bernier, the sati does not freely choose a course that will bring her merit, but is conditioned to believe that it is the only course that will avoid demerit. The dire consequences of not performing sati are recognized by Bernier as an insidious form of coercion, but not all observers saw it as such. The Dutch factor, Francisco Pelsaert, denied the existence of such pressure altogether. Having extolled the primacy of love as the motivating force behind sati, he goes on to say, 'At the same time there are hundreds, or even thousands, who do not do it, and there is no such reproach as is asserted by many that those who neglect it incur the reproach of their caste.'[87] Pelsaert is unusual in his outright rejection of the element of duress in the act. However, the majority of observers appear to have recognized both a degree of agency and a degree of coercion. Indeed, the very fact that Pelsaert felt the need to make his rejection of coercion explicit suggests that he recognized the existence of doubt in this head.

For those who did recognize a degree of coercion, its nature and extent was the subject of differing interpretations. Albert de Mandelslo follows Della Valle and Hawkins in ascribing free choice to the practice of sati, but in the same sentence touches on the very circumstance that negates the idea of pure volition:

I say this obligation of dying with their husband was imposed only on those women who stood upon a reputation of honesty, yet so as they were engaged thereto only by a principle of honour, there not being any punishment to be inflicted on such as refused to follow them on that dreadful journey, other than that they were not admitted to the company of persons of quality, as being looked on as infamous women.[88]

Mandelslo here devalues the punitive nature of the treatment of widows, reducing the severity of its dictates in the eyes of his readers with the casual nature of his reference to it; seemingly he is able to reconcile in his own mind the freedom of choice and the punishment for nonconformity.

This concern with the coalescent nature of apparent free agency and implied coercion featured in many of the early accounts of sati. Concern with the widow as the central actor in the drama of sati created space in this period for a much clearer and less cluttered appreciation of the human motivations at work than was possible in the early nineteenth century, when concern over sati was shifted into the public realm and the experience of the individual became submerged in a legalistic reinterpretation of the rite itself.[89] Indeed, the suggestion that the degraded status of the widow who did not commit sati acted as an incentive for sati, foreshadows the late nineteenth-century feminist arguments and remains an important aspect of the feminist debate on sati today.[90] In the early modern period, however, the austerities imposed upon the widow were not conceived to totally negate the possibility of free will in the widow's choice, as they were in later feminist constructions, but were rather seen as coexisting in an uneasy relationship with it, the dynamics of which were the source of some consideration. When Caesar Frederick comments 'when there is any Noble man or woman dead, they burne their bodies: and if a married man die, his wife must burne herselfe alive, for the love of her husband, and with the body of her husband',[91] he implies both the motivation of love and the implied coercion of 'must'. Pietro Della Valle, an ardent admirer of the conjugal devotion of the sati, is more direct in recognizing the coercive potential of societal expectation. He comments:

Nevertheless,' tis possible too that many Widows being in the height of their passion taken at their word by their kindred who desire it, go to it afterwards with an ill will, not daring to deny those who exhort them thereunto, especially if being obliged by their word; nor to discover their own mind freely to the Governor, things, which amongst Women, through their natural fearfulness and modesty, easily happen. And I would to God that in our Countries, in sundry cases, as of marrying or not, and the like matters, we had not frequent examples which Woman not seldom give of great resolutions, not forc'd in appearance, but indeed too much forc'd in reality, for avoiding displeasure and other inconveniences.[92]

For Della Valle the inherent nature of woman, which he conceives as being shared by women across the globe, makes her susceptible to outside pressure and negates her ability to exercise her free will in the face of societal pressure. Despite his assumptions about female frailty, Della Valle here shows an unusual flash of insight into the dynamics of a decision to commit sati that may appear wholly voluntary on the surface. Unfortunately, he does not allow this insight to inform his own reaction to a sati, but, as we have seen, rather reverts to lauding her conjugal fidelity instead of considering a bravery of another kind— the stoic acceptance of what society forces upon her.

The Basest Slave: Sati and Widowhood

The European understanding of the forces acting on the widow was not clearcut during this period. Assessments of the level of coercion present vary between accounts, but a recurrent theme is the juxtaposition between the honoured sati and the ascetic widow. European understanding of the nature and severity of impositions on the widow differ. Mandelslo, as we have seen, sees the social stigma attached to surviving the husband as barely a punishment at all, but others repre-

sent it as a tangible retribution for failing to comply with socially
expected norms. The dramatic foil to the heroic sati is the widow
who, having failed to comply with expectations, is despised for her
failure and marked out by physical signs. East India Company surgeon
John Fryer, writing in the late seventeenth century, states:

> Those who have buried their husbands, or rather burned them, are rifled of
> all their jewels, and shaved, always wearing a red lungy, whereby to be
> known that they have not undergone the conflagration; for which cause
> they are despised, and live more uncomfortably than the meanest servant.[93]

For many, but not all, European observers in this period, sati was seen as
normative and ascetic widowhood as punitive: not a removal of choice, but
retribution for making the wrong one. Robert Corverte tells us:

Fig. 4. Illustration from Francois Bernier, *Histoire de la dernier revolution des
Etats du Gran Mogol* (Paul Marrat: Amsterdam, 1699), facing p. 113. By
permission of the British Library, 673. a 18.

The Pythagoreans in former times...had a law that when the husband died the wife should also be burnt, which is holden till this day, though not in so strict a manner; for now she may refuse it, but then her head is shaved and she is clad in a black vesture or garment, which among them is reputed most vile and hateful; that the basest slave in the country will not succour or relieve her, though she should starve.[94]

Similarly Duarte Barbosa observed, 'All perform this in general, and if any women do not choose to do this, their relations take them, shave their heads, and turn them out of their houses and families in disgrace. And so they wander through the world as lost ones.'[95] He implicitly suggests the severity of widowhood when he refers to the widows as 'lost ones', a phrase that has unmistakable resonances with 'lost souls'. By echoing the terminology usually used to refer to suicides (whose souls were perceived in popular European culture to be restless and prone to nightly wanderings[96]), he makes a number of interlocking suggestions. He removes the widow from the interactive world of the living and places her within a purgatory of living death, thus implicitly recognizing the complete negation of the 'self' in-volved in ascetic widowhood. Moreover, he suggests the nature of the non-choice presented to the widow: physical death (and in the Chris-tian conception eternal spiritual damnation), or a living death involv-ing social and ritual damnation. The widow, it seems, commits suicide whatever choice she makes.

For the above observers, sati is deemed normative and ascetic widowhood viewed as a punishment for failing to comply with expec-tations. Others, however, viewed the rigours of widowhood as the cause, rather than the effect, of sati. Tavernier, for example, writes:

It is also an ancient custom among the Indians that the husband happening to die, the wife can never marry again. So that as soon as the man is dead, the wife retires to bewail her husband; some days after that they shave off her hair; she lays aside all ornaments of her apparel; she takes from her arms and legs the bracelets her husband put on when he espoused her, in token of her submission and of her being chained to him: and all the rest of her life she lives slighted and despised, and in a worse condition than a slave in the very house where she was mistress before. This unfortunate condition makes them hate life so that they rather choose to be burned alive with the body of their deceased husband than live in the scorn and contempt of the world.[97]

In doing so he comes very close to later interpretations of the causes of sati. The variation in interpretations of cause and effect in understanding the widow's motivation is a recurrent anomaly in the European understanding of sati. By the nineteenth century, the majority of observers tended to take Tavernier's position and viewed sati as an exceptional act of desperation borne out of reprehensible societal subjugation of the widow. In this earlier period, however, the majority of observers appear to have viewed sati as normative (even while accepting that only a minority had the supposed courage to carry it through to its fatal conclusion) and ascetic widowhood as a form of punishment for noncompliance; a perspective that is perhaps indicative of an attitude to women that constructed their virtue primarily in terms of their relationship to men.

Never Known of Man: Sati and Sexuality

Tavernier, above, directly relates the indignities inflicted on the widow to the interdiction against widow remarriage. The double standard that allows a husband the freedom to remarry but denies the same to the wife is repeatedly stated, though unsurprisingly it is rarely condemned in itself. Rather, it was the severity with which the rule was applied and the practical and moral outcome of a surplus of unmarried females that evoked a response. As we have already seen, the European construction of ideal behaviour for a widow was not so very different from Hindu prescriptions, except in the degree to which it was enforced and the severity of its dictates. While the degree of degradation to which the widow was subject was the source of censure, it is also clear that concerns about the widow's conduct were understood and appreciated. English traveller William Methold comments:

If the husband dieth, the wife may not marry again, and which is most unreasonable not the young ones though never known of man, who happening to be widows in their infancy, must not only continue so, but be made the drudge to the whole Family, not permitted to wear their Jewels, good or clean clothes, or upon occasion to go abroad (at least upon pleasure) & this with most of them, together with a reverend respect they bear to the reputation of their house, mortifies them after a strange manner, yet some it cannot contain, but they fly out, & forsaking their father's house, brand it with a lasting obloquy by their looser lives, keeping themselves at a distance, for if conveniently their kindred would poison them.[98]

Methold here picks up on the important issue of the widow's sexuality and how to control it. He recognizes that the rationale behind the austerities imposed on the widow is to 'contain' her and thus prevent her bringing shame on her family by forming a second alliance. That woman's flawed nature would not be equal to the constraints of chastity is an idea shared by both Europeans and Hindus in this period. Both cultures believed that woman's sexuality is stronger and more capricious than man's and the image of the lusty widow was a stock stereotype in the European arsenal of women's depravity. There was a shared belief that a widow, having been initiated into the joys of the flesh, would be unable to control herself, should the opportunity arise to experience them again (men of both cultures obviously having a very high opinion of their collective prowess). The concern that widows were behaving in an unseemly manner is what prompted Richard Braithwaite to advise against them frequenting court-resorts, but it was also beginning to inspire more liberal souls to look more favourably on remarriage as a means of normalizing sexual behaviour. Methold's disapprobation of the ban on widow remarriage is expressed in terms of the severity of its implementation—even young widows who have not yet become sexually active were subject to it—rather than with the principle of fidelity to the dead husband itself. In the latter respect, the framework of interpretation, if not the conclusion drawn from it, is not dissimilar to that which informs the Hindu position on the matter. Pietro Della Valle exhibits the same concern when he writes:

When the Wife dyes, they marry another if they please; but if the husband dye, the woman never marries more; were she so minded, nor could she find any of her race who would take her, because she would be accounted as very bad as infamous for desiring second Marriage. A very hard Law indeed, and from which infinite inconveniences arise; for not a few young Widows, who in regard of their Reputation cannot marry again, and have not the patience to live chastly, commit disorders in private, especially with men of other Nations and Religions, and with any they find, provided it be secret.[99]

The widow is not expected to be able to maintain her chastity and so remains a constant threat of sexual impropriety to her family. John Fryer makes the choice between chastity-ensuring death and the lapse into sexual immorality explicit when he comments that '...in the husband's flames the wife offers herself a sacrifice to his manes, or else she shaves and turns whore for her livelihood, none of her friends looking upon her.'[100] The sati then represents one extreme of female behaviour, the widow-turned whore the other.

In their concern for the chastity, or lack thereof, of the widow, the European observers were finding analogies with their own ideas about female nature and attempting to explain sati in familiar terms. They were also reintroducing the issue of sex into the discussion of sati. The act of immolation, the complete negation of the physical, and therefore the sexual, self, has thus far been represented in asexual terms. Indeed, Kate Teltscher points to sati as the only instance in which European men do not represent Indian women primarily in terms of their sexuality.[101] I would argue that European concern with the widow's potential for impropriety makes it clear that this asexuality is achieved only through the physical negation of the natural sexuality deemed intrinsic to her gender, regardless of race. As Lucy Hughes-Hallett points out, for European men of this period, 'The only good woman is a chaste woman, and the only chaste woman is a dead one.'[102]

The Violence of Others: The Use of Physical Force

The great merit that the sati bestowed upon her family, combined with the economic burden the widow represented and the fear that she might be the cause of dishonour, meant that it could be in a family's interest to see sati occur. Early modern observers certainly recognized the existence of forms of coercion that went beyond societal pressure. Manucci, for example, succinctly marries the attraction of personal honour with the threat of physical force when he notes:

The Hindus think so highly of those who are burnt in this way that they assert their reincarnation as goddesses in the heaven of Vishnu. This is done equally for the husband. They assume that men blessed with wives of such great virtue as to sacrifice their life for their honour, must without fail be placed among the gods. But if any wife be found to have a greater love for life than for honour, her relations do not leave her to enjoy it for very long, for they throw her into the fire by force, where she ends by undergoing the same suffering without acquiring the same laudations. Thus it is much better for them to endure this hard penalty with firmness and equanimity than to be subjected to it by the violence of others.[103]

European understanding of the reasons for and timing of the use of physical force was varied. Some apparently believed that sati was essential for the honour of the deceased, and so would be insisted upon from the outset, by fair means or foul. Manucci states: 'Among the caste of Rajahs it is imperative that on the husband's death the wife be burnt alive with the body, for should regard for her own honour even not force her to this act, the relations will force her to it, it being an inviolate custom of their caste.'[104] Here the rite is insisted on from the start and if necessary the entire affair coerced. More common in the European reports, however, is the application of force to prevent a widow retracting an originally voluntary intention at the last minute. Tavernier, for example, suggests that narcotics are employed to prevent the widow recoiling at the sight of the flames, saying:

The Bramins that accompany her exhort her to give public testimonies of her constancy and courage: and many of our Europeans are of the opinion, that to take away the fears of death that naturally terrify humanity, the priests do give her a certain beverage to stupefy and disorder the senses, which takes from her all apprehension of her preparations for death.[105]

Several years before they outlawed the custom completely, the British would prohibit the use of drugs in the ceremony, animated by this image of the intoxicated widow being hurried senseless to her death. Some earlier observers interpreted the use of drugs differently, however, seeing it rather as a choice made by the widow to alleviate the suffering that she has herself elected to undergo. Mandelslo explains the fortitude of the widow thus:

She was not above 20 years of age, yet we saw her come to the place of her execution with so much confidence and a cheerfulness so extraordinary to those who go to present and inevitable death, that I was much inclined to believe that she had dulled her senses with a dose of opium, which is as commonly used in India as in Persia.[106]

The agency that many early modern observers ascribed to the widow in choosing sati, something often denied her by later interpretations of the rite, meant that they could also ascertain her agency in the use of what would later be unambiguously deemed the implements of coercion.

For some, then, the widow having chosen sati makes prior arrangements to preclude the possibility of dishonouring herself when faced with the flames. This is the exception, however, and once the ceremony began the impetus for ensuring its completion was usually shifted from the widow to the family. Della Valle reports:

...divers men stand about the pile with staves in their hands to stir the fire, and to pour liquors on it to make it burn faster; and that if they should see the Woman offer to come out, or avoid the flames, they would knock her on the head with their staves and kill her, or else beat her back into the fire; because 'twould be a great shame to the Woman and all her kindred, if she should go to be burned, and then through fear of the fire and death, repent and come out of it.[107]

In this representation, though the widow makes the initial decision, her family then constrains her to honour it by the threat of physical force.

This image of the widow being forcibly burned against her will underpins a recurring theme in the European image of sati—the rescue fantasy. Gayatri Spivak encapsulates the idea in a sentence, saying, 'White men are saving brown women from brown men.'[108] Later this idea would provide moral impetus to the campaign to outlaw sati legally. In this earlier period, it could only be realized by personal intervention. The following account by Manucci is a classic example:

During my stay in Agrah, I went one day to make an excursion into the country on horseback, in the company of a young Armenian. We came to where a Hindu woman had just begun to move round her pyre, which was already blazing; she rested her eyes upon us, as if she appealed to us for help. The Armenian asked if I would join him in saving the woman from death. I said I would. Seizing our swords, and our servants doing the same, we charged with our horses into the midst of the crowd looking on, shouting 'Mata! Mata! (Kill! Kill!), whereat the Brahmins being frightened, all took flight and left the woman unguarded. The Armenian laid hold of her, and making her mount behind him, carried her off. Subsequently having had her baptised, he married her. When I passed through Surat I found her living there with her son, and she returned me many thanks for the benefit done to her.[109]

This account incorporates all the conventional constituents of the rescue fantasy. The woman makes an appeal for help, albeit an implied one. The virile Europeans frighten off the craven Brahmins without recourse to actual violence, the woman is rescued from the flames, married (thus also saved from her own uncontrolled sexuality) and converted to Christianity (the ultimate form of salvation). Finally the moral rectitude of the European intervention is affirmed by the grateful thanks of the intended victim.

Not all intended rescues fitted this pattern so neatly. In a period before colonial domination had been implemented, the 'virile' European was not always in a position to intervene. Bernier recounts the following obviously coerced sati.

At Lahore I saw the most beautiful young widow sacrificed, who could not, I think, have been more than twelve years of age. The poor little creature appeared more dead than alive as she approached the dreadful pit: the agony of her mind cannot be described; she trembled and wept bitterly; but three or four of the Brahmans, assisted by an old woman, who held her under the arm, forced the unwilling victim towards the fatal spot, seated her on the wood, tied her hands and feet, lest she should run away, and in that situation the innocent creature was burned alive. I found it difficult to repress my feelings and to prevent their bursting forth into clamorous and unavailing rage; but restrained by prudential considerations, I contented myself with silently lamenting the abominable superstition of these people....[110]

Bernier excuses his presence at such a reprehensible event by emphasizing his instinctive impulse to intervene. At the same time, however, he explicitly recognizes his own impotence in the situation. He can only recover his potency by asserting his superior morality over the surrounding Brahmins. Bernier's sense of impotence in the face of sati is mirrored more than a century later in the accounts of British observers who were prevented from intervening by the government's instructions on sati. Thus, although the rescue fantasy was on the surface a classic example of European masculinity and potency comparing favourably with Indian effeminacy and barbarity, in reality the failure to act often reaffirmed individual powerlessness. Even when Europeans did seek to intervene physically in events, they sometimes found their interference unwanted. William Methold recounts the story of an English factor who attempted to rescue a sati having

...espied not far out of his way a concourse of people unto whom he made, and being come near he was informed by his Servants that it was a woman about to burn with her dead husband: he presently drawing his Sword rode in amongst them, whereupon they all fled but the woman her self, whom he persuaded to live, promising to secure her against her friends, if their importunities had wrought her to this course: but she besought him not to interrupt her, it was her own most earnest desire, wherein we did constantly persist, whereupon he put up, and her friends came in, and presently in his sight with the like ceremony and duty formerly recited; she became the same ashes with him, to whom she had been one flesh.[111]

Here the factor was prevented in his intentions not by physical impotency, but by the will of the widow herself. In this variation, Spivak's 'brown woman' needs saving not from brown men, but from herself—a feat which European men were not yet always arrogant enough to attempt.

The strength of the widow's desire to perform sati was put forward as confounding not only individual European observers, but also the Mughal governors. The Mughal rulers during this period followed a policy on sati not dissimilar to that that was to be adopted by the British in the years before their abolition of the custom. Tavernier notes that

...there is no woman who can burn her husband's body, till she has leave of the Governor of the place where she inhabits, who being a Mahumetan, and abhorring that execrable custom of self murder, is very shy to permit them. Besides, there are none but widows that have no children, which lie under the reproach that forces them to a violent death. For as for the widows that have children, they are by no means permitted to burn themselves; but quite the contrary, they are commanded to live for the education of their children....[112]

The Muslim rulers, while not abolishing the custom outright, regulated it and attempted to ensure that the sati was voluntary and that certain conditions were met, while also trying to prevent the immolation by means of persuasion. Although the British later conspicuously shied away from actually granting permission, for fear that this would be read as tacit approval of the rite, a sati had by law to be reported so that government officials could be present to ascertain the validity of the voluntary act.

The emphasis placed on the widow's determination in the early modern period was in striking contrast to the early nineteenth-century interpretation of her as a passive victim. In these earlier accounts, far from being stripped of all agency, the widow's determination sometimes bordered on the supernatural. Tavernier, for example, reports:

I observed a strange passage at Patna, being then with the Governor, a young gentleman of about twenty-four years of age, in his own house. While I was with him, in came a young woman, very handsome, and not above two and twenty years old, who desired leave of the Governor to be burned with the body of her deceased husband. The Governor compassionating her youth and beauty, endeavoured to divert her from her resolution; but finding he could not prevail, with a surly countenance he asked her whether she understood what a torment the fire was, and whether she had ever burned her fingers? No, no, answered she more stoutly than before, I do not fear fire, and to let you know as much, send for a lighted torch, hither. The Governor, abominating her answer, in great passion bid her go to the devil. Some young lords that were with the Governor, desired him to try the woman, and to call for a torch; which with much ado he did, and a lighted torch was brought. As soon as the woman saw the lighted torch coming, she ran to meet it, and held her hand in the flame, not altering her countenance in the least; still searing her arm along to the very elbow, till her flesh looked as though it had been broiled; whereupon the Governor commanded her out of his sight.[113]

Hindu tradition suggests that the true sati, divinely inspired, does not feel the torment of the flames (and thus also, one would think, would not need the assistance of narcotics) and this story, as well as those which recount the sati's patient tolerance on the pyre, perhaps draw on this idea. It is significant that while the British accounts of the early nineteenth century suppress almost all suggestion of the widow's agency, the emphasis on both her willingness and on the supernatural aspects of the sacrifice that appear in some of these earlier accounts remerge in the later nineteenth century when the British come to deal with the question of sati in Rajasthan. Perhaps then the view of the sati as passive victim that predominated in the early nineteenth century and which has informed Western interpretations of the rite in modern times was not actually representative of Western ideas on sati, but rather was an atypical construction—the product of a specific historical juncture and its imperatives.

Poisoners and Paramours: Explaining Sati

Because of the nature of the narratives they appeared in, European interpretations of sati in this period tended to concentrate on eyewitness accounts and rarely ventured into any extended discussion of the theoretical or ideological basis for sati. When early modern observers did seek to explain the sati's motivations it was usually in terms of sociological factors rather than religious principles. Whether she is lauded or condemned and whether her actions are viewed as the result of her own autonomous agency, coercion, or a combination of both, it is the socio-cultural aspects of sati that are discussed in detail. This lack of concern with the religious aspects of the rite is perhaps one of the most striking ways in which these accounts differ from later interpretations of sati. As we have seen, there was a general under- standing that sati bestowed religious merit and honour on the de- ceased, the widow and their families. But this was a relatively generalized conception in comparison to the detailed discussion of the immediate social causes of the rite. Bernier, for example, is un- usual when he tells us that the Muslim rulers did not intervene further because, '…it is part of their policy to leave the idolatrous population, which is so much more numerous than their own, in the free exercise of their religion',[114] as it had not been the common practice up to this point to refer to sati specifically as a religious rite. Bernier here attributes to the Muslim rulers the same concerns that were later to so impede British attempts to outlaw the custom. Indeed, the logic is so similar that the passage might have been taken from nineteenth- century parliamentary papers on the subject. In both cases, a powerful minority's hand was stayed by fear of provoking the majority popula- tion by attacking what was deemed to be their dearest institution: religion. This position is representative of ideas that would emerge with more force in the eighteenth century as a new construction of sati, as a religious issue came to the fore.

The relative lack of a religious context in understanding sati in this earlier period is particularly clearly illustrated by the widely prevail- ing view, expressed over and over again in these narratives, that the practice of burning widows originated in a desire to prevent other women from poisoning their husbands. This (highly misogynistic) explanation dates back to the Greek encounter with sati and can be found in the accounts of Strabo. It achieved almost universal accep- tance among the writers of this period and appears repeatedly, in slightly varying forms, in narrative after narrative. John Huygen van Linschoten deals with the issue at some length, saying:

The first cause why the women were burnt with their husbands, was (as the Indians themselves do say), that in time past the women, as they are very lecherous and inconsistent both by nature and complexion, did poyson many of their husbands, when they thought it good (as they are likewise very expert in) thereby to have the better means to fulfil their lusts. Which the King perceiving, and that thereby his principal Lords, Captains and soldiers, which upheld his estate and kingdom, were so consumed and brought unto their endes by the wicked practices of women, sought as much as he might to hinder the same: and there upon he made a law and ordeyned, that when the dead bodies of the men were burned, they should also burn their wives with them, thereby to put them in fear, and so make them abstain from poysoning of their husbands: which at the first was very sharply executed, only upon the nobles, soldiers, as also the Bramenes (for that the common people must bear no arms, but are in a manner like slaves). So that in the end it became a custom among them, and so continueth: at this day they observe it as a part of their law and ceremonies of their devilish idols, and now they do it willingly, being heartened and strengthened thereunto by their friends.[115]

The motivation for instigating the custom of sati is here defined in secular terms, an issue of crime and punishment that has mutated into a religious tradition. Of course, it is hardly surprising that no attempt should be made to uncover the scriptural origins of sati by European travellers at this time. Very few had more than a smattering of pidgin Hindi and the Hindu scriptures were not easily available for study by non-Brahmins. Even so, it seems incredible that this explanation should be so widely believed. Even Henry Lord, whose account of religion of the 'Banians' was supposedly based on a study of Hindu texts undertaken with the help of an interpreter, falls back on the Classical explanation of the custom's origins, saying:

But though Propertius makes this to be a witness to their conjugal fidelity, yet Strabo makes the ground thereof to be the Indian women's disloyalty to their husbands; who in former times by secret means untimely poisoned them to enjoy their paramours. The Rajahs therefore to restrain this practice did procure the Brahmins to make it an act of religion to interdict second marriages to the women; and that after the decease of the husband, the woman should no longer survive, that so they might become more careful of their preservation. The chaster sort, to gain honour from the infamy cast upon their sex, did by voluntary sufferance remove all superstition of such machination of evil, since they were so ready to cope with the terror of death, to confirm their love....[116]

The widespread acceptance of this quite unfeasible story of the origin of sati requires some explanation. As we have already commented, it would have been difficult for Europeans to garner any authentic historical or scriptural material on the custom (this breakthrough belonged to the late eighteenth century). Moreover, the classical authors still enjoyed a considerable degree of authority in this period, but for this basically unsupported story to be so widely accepted at a time when other assumptions were being tested by personal experience, there must have been aspects of it that appealed to the European imagination. Perhaps the most striking feature is its blatant misogynism, as it accepts as inconvertible truth the idea that women are wicked and licentious. Thomas Herbert is a fine exponent of this chauvinistic point of view, claiming that sati was

...a just revenge, for their [wives'] former too much abused liberty, growne so audaciously impudent, that upon the least distaste nothing but the harmlesse lives of their too much loving Husbandes, would satiate their lustful boldness, procured by poison, till by Parliament this course was taken (to burn their wives with their dead bodies) to secure themselves from future dangers.[117]

Herbert is perhaps the most direct in his inversion of the ideal of the pure and virtuous sati. Under his interpretation, the rite becomes an emblem for female incontinence. The roles of oppressor and oppressed are inverted and the Hindu female becomes the perpetrator of violence while the 'too much loving Husbandes' are portrayed as the passive victims. Even in the passing of the law that condemns women to burn, whether guilty of murder or not, the figure of the husband is exonerated of all blame. It is the 'Parliament' who hands down the law and while it is safe to assume that this 'Parliament' would have been understood as a male-dominated power structure, still the dispensation of this tough 'justice' is depersonalized and distanced from the supposed figure of the long-suffering husband.

In today's gender-conscious environment, with the experience of 400 years of writings on sati that would serve to effectively turn this consideration on its head, it seems incredible that such an explanation should be either tendered or believed. To the English observer of the period it must have had a certain familiarity, however. Certainly there were aspects of this interpretation that would have struck a chord with the sixteenth- or seventeenth-century male. The English law of that period held a husband's power over his wife to be almost feudal in nature and the wife who murdered her husband, like the servant who turned on his master, was deemed guilty of treason and subject to the most extreme form of the death penalty then available—being burnt alive. As Kate Teltscher puts it, 'The belief in sati as a penalty for

husband murdering is a satisfying interpretation for the European
mind: it explains a disturbing rite in familiar terms of crime and
punishment and coincides with the Christian sense of the sinfulness
of women.'[118] For those who subscribed to the idea that women were
essentially fallen and sinful, the courage, devotion, and self-sacrifice
perceived in the sati was an anomaly best explained not as a result of
her inherent virtue, but as a punishment for her inherent vice. Europeans in this period did not have the resources to search for culturally
specific origins of sati (an issue which is still perplexing historians),
so rather chose to adopt a classical explanation that at once fitted with
their assumptions about women in general and about Indian women
in particular and allowed them to negate the 'virtue' of the sati, whose
action might otherwise be used to make unflattering comparisons
with European women's devotion to their husbands.

The tensions apparent in a body of writing that view the sati at once
as diabolical suicide, martyr, devoted wife, and licentious murderer
suggest that European attempts to understand sati in this period were
not entirely preconditioned by a consistent set of assumptions about
the nature of Hindus. Rather, these observers were trying to find ways
of interpreting the customs of this strange new land through familiar
frameworks. The diversity of both texts and travellers during this
period meant that the analogies that they chose to make, and the moral
value that they placed upon them, differed widely and depended very
much on personal subjectivity. Underlying these variations, however,
are areas of similarity in terms of the tendency to view the widow as
central to the rite and to understand it in terms of sociological forces
that could be contrasted, if not conflated, with European ideas. Thus,
while sati was overtly projected as an example of Indian 'difference',
the ways in which European observers attempt to explain the rite
suggests a tendency to understand it through the location of similarity
with their own societies. Far from constructing India as fundamentally 'other', their attempts to interpret sati through the framework of
their own cultural understanding suggests that they viewed Indian
society more as a mutation or variation of their own, rather than
something diametrically opposed to it. This is not, of course, to
suggest that this early period of interaction with India was entirely
free from either the imperatives of power, or the influence of essen-
tialism and racism, but rather that these imperatives of difference,
even at this early stage, were cross-cut by what has been referred to
as the 'construction of affinities.'[119] Of course, the heterogeneity of the

early modern response and the concentration on equivalences was to a great extent the product of the circumstances in which these accounts were produced, when knowledge of India was both sporadic and informal, based primarily on individual interpretation. As both the political position of Europeans in India and their knowledge of it became more formalized and coherent in the eighteenth century, so to did the prevalent understanding of sati become more homogenous, as an understanding based on the essential nature of Hindus and their religion began to take precedence over the multifaceted socio-cultural imperatives that informed this earlier period.

Notes

1. Cited in A. Sharma, *Sati*, pp. 2–3.
2. William Methold, 'Relations Of The Kingdom Of Golchonda', in Samuel Purchas, *Purchas His Pilgrimage Or Relations Of The World And The Religions Observed In All Ages And Places Discovered From The Creation Unto This Present* (London: William Stansby For Henrie Fetherstone, 1626), p. 1001.
3. Travellers of this period came from a variety of countries including England, Scotland, France, Germany, Holland, Spain, Portugal, Italy, and even Iceland.
4. English awareness of a semi-mythical land from which they purchased spices and other commodities via their trading links with the Levant is thought to pre-date the Celtic invasions. R.C. Prasad, *Early English Travellers in India* (Delhi: Motilal Banarsidass, 1965), p. xix.
5. Thomas Metcalfe, *Ideologies of the Raj* (Cambridge: Cambridge University Press, 1998), p. 4.
6. For more on India as the possible location of Paradise, see John Drew, *India and the Romantic Imagination* (New Delhi: Oxford University Press, 1987).
7. Polo's narrative is by no means free from romantic interpolations itself, although many of these were thought to be the work of his editor, Rustichello of Pisa, who seemingly could not resist the urge to conform to romantic literary convention. For more on early interpretations of the East, see M.B. Campbell, *The Witness and the Other World: Exotic European Travel Writing 400–1600 AD* (Ithaca: Cornell University Press, 1988).
8. Marco Polo, *The Travels of Marco Polo*, vol. 2 (London: John Murray, 1875), p. 325.
9. Odorico da Pordenone, 'The Journal Of Friar Odoric', in A.W. Pollard (ed.), *The Travels of Sir John Mandeville* (London: Macmillan, 1900), p. 332.

10. This explanation is not as simplistic as it may seem, as early twentieth-century historians and anthropologists would come to associate the earliest origins of sati with prehistoric death rites that supplied the dead man with things he might need in the next life—wealth, horses, wives, etc.

11. This description appeared in *Bengal Past and Present* on the sale of the document at Sotherby's in 1930. It is cited in O.P. Kejariwal, *The Asiatic Society of Bengal and the Discovery of India's Past* (New Delhi: Oxford University Press, 1988), p. 9.

12. John Mandeville, *The Travels And Voyages Of Sir John Mandeville* (London: J. Osborne, 1700), p. 82.

13. Cited in J. Winter Jones (ed.), *Travellers in Disguise* (Cambridge, Mass.: Harvard University Press, 1963), p. 28.

14. It is out of the fragmentation of the Reformation and the Counter-Reformation that the impulse to proselytizing and the necessity to convert the heathen first emerges—a form of religious mercantilism that was used to justify the forcible conquests, conversions, and confiscation of wealth.

15. Barbara Korte, *English Travel Writing* (Basingstoke: Macmillan, 2000), p. 6.

16. In William Foster (ed.), *Early Travels in India, 1583–1619* (London: Oxford University Press, 1921), p. 14.

17. Arnold Wright as cited in Prasad, *Early English Travellers*, p. 31.

18. Ibid.

19. Korte, *English Travel Writing*, p. 6.

20. Jenny Mezciems, "'Tis Not to Divert the Reader': Moral and Literary Determinants in Some Early Travel Narratives', in P. Dodds (ed.), *The Art of Travel* (London: Frank Cass, 1982), p. 1.

21. Ibid., p. 3.

22. W.T. Jewkes, 'The Literature of Travel and the Mode of Romance in the Renaissance', in W.G. Rice (ed.) *Literature as a Mode of Travel* (New York: New York Public Library, 1963), p. 14.

23. Charles Dellon, *A Voyage To The East Indies* (London: Roper, T. Leigh, D. Browne, A. 1698), p. 49.

24. J.A. Mandelslo, 'The Voyages And Travels Of J. Albert De Mandelslo Into The East Indies 1638–40', in Adam Olearius (ed.), *Voyages And Travels Of The Ambassadors* (London: John Starkey and Thomas Basset, 1669), p. 31.

25. Francois Bernier, *Travels In The Mogul Empire, AD 1656–1668* (Delhi: S. Chand and Co., 1969), p. 311.

26. In this story, a widow, having murdered her husband in favour of her lover, is jilted by the lover and so commits sati. At the last moment she pulls the lover with her into the flames.

27. Niccolao Manucci, *Storia Do Mogor, Or Mogul India, 1653–1708* ed. W. Irvine (Calcutta: Indian Edition, 1966), vol. 2, p. 89.
28. Bernier, *Travels,* p. 306.
29. Mandelslo, *Voyages And Travels*, p. 31.
30. Duarte Barbosa, *A Description of the Coasts of East Africa and Malabar in the Beginning of the Sixteenth Century* (New York: Johnston, 1970), p. 92.
31. Manucci, *Storia Do Mogor*, vol. 3, p. 62.
32. Barbosa, *Description*, p. 93.
33. Mandelslo, *Voyages And Travels*, p. 31.
34. Jean Baptiste Tavernier, *Tavernier's Travels In India, 1676* (Calcutta: Bangabasi, 1905), p. 410.
35. Bernier, *Travels,* pp. 312–13.
36. Nicolas Witherington, 'A Brief Discoverye Of Some Things Best Worth Noteinge In The Travells Of Nicholas Witherington', in *A Journey Overland From The Gulf Of Honduras To The Great South Sea Performed By John Cockburn And Five Other Englishmen* (London: C. Rivington, 1735), p. 315.
37. See Mani, *Contentious Traditions*.
38. Pietro Della Valle, *The Travels Of Pietro Della Valle In India*, E. Grey and G. Havers (eds) (New Delhi: Asian Educational Services, 1991), p. 267.
39. See Teltscher, *India Inscribed: European and British Writing on India, 1600–1800* (New Delhi: Oxford University Press, 1995).
40. Edward Terry, 'A Voyage To East India' in William Foster (ed.), *Early Travels In India, 1583–1619* (London: Oxford University Press, 1921), p. 328.
41. St Augustine considers the implications of suicide at length in his *City of God Against the Pagans*, written in *c.* AD 410, and declares it to be a sin. See *City of God*, Book 1 (Harmondsworth: Penguin Books, 1972).
42. Cited in Lucy Hughes-Hallet, *Cleopatra: Histories, Dreams, Distortions* (London: Pimlico, 1990), p. 153.
43. Both these pictures, as well as the reading of them as representing the descent into hell, appear in Teltscher, *India Inscribed*, pp. 56–9.
44. Her nakedness, of course, almost certainly owed a lot to 'artistic impression'!
45. Abbe Carre, *The Travels of Abbe Carre in India and the Near East, 1672–1674,* C. Fawcett (ed.), (New Delhi: Asian Educational Services, 1990).
46. Quoted in Teltscher, *India Inscribed*, p. 56.
47. Not only did contemporary European ideas about the diabolical nature of suicide inform some in their construction of the sati's actions, but the example of sati itself entered a debate on suicide in Britain as an example of a certain sort of self-murder. Rev. John Sym picks up this thread in his famous 1637 work on suicide, using the sati as a cautionary tale: 'The external motives of self-murder I will for memory and

for method reduce to eight ranks. The first whereof is error of judgement; when men think and believe upon deceitful grounds, that they
ought or may lawfully kill themselves. As among the heathens and
Indians; whereby custom and law, servants and wives, in testimony of
love to their masters and husbands were want to cast themselves into
the fire to be burnt....' [Rev. John Sym, *Life's Preservative against self-
killing* (London, 1637)]. As we shall see, this practice of using sati as
a moral tale to discourage suicide at home would become even more
marked in the eighteenth and nineteenth centuries and is an example
of the multidirectional nature of the colonial encounter.

48. Michael MacDonald tells us that the years between 1660 and 1800 saw
a move away from the diabolical interpretation of suicide to one that
concentrated on the mental health of the person involved. This interpretation will be of importance later when we look at changing attitudes
to sati in later periods, but for our purposes here, we assume that writers
during this period would certainly have been influenced by the former
interpretation. See Michael MacDonald, 'The Secularization of Suicide
in England 1660–1800', in *Past And Present*, 3:2, May 1986, p. 76.

49. John Cockburn, *A Discourse on Self Murder* (London: 1716), p. 2.

50. Cited in M.J. Boxer and J.M. Quataert (eds), *Connecting Spheres:
Women in the Western World, 1500 to the Present* (Oxford: Oxford University Press, 1987), p. 33.

51. Partha Mitter, *Much Maligned Monsters: History of European Reactions to
Indian Art* (Oxford: Clarendon Press, 1977).

52. Ibid., p. 21.

53. Ludovico de Varthema, 'The Itinerary Of Ludovico de Varthema', in
J. Winter Jones (ed), *Travellers In Disguise* (Cambridge, Mass: Harvard
University Press, 1963), pp. 173–4.

54. Ibid.

55. Mitter, *Much Maligned Monsters*, pp. 16–17.

56. Bernier, *Travels*, p. 308.

57. Ibid., pp. 307–8.

58. Poompa Banerjee, *Burning Women: Widows, Witches and Early Modern
European Travellers in India* (New York: Palgrave, 2003).

59. M. Gaskill, *Crime and Mentalities in Early Modern England* (Cambridge:
Cambridge University Press, 2000), pp. 34–5.

60. Ibid., p. 36.

61. Ibid.

62. If she was burned by force, of course, she remained a blameless victim.

63. In England witches were hung rather than burnt, as their crime was
considered a felony rather than a heresy, although there would still
have been a strong correlation between magical powers and diabolical
involvement, and popular superstition seems to have preferred that
witches be burnt, as this would prevent their evil passing on to their

children. In Scotland and on the Continent, burning was normal punishment for heresy, and thus for all forms of witchcraft.

64. Poompa Bannerjee refers to the burning of heretics as the other great silence in early modern accounts of sati, but, as with her arguments about witchcraft, this is based on a lack of explicit comparisons and fails to take into account the numerous implicit or indirect references and images.

65. Teltscher, *India Inscribed*, p. 56.

66. Cited in Hughes-Hallet, *Cleopatra*, p. 156.

67. Cited in Antonia Fraser, *The Weaker Vessel: Women's Lot in Seventeenth Century England* (London: Weidenfeld and Nicholson, 1984), pp. 81 and 99.

68. Fraser tells us that in England during the seventeenth century about one-quarter of all marriages were remarriages. Ibid., p. 84.

69. Ibid. For more about changing social attitudes to widow remarriage, see Barbara Todd, 'The Remarrying Widow: A Stereotype Reconsidered', in M. Prior (ed.) *Women in English Society* (London: Methuen, 1985).

70. Della Valle, *Travels*, p. 267.

71. Henry Lord, *A Discovery Of Two Foreign Sects In The East Indies, Viz. The Sect Of Banians, The Ancient Inhabitants Of India And The Sect Of Persees, The Ancient Inhabitants Of Persia, Together With The Religion And Manners Of Each Sect* (London: s.n., 1630).

72. Teltscher, *India Inscribed*, p. 65.

73. Robert Coverte, 'The Voyage And Travels Of Captain Robert Coverte', in T. Osbourne (ed.), *A Collection Of Voyages And Travels*, (London: Thomas Osborne Of Grays Inn, 1745), p. 253. Wealthy relatives of the condemned in Europe would often bribe the executioner to place gunpowder in the pile so that they would die quickly from asphyxiation rather than suffer a drawn out death by burning. Conversely, should someone with influence wish to increase the agonies of the victim, green or slow-burning wood could be used on the pyre.

74. John MacDonald, *Memoirs Of An Eighteenth Century Footman, Travels 1745–1779* (London: Routledge, 1927), p. 160.

75. Terry, 'A Voyage to East India', p. 328.

76. Boxer and Quataert (eds), *Connecting Spheres*, p. 36.

77. Shakespeare's *Romeo And Juliet*, for example, expresses the possible passion of a temporal love that transcends the bounds of death in a sympathetic, if ultimately tragic, manner.

78. John Ovington, *A Voyage To Surat In The Year 1689* (New Delhi: Asian Educational Services, 1994), pp.189–90.

79. Ibid., p. 201. Immediately after this he concedes that '...this was seldom. For it generally fell to the Wives lot to be committed to the Flames with the dead Husband.'

80. Fransisco Pelsaert, *Jehangir's India: The Remonstrantie Of Francisco Pelsaert* (Cambridge: Heffer and Sons, 1925), p. 80.
81. Cited in Teltscher, *India Inscribed*, p. 61.
82. Ibid.
83. Pietro Della Valle, *The Travels Of Sig. Pietro Della Valle: A Noble Roman, Into East India And Arabia Deserta In Which The Several Countries, Together With The Customs, Manners, Traffique, And Rites Both Religious And Civil, Of Those Oriental Princes And Nations Are Faithfully Described In Familiar Letters To His Friend Sig. Mario Schipano* (London: J. Mattock For John Place, 1665), p. 44.
84. William Hawkins, 'Hawkins' Voyages', in William Foster (ed.), *Early Travels In India, 1583–1619* (London: Oxford University Press, 1921), p. 119.
85. Tavernier, *Tavernier's Travels*, p. 406
86. Bernier, *Travels*, pp. 310–11.
87. Pelsaert, *Jehangir's India*, p. 80.
88. Mandelslo, *Voyages And Travels*, p. 31.
89. See Teltscher, *India Inscribed*, p. 53.
90. Ibid.
91. Caesar Frederick, 'Extracts of Master Caesar Frederike of Venice, his eighteen yeeres Indian Observations', in Samuel Purchas, *Purchas his Pilgrimes, the second part* (London: William Stansby For Henrie Fetherstone, 1625), p. 1704.
92. Della Valle, *Travels Of Pietro*, pp. 44–5.
93. John Fryer, *A New Account of the East Indies and Persia, Being Nine Years Travels, 1672–1681* (New Delhi: Asian Educational Services, 1992), p. 117.
94. Coverte, *Voyage And Travels*, p. 253.
95. Barbosa, *Description*, p. 93.
96. The medieval European custom of burying the corpse of a suicide at a crossroads with a stake through the torso was aimed at preventing the deceased's ghost from haunting the neighbourhood—the heavy traffic of a junction passing over the grave, and the stake itself, were both thought to keep the soul in the grave.
97. Tavernier, *Tavernier's Travels*, p. 406.
98. Methold, 'Relations', pp. 1000–1.
99. Della Valle, *Travels*, p. 41.
100. Fryer, *New Account*, p. 18.
101. Teltscher, *India Inscribed*, p. 51.
102. Hughes-Hallet, *Cleopatra*, p. 168.
103. Manucci, *Storia Do Mogor*, vol. 3, p. 62.
104. Ibid.
105. Tavernier, *Tavernier's Travels*, p. 408.
106. Mandelslo, *Voyages And Travels*, p. 31.

107. Della Valle, *Travels Of Pietro*, p. 44.

108. Gayatri Spivak, 'Can The Subaltern Speak? Speculations On Widow Sacrifice', in *Colonial Discourse and Post Colonial Theory* (Hemel Hempstead: Harvester Wheatsheaf, 1994), p. 94.

109. Manucci, *Storia Do Mogor*, V. 2, p. 89.

110. Bernier, *Travels*, p. 314.

111. Methold, *Relations*, p. 1002.

112. Tavernier, *Tavernier's Travels*, p. 407.

113. Ibid., p. 415.

114. Bernier, *Travels*, p. 306.

115. Van Linschoten, *Voyages*, pp. 250–1.

116. Lord, *Discovery*. In suggesting that the rajas asked the Brahmins to make sati an act of religion, Lord foreshadows eighteenth-century interpretations of the rite's origins in which civic and religious roots are conflated. The majority of seventeenth-century observers miss this connection, however.

117. Cited in Teltscher, *India Inscribed*, p. 53.

118. Ibid.

119. Cannadine, *Ornamentalism*, p. xix.

3

PIOUS PRINCIPLES

Sati, Orientalism, and Enlightenment

CRSO

...a contempt for death is not peculiar to the women of India, it is the characteristic of the nation; every Gentoo meets that moment of dissolution with a steady, noble and philosophical resignation, flowing from the established principles of their faith.[1]

The eighteenth century saw both a quantitative and, more importantly, a qualitative shift in the material about sati that was available to the reading public in Europe. The most obvious locus of change occurred in the last quarter of the century, when the work of 'orientalist' scholars in learning Sanskrit and translating ancient Hindu texts brought a new dimension to the European understanding of India, its religions and customs. Personal observation was replaced with textual authority in explaining the practices of the Hindu population and the authenticity of a particular tradition or rite came to be measured not by personal experience, but by reference to a codified body of literature believed to outline the immutable principles of the Hindu religion. As momentous as these developments were in terms of the way in which Europeans in general, and the British in particular, sought to understand and deal with sati, they should not be viewed as representing a radical and unilateral change of direction. In ideological terms they augmented, modified, and accelerated certain shifts in the way in which sati was presented to the European audience, that had begun in the preceding decades of the century. Prolonged and increasing contact with the Subcontinent broadened the base of knowledge available, while the intellectual developments had a profound effect on the ways in which this information was processed and formulated into an image of India. The eighteenth century was a transitional period that linked the explorative impulses of the preceding centuries to the imperial imperatives of the later ones, both in terms of the political and economic relationships between India and Europe and the ideological constructs that underpinned them. In terms of the European understanding of sati, it linked the individual accounts of travellers and traders to the official attitudes of administrators and rulers, and saw the genesis of many of the preconceived ideas and assumptions that informed the nineteenth-century debate on sati and its abolition. The second part of this chapter will look at the ideas that emerged in the period after the East India Company stood forth as *diwani* of Bengal, the period of the orientalists, and of the formation of a British government in India; but first it will consider the ways in which Enlightenment thought had by this time modified the European understanding of sati in the first three quarters of the eighteenth century.

A Well-known and Well-authenticated Custom: Sati and Travel Literature in the Eighteenth Century

As European influence in the Subcontinent consolidated its foothold and the number of Europeans living and working in India increased, so too did the stream of travel narratives and general accounts on Indian themes that found their way back to the West. The eighteenth century saw the zenith of travel writing as a genre, with accounts reaching a far wider audience than ever before. Interest in the wider world, both to the east and west of Europe, was burgeoning among the general public and among intellectuals who, by the middle of the century, were beginning to apply new ways of thinking to the study of other cultures, inspired by the intellectual trends of Enlightenment. Those going abroad were encouraged to report on what they found there, and to do so in a scientific manner, while those who remained at home were bombarded with opinions extolling the virtues of the travel narrative, which was increasingly being viewed as educational as well as diverting.

In addition to the influx of new material, accounts from the sixteenth and seventeenth centuries were resurrected for inclusion in larger collections that grouped together various travel narratives, often under the auspices of a well-known editor.[2] The aim of most of these compendia was not to showcase new material, but to bring together what was considered to be the most reliable of what was already available. The poorer sections of the reading public were catered to by cheap pamphlets and tracts, in which only the most exciting or interesting aspects of any account were retained, and collections of voyages were often serialized so as to be within the means of a wider range of consumers. Journals such as the *Annual Register* and *Gentleman's Magazine*, and later the more specialized *Monthly Review* and *Critical Review*, carried material on other countries and reviews of books that often included substantial quotations from the text. Moreover, the growth of libraries of every kind facilitated access to expensive, multi-volume works and brought them to a wider audience than would have previously been possible. There was considerable competition between publications and supporters of one compendium or travelogue would not hesitate to denounce the authenticity of a rival while extolling the veracity of their own publication. In truth, the desire to make their offerings appealing to an ever-expanding audience meant that compilers would engage in editing and rearranging their material in order to maximize its impact, with the result that many works were of haphazard arrangement and dubious reliability.[3] Editorial intervention and authorial embellishment were acceptable parts of the writing process in the eighteenth century and most would have agreed with the famous novelist Henry Fielding that '...to make a traveller an agreeable companion to a man of sense it is necessary not only that he should have seen much, but that he should have overlooked much of what he had seen.'[4] Certain levels of plagiarism, exaggeration, and embellishment were expected, as were the unintentional errors that sprung from a poor or distorted memory. The result was that while 'Men with one foot, indeed, cyclops, sirens, trogladites, and suchlike imaginary beings, have almost entirely disappeared from this enlightened age...'[5] there was still a general consensus that travel accounts, though undoubtedly useful and entertaining, were not always as reliable as one might wish.

The growing incredulity of the reading public as regards improbable creatures and events meant that travellers who reported their own encounters with sati retained the practice, common in an earlier period, of strenuously attesting to the truth of their account, despite the fact that sati was one of the most widely reported of Indian customs. The Abbe de Guyon, for example, commented that 'There are none of the almost infinite number of travellers who have gone through that country, who do not mention the abominable custom which women have to burn themselves publicly on the death of their husbands....'[6] A report of sati, whether witnessed personally or pla- giarized from another's account, was an indispensable incident in any Indian travel narrative. Despite this, many eighteenth-century writers tended to justify their presence at a sati in terms of ascertaining the truth of previous reports. Scottish traveller Donald Campbell, for example, tells us '...this spectacle was most melancholy, and naturally struck me with horror...I had only gone there to assure myself of the truth of such sacrifices being made....'[7]

The emphasis on 'scientific' inquiry into the truth of sati meant that the rhetoric of rational inquiry permeated accounts of this period. Eyewitnesses observed sati with an almost clinical precision; ele- ments of ritual are described in detail and every aspect of the widow's deportment was subject to close scrutiny, that the observer might give a definitive account of the process of a sati. Great emphasis was placed on the reliability of the observer and his memory of events. Donald Campbell, for example, tells us: 'As this is a point that has occasioned some speculation and some doubt among some Europeans, I enclose

Fig. 5. 'Procession of a Hindu Woman to the Funeral Pile of her Husband' from William Hodges, *Travels in India During the Years 1780, 1781, 1782 and 1783* (London J. Edwards, 1793). By permission of the Edinburgh University Library.

you an accurate account of that ceremony as minuted down at the time that it happened....'[8] Englishman William Hodges, who has left behind a detailed account of his travels in India in the early 1780s, went as far as to record the sati that he witnessed in pictorial form (Fig. 5). He recalls: '...the event that I had been witness to was such, that the minutest circumstance attending it could not be erased from my memory; and when the melancholy which had overwhelmed me had somewhat abated, I made a drawing of the subject, and from the picture since painted the annexed plate was engraved.'[9]

The rationalistic bent of Enlightenment thought certainly would have predisposed many educated observers of sati to attempt to deal with it in a scientific manner, with the purpose of providing an objective account for the information of their readers. One senses, however, that the preoccupation of many with verifying the custom by observing it may also have helped to disguise a voyeurism that it was no longer acceptable to openly acknowledge. Executions in Europe were still public, of course, but cessation of the witch craze and of the burning of heretics meant that public burnings were now a rarity in Europe. Moreover, the Enlightenment rejection of barbaric justice and shifting attitudes towards corporal punishment meant that many of liberal bent might have wished to disguise a morbid curiosity in sati with the rhetoric of scientific observation.[10] William Hodges hints at this when he comments:

Whatever is the means, reason and nature so revolt at the idea, which, were it not a well known and well authenticated custom, it would hardly obtain credit. In truth, I cannot but confess, that some degree of incredulity was mingled with curiosity on this occasion; and the desire of ascertaining so extraordinary a fact was my great inducement to be a spectator.[11]

Hodges here acknowledges that the custom is well authenticated, but still manages to subordinate his own curiosity to the more worthy goal of ascertaining truth. Just as in a later period the professed desire to dissuade the widow, or at least to ensure she received fair play, would be used to justify the European's presence at the sacrifice. So in this period, the rationale of scientific observation is invoked as a validation for European attendance.

Hodge's expression of disbelief over the existence of sati was not unusual. Despite the widespread consensus that sati was indeed an authentic custom, many observers still felt the need to express their

amazement and feign empathy with their readers' projected incredulity. English merchant Abraham Caldecott wrote of sati as:

...a circumstance so widely differing from the tenets of our Religion and so
repugnant to human nature that had I not seen it with my own eyes, I
certainly would have been apt to doubt the veracity of it, but the fact is so
well established and so many instances of the like nature have occurred since
writing my letter as leaves no doubt of the generality of the practice all over
Bengal....[12]

Emphasizing their tendency to disbelief allowed the narrator to
share in the projected sentiments of his reader, and to emphasize his
difference in relation to the Hindu crowd. As mentioned above, this
may have been in part due to the changing attitudes that made public
displays of brutality less acceptable parts of everyday life for educated
Europeans. It also represented a growing tendency to divorce European experience from Indian life. Indeed, the frequency with which
eighteenth-century observers prefaced their accounts with protestations of disbelief suggests a shift away from understanding sati through
reference to European attitudes and assumptions, which had been the
norm in the early modern period, and towards viewing it as part of an
alien culture that had its own specific and inherent characteristics.
This is not to suggest that European ideas and assumptions with
regards to issues such as gender, suicide, and religion did not still play
an important part in shaping attitudes to sati—they did—but these
underlying forces were to an extent submerged in an overt rhetoric
that explained sati in terms of emerging ideas about Indian society
rather than through analogy with Europe.

The tendency to view sati as part of a broader picture of Indian life
was exacerbated by the emergence of more 'scholarly' accounts of
other countries and peoples, a genre that attempted a broader task than
the mere recitation of personal experience and which might in fact be
attempted by authors who had not even set foot in the countries they
were writing about. These works of synthesis were aimed at collect-
ing, cataloguing, and classifying the characteristics of the various peoples
of the newly expanding world. This embryonic form of anthropology
was not entirely new, of course. It was in many ways an offspring of
the geographies and cosmologies of earlier eras,[13] but the Enlightenment fixation with scientific method in the search for universal truths
gave it a new impetus and direction. The writers of this period were
no longer the pioneers of new information—most of what they re-

ported had been seen before—and there was a wealth of recent accounts for them to draw on for information and ideas, allowing them to concentrate on the interpretation rather than the collection of material. The result was that while some of the stereotypes of the classical and medieval periods were rejected, they were replaced by new ones born out of the Enlightenment tendency to classify, categorize, and present grand explanations. Increasingly, sati was explained less in terms of what the author or his sources had seen, but rather in terms of how the act conformed to a picture of India and Indians that was by this time consolidating in the European imagination; of which it was a constituent part.[14]

A Mischief So Very Common: Changing Ideas about the Origins of Sati

The Enlightenment concern with method and with universal laws, mentioned above, was in part responsible for two interrelated changes in the way in which sati was understood in the eighteenth century; the repositioning of sati as a religious act and the accompanying shift in critical focus away from the individual widow. Whereas early modern travellers tended to discuss sati in terms of its specific social context and saw the widow as the central actor in the sacrifice, Enlightenment accounts of sati increasingly fit it instead into a framework of assumptions about India more generally. Changing attitudes to the wider world and the influence of the work of Baron de Montesquieu, among others, helped reinforce the idea that continents and peoples had their own intrinsic qualities and characteristics that defined them in relation to others. These qualities were believed to be the result of climate, religion, form of government, and so on, and constituted the immutable essences of a race. The disgrace and discomfort of the widow who survived her husband was still occasionally alluded to, but for the most part these considerations were subsumed in eighteenth-century rhetoric about the nature of India, its people and religion. Increasingly, the sati is portrayed as acting as she does not as the result of a rational (or even irrational) decision-making process, rather because it is her nature to do so. The process of constructing sati to coincide with a predetermined image of India was self-reinforcing; sati both helped to create and was explained by certain assumptions. This process is perhaps best illustrated by the two main explanations for sati that became current in this period: that it was a religious rite followed as an article of faith by an intensely devout population and that it was a result of the Hindu woman's inherent predisposition for devotion to her husband. These assumptions increasingly supplanted earlier interpretations, both of the contemporary motivations for sati and of its distant origins.

The explanation that sati was part of a civic solution to wives murdering their husbands did not disappear immediately, though it was increasingly being treated with incredulity. As late as 1757, Abbe de Guyon could write:

If we believe the ancients, they themselves had given occasion to this cruel alternative. It had been found, that many were so cruel as to poison their husbands in the hope of espousing others. The necessity there was to put a stop to an abuse, which began to grow as common as it was enormous, occasioned the magistrates to make an order that every woman who survived her husband should be obliged to follow him to the pile. Thus what in its original was only a testimony of friendship or greatness of soul, became afterwards and inviolable law; and is at this day an article of religion.[15]

In the absence of an alternative explanation for sati, de Guyon falls back on the hackneyed classical account. While doing so, however, he disassociates himself from it, leaving it to the reader to decide on its veracity. More importantly, even in his hesitant allusion to Strabo, de Guyon combines the classical myth of civil injunction with the more recent understanding of sati as a religious rite. This tendency was not uncommon, as from the late seventeenth century those who explained sati usually did so primarily in terms of a secular law that had mutated in religious tradition. Frenchman Charles Dellon, writing in 1698, for example, reiterated the idea of a law that made sati a deterrent to murder, and claimed:

To give better colour to this cruel decree, it was backed by the specious pretext of religion, promising a large share of enjoyment to those creatures in the other world. Besides that, the Brahmins paid them very near the same reverence as to their deities, by which vain glory the crafty priests having gained upon the weakness of their sex, they frequently chose to make a virtue of necessity, and by a voluntary act to render their deaths more glorious.[16]

Niccolao Manucci's eighteenth-century editor F.F. Cattrou, made the connection between the secular and religious origins of sati even more explicit, claiming:

Brahma enacted this law to put a stop to a crying iniquity. The women grown weary of their husbands had frequently made them away by poison. The most effectual means that Brahma could think of to prevent a mischief so very common was placing the glory of women in burning themselves on the bodies of their husbands, or living after their decease in a perpetual state of widowhood. Thence arises that care and tenderness of wives for those to whom providence has once assigned them. Their lives and liberties depend on the lives of their husbands.[17]

In doing so he combined the classical account of the origins of sati with the Enlightenment construction of the founder of 'Hinduism'[18] as a historical figure, Brahma. This mode of interpreting the origins of Hinduism, as with other non-Christian religions, was a result of the tendency of Enlightenment thought to view other religions within the teleology of Christian tradition. Europe's own religious experience was projected on to other parts of the world and 'new' religions were for the most part understood by ascribing their origins to historical founding figures. As Williams and Marshall point out, Europeans believed that 'Scriptures had been written and patterns of worship devised by a Mohammed, a Zoroaster, a Confucius or a historical Brahma.'[19] By attributing the origins of sati to Brahma himself, Cattrou conflates the secular and religious argument. The civic enactment to prevent conjugal fatalities is automatically encompassed within the religious sphere, by being instigated by the founder of the religion.

While some tried to incorporate Strabo's account of sati's origins with the new ideas about its religious status, others refuted it wholly. John Zephaniah Holwell, writing in 1767, for example, denounced this explanation, for which he said he could not '...trace the smallest semblance of truth'.[20] He argued that the purely voluntary nature of the rite precluded the possibility of it having been instituted by a civic enactment. His reasoning was somewhat flawed, as the majority of proponents of Strabo's explanation viewed it as being arbitrary only in the distant past. He did, however, go on to offer his own account of the origins of sati, suggesting:

At the demise of the mortal part of the Gentoo's great law-giver and prophet Brahma, his wives, inconsolable for his loss, resolved not to survive him, and offered themselves voluntary victims upon his funeral pile. The wives of the chief Rajahs...being unwilling to have it thought that they were deficient in fidelity and affection, followed the heroic example set them by the wives of Brahma...the wives of every Gentoo caught the enthusiastic, now pious flame.[21]

Holwell here echoes Cattrou in ascribing the origins of the custom to events surrounding a historical figure, Brahma. In literal terms Holwell's story is as unfounded as the poisoning explanation, but it does have certain interesting resonances with more modern thought on the subject, as many twentieth-century scholars have suggested that sati may have begun as a practice among warrior castes, which was then adopted by other groups in an attempt to improve their ritual status.

A Union of Hearts: Conjugal Fidelity and the Hindu Widow

John Holwell attempted to present an alternative explanation for the origins of sati, but for the most part Strabo's account was rejected, not on the basis of new information, but upon the supposition that the inherent chastity and conjugal devotion of Hindu women precluded the possibility of their being guilty of so heinous a crime. Englishman John Henry Grose, for example, claimed that the story was:

...an over refinement of conjecture, as false as it is injurious to the women of this country, no such practice being either attested by creditable tradition, or warranted by the behaviour of the other Indian women not subject to this custom, who are generally of a mould of mind too soft and tender to incur even the suspicion of such a detestable barbarity.[22]

Not only did the assumption of Indian women's honour undermine the suggestion that she was, or had ever been, a husband-murderer, but for many eighteenth-century observers this very virtue was sufficient in itself to explain the practice of sati. French orientalist Pierre Sonnerat, for example, commented that '...however extravagant and atrocious this custom may appear, it is easy to give a reason for it. The extreme love of some women for their husbands, the despair at their loss, and the desire to follow them, was the first cause of this sacrifice, which custom authorised and time made universal.'[23] The emphasis on conjugal fidelity in motivating sati was not new, of course; many early modern travellers had seen the rite in precisely this context. What was new was that rather than being an example of individual devotion, it is increasingly—in the eighteenth century—being taken as representative of Hindu women's character generally. This is reinforced by the disappearance of the image of the sexually dangerous widow, so prominent in the early modern period, from eighteenth-century accounts. Rather than understanding sati as the extraordinary negation by some widows of their natural sexuality, sati is increasingly seen as the natural outcome of their innate virtue and devotion.

The rationale behind the depiction of Indian women as totally devoted to their husbands was made up of several strands. For some the very act of sati itself proved an unprecedented level of devotion. Luke Scrafton for example tells us that '...no women are more remarkable for their conjugal fidelity, in which they are distinguished beyond the rest of their sex, by that remarkable custom of burning with their husband'.[24] More than this, however, changing attitudes to Hindu women's sexuality also seem to correlate to changing ideas about femininity in the West. Eighteenth century saw the resolution of the *querelle des femmes* in favour of woman's inherent virtue rather than her inherent vice. This is not to suggest that eighteenth-century thinkers accorded women equality, but rather that they viewed her as possessing her own particular excellences, among which were her spirituality and morality. As Elizabeth Fox-Genovese points out; '...they exalted women above the political world of men and relegated them to a "higher" sphere of morality, establishing the next century's ideology that put women on a pedestal'.[25] This shift in attitudes to women sprang in part from the changing medical ideas that redefined women as 'perfect in themselves' rather than as imperfect men.[26] The shift away from Galenic medicine further undermined the idea of women as inherently more sexually driven, an assumption previously based on the supposed craving of their cold wet constitutions for the dry heat of the male.[27] Gradually this image was reversed and women were increasingly constructed as sexually passive—physically and mentally the weaker or softer sex. Under these circumstances it is hardly surprising that eighteenth-century observers, drawing on their own assumptions about the nature of women, should begin to characterize the sati less in terms of capricious sexuality and infidelity and more in terms of conjugal fidelity and spirituality.

This shift in the perception of women, both in Europe and in India, was also implicated in the common contemporary concern with the state of the society, as decadence and luxury were often linked with female sexuality. Aristocratic women in particular were often portrayed as having 'slipped through the cracks of traditional restraints'[28] and into illegitimate sexual activity. The new model of female domesticity and her role as moral conscience and spiritual helpmeet of man was in part a response to these fears. The stress on Hindu women's conjugal devotion can therefore be seen as the result of changing ideas about the inherent nature of women in general, as comparisons between Indian women's fidelity and European women are both explicitly and implicitly made. The aristocratic Hindu woman's virtuous self-sacrifice could, in sentiment if not in practice, be used to represent an ideal of female behaviour that the contemporary European nobility were not living up to. Rev. William Tennant suggests the potential for aristocratic virtue in 1803 when he comments:

Human nature is not always consistent; nor are the efforts of the mind always proportioned to our opportunities for exertion. Bred in scenes of the most voluptuous sensuality, these Indian ladies exhibit on occasion the most magnanimous exertion of fortitude of which history records any example.... There is hardly an instance of any individual of these ladies, nursed in the lap of pleasure, having shrunk from this horrid trial of their fortitude, after it was undertaken; and incredible as it may seem, hardly any instance of their betraying symptoms of fear, hesitation or pain.[29]

This image of a heroic Hindu lady would have provided a striking contrast to the popular image of debauched European ladies, as epitomized by the Marquise de Merteuil in Chouderlos de Laclos's *Les Liasons Dangereuses*.

As important as these changing ideas about women were in shaping the image of the Hindu woman as inherently chaste, they were also reinforced by culturally specific assumptions about Hindus. The conjugal fidelity, which is increasingly seen as Hindu woman's defining characteristic, was to a large extent premised on the supposition of the combined force of religious injunction and social conditioning. Early marriage was viewed as contributing to a devotion that sprang from total dependence on the husband, while religious dictates imposed punishments for infidelity. John Henry Grose elaborates on this theme, saying:

Another reason too for their prodigious affection and veneration for their husbands, is their early marriage.... After which, the parties, in the tenderness of that ductile age, are bought up until that of consummation, in the constant inculcation to them of mutual dearness, as a sacred point of religion. And the women especially entertain such a strong impressions of this doctrine, that, notwithstanding the influence of a climate far from favourable to chastity, instances of infidelity are at least as rare among them as in any people of the world besides.[30]

Grose thus combines the idea of the influence of early marriage in encouraging bonds of conjugal affection with the idea that this affection is imposed on women as a religious duty. Previously in his narrative, Grose has given a graphic example of the power of religious dictates in enforcing fidelity, by recounting a story of a Brahmin woman. Having been abducted and raped by a Muslim man, she is told that she cannot regain her caste and go back to live with her husband, even though he is willing to receive her. In despair she agrees to be purified by having molten lead poured down her throat, that she might at least die in her caste. Grose goes on to comment:

But whether this story be true or false, it is certain that it contains nothing but what the law of the Gentoos renders probable, and as certain, that an article of it annexing an expulsion from their communion to any violation of the conjugal faith.... In short the wives of the principle Gentoos, with all their apparent freedom of showing themselves, are, by their never going abroad unless accompanied by their superstition, as effectually defended from the approaches of strangers as those of the Moors are by their walls, bars, lattice windows and impenetrable veils.[31]

The conjugal fidelity of Hindu women was thus the joint result of social institutions and religious dictates that combined to lead them to the pyre. For some observers the influence of this devotion in motivating sati was supplemented by the promise of posthumous rewards that combine religious merit with reunion with the husband. Scrafton suggests:

Let it be considered, they are brought up together from their infancy; the woman has no opportunity of ever conversing with any other man; her affections are centred solely in this one object of her love; she is firmly persuaded that by being burnt with him, she shall be happy with him in another world; that if she neglects this last token of affection, he may take another wife, and she be separated from him forever. However false these principles, yet, if those poor women are persuaded that they are true, you must allow that they are powerful motives.[32]

Not all Europeans viewed inherent chastity as the motivating force for sati. French editor Bernard Picart, for example, having lauded the sati's courage in the face of the flames, questioned the influence of conjugal devotion as a motive, saying:

...the Indies afford us a thousand instances of the like nature in favour of the weaker sex, who are so fickle and inconstant that in one and the same moment almost, they'll be all fondness and all disdain? 'Tis not therefore a sincere and unaffected conjugal love; for were that the case the women of other countries would in that respect by far excel them. 'Tis ambition, a thirst after glory, that prompts them to this compliance. Their law has inseparably connected these two irresistible inducements with this inhuman sacrifice.[33]

He here inverts the image of sati as the ultimate expression of a fidelity specific to her race and instead suggests that other women would outdo her if this alone was the criteria. In his explicit comparison between Hindu and European women, however, he conforms to the general tendency to understand sati not solely through racial characteristics but in terms of a wider debate about the nature of women generally.

Picart's attack on the popular interpretation that sati was the result of excessive conjugal devotion appeared as early as 1733, but it is towards the end of the eighteenth century that we find the belief in the conjugal fidelity of Hindu women as the cause of sati really being challenged. Abbe Dubois, for example, whose famous work on India was used as a teaching aid at Fort William College in the early nineteenth century, rejected not only marital fidelity as a motivation for sati, but the very idea of Indian women's conjugal devotion itself, saying:

I am by no means inclined to attribute these voluntary sacrifices to an excess of conjugal affection. We should, for instance, be greatly mistaken were we to allow ourselves to be deceived by the noisy lamentations that wives are accustomed to raise on the death of their husbands, and which are no more than rank hypocrisy. During the long period of my stay in India, I do not recall two Hindu marriages characterised by a union of hearts and displaying a true mutual attachment.[34]

Dubois's manuscript was composed between 1792 and 1823, and its wide circulation among English ensigns in India meant that it had a considerable impact on ideas about Indian society and on the way in which sati was understood.

Eliza Fay, one of the earliest British women to mention sati, also attacks the idea that the widow acts out of love for her husband, although her understanding of a sati's actions is informed by considerations of gender as much as of race. She comments:

I cannot suppose that the usage originated in the superior tenderness, and ardent attachment of Indian women towards their spouses, since the same tenderness and ardour would doubtless extend to his offspring and prevent them from exposing the innocent survivors to the miseries of an orphaned state, and they would see clearly that to live and cherish these pledges of affection would be the most rational and natural way of showing their regard for both husband and children. I apprehend that as personal fondness can have no part here at all, since all matches are made between the parents of the parties who are betrothed at too early a period for choice to be consulted, this practice is entirely a political scheme to ensure the care and good offices of wives to their husbands, who have not failed in most countries to invent a sufficient number of rules to render the weaker sex totally subservient to their authority.[35]

Fay here brings the emotive response of a mother and the fate of the orphaned children into the equation, issues that would gain in importance in early nineteenth-century interpretations of sati. Her comments also reflect an incipient feminism that was beginning to emerge in the eighteenth century and which allowed her to reject the male-imagined stereotypes of Indian women and concentrate instead on the influence of a 'global' patriarchy that seeks the same goals, if by different means, in various regions of the world. Fay seems to view the influence of this patriarchy as uniting women in their responses to it. She goes on to comment:

I cannot avoid smiling when I hear gentlemen bring forward the conduct of Hindoo women, as a test of superior character, since I am well aware that so much are we slaves to habit *everywhere* that were it necessary for a woman's reputation to burn herself in England, many a one who has *accepted* a husband merely for the sake of establishment, who has lived with him without affection; perhaps thwarted his views, dissipated his fortune and rendered his life uncomfortable to its close, would yet mount his funeral pile with all imaginable decency and die with heroic fortitude. The most specious sacrifices are not always the greatest, she who wages war with a naturally petulant temper, who practices rigid self denial, endures without complaining the unkindness, infidelity, extravagance, meanness or scorn, of the man to whom she has given her tender and confiding heart, and for whose happiness and well being in life all the powers of her mind are engaged, is ten times more of a heroine than the slave of bigotry and superstition, who affects to scorn the life demanded of her by the laws of her country or at least by that country's custom; and many such we have in England, and I doubt not in India likewise: so indeed we ought, have we not a religion infinitely more pure than that of India?[36]

Fay's stance on sati can be seen in many ways as reflecting her own experience with a husband who ran them into debt, alienated his professional friends, engaged in intrigue against the then Chief Justice of Calcutta, Elijah Impey, fathered an illegitimate child, and whom she eventually left. Her recognition of a universal subjugation of women to men, and of women to established custom, resonates strongly with her own experience in rejecting an unhappy marriage and attempting to become an independent business woman; a move which was both brave and unusual at the time. It is interesting to note, however, that her ideal of sacrifice is the very life of submission to the husband which she herself has rejected and which she deems far more heroic than a hypocritical sati.

The Specious Pretext of Religion: Sati as an Article of Faith

If the European construction of the Hindu woman as being inherently chaste was increasingly being challenged by the late eighteenth century, one of the assumptions on which it was based remained current, and even gained force throughout the century. The desire to represent the Hindu woman's devotion to her husband in terms of religious injunction was illustrative of the degree to which religion was increasingly seen as regulating all aspects of Hindu life, even personal emotive bonds. The emerging European understanding of sati was deeply implicated in this construction of Hindu society as inherently devout and there was a general consensus that sati was, in the present at least, followed as an article of religion. This location of sati firmly within the religious sphere was extremely significant as it laid the foundations for the debate over the rite's scriptural authenticity that dominated British discussions on abolition during the first three decades of the nineteenth century. It was a significant break from previous interpretations of the sati, however. For although some early modern observers had commented that the act was thought to be meritorious in the next life, and while Brahmin priests were often described as instigating or overseeing the sacrifice, the majority had tended to view sati in its social rather than its religious context. The new emphasis on sati as a religious rite was in part the result of greater access to information on the subject. It was also reflective of new ideas, both about the nature of Indian society specifically and of non-Christian religions more generally.

The medieval belief that the pagan deities were incarnations of demons and devils had largely been discredited by the eighteenth century, as had the idea that Hindus were simply followers of the Pythagorean doctrine (of reincarnation), or descendants of the original Gentiles of the Old Testament. The precise nature of India's religions, and indeed of all the 'newly discovered' faiths of the 'East', was the subject of considerable debate. It was generally assumed that the various different belief systems of the non-European world could be neatly compartmentalized into separate religions, all of which were assumed, like Christianity, to have their own historical tradition and their own body of doctrine preserved in their sacred writings. Thus Hinduism, Buddhism, Confucianism, and Taoism were all supposed to represent unified and coherent belief systems, despite the considerable regional diversity evident in their actual practice. This mode of interpretation led to a growing tendency to view all the non-Muslim peoples of India as adherents to a single overarching devotional system that could be understood as a coherent religion, comparable to Christianity.

As far as Hinduism was concerned, the 'enlightened' European view discerned a significant distortion between what it deemed to be the true essence of the religion as stated in the religious texts and preserved by the higher castes, and the rites and customs practised by a majority of the population. In its purest form, Hinduism was considered to be a monotheistic religion, believing in retributive justice and transmigration of the soul. Although the later doctrine was anathema to Christian belief, the moral integrity of 'scriptural' Hinduism meant that it gained considerable approbation from certain sections of the intellectual community.[37] The Hinduism practised by the majority of the populace was deemed to be a very different beast entirely: polytheistic, idolatrous, and steeped in superstitions fostered by an unscrupulous priesthood in the people to keep them in subjugation. While some sections of the European intellectual elite generously chose to view popular Hinduism as allegories for the inner truth guarded by the Brahmins, the majority expressed little but disapprobation for the outward trappings of Hinduism. Customs such as sati were viewed as the self-interested impositions of an almost omnipotent priesthood. John Holwell, for example, explains the transmutation of sati into a religious rite as follows:

...the Brahmins had given it the stamp of religion, they foisted it into the *Chartah* and *Aughtorrah Bhades* and instituted forms and ceremonials which were to accompany the sacrifice, straining some obscure passages of Bramah's *Chartah Bhade*, to countenance their declared sense of the action, and established it as a religious tenet throughout Indostan....[38]

This passage is fascinating for the way it foreshadows, by nearly a hundred years, the discovery by Horace Hayman Wilson of the ontological error that underpinned the supposed Vedic authority for the rite. Holwell here casts doubt on the authenticity of sati as a religious act by questioning the reliability of the Brahmins who consecrated it as such. Of course, the Brahmins had long been seen as active instigators and beneficiaries of the rite, and the purity of their motives in encouraging the widow to the pile had often been called into question, but the supposed dynamics of the Brahmins' involvement in transforming a custom into a religious rite, though previously hinted at, had never so clearly been expressed.

That the Brahmins imposed their will on a credulous population through their religious dictates is a recurrent theme in the eighteenth century. Whatever the origins of the custom's religious status, few observers doubted that a majority of the population held it to be an act of considerable religious merit, a belief supposedly carefully cultivated by the Brahmins. Even John Holwell, who was for the most part sympathetic to sati, could note that '...the Bramins take unwearied pains to encourage, promote and confirm in the minds of the Gentoo wives this spirit of burning...they seldom lose their labour....'[39] Similarly, Pierre Sonnerat tells us:

The Brahmins encourage her to sacrifice herself with assurances that she is going to enjoy eternal felicity in paradise, where she will become the wife of some god, who will espouse her as a reward for her virtue. They further promise her that her name shall be celebrated throughout the earth, and sung in all their sacrifices, which is still a further inducement for some women to burn themselves; as there is no legal obligation.[40]

Whereas early modern observers had for the most part concentrated on the sociological factors that 'pushed' a widow into sati, by the eighteenth century the order had been reversed and promises of spiritual benefit in the hereafter were seen as 'pulling' her towards the pyre. Although these promises were widely believed by the Europeans to be spurious and imposed on the credulous by the priests, there is little doubt expressed that in her characteristic religiosity, the Hindu widow believed them implicitly. Bernard Picart, for example, de-

scribed the religious benefits promised to the sati in detail, then
added:

Tis very difficult for persons who are buoyed up with such pleasing hopes,
to be guided by the right dictates of cool reason: and how indeed should they
when not only their intellects are so weak, but they so implicitly believe every
doctrine which their designing priests are pleased to impose on them? Thus
it is that conscience turned topsy-turvy runs such exorbitant lengths, and
even the most flagrant crimes are deemed the most virtuous and heroic
actions.[41]

The prevalent understanding of the caste system, combined with
the belief in essences that dictated the characteristics of non-European
peoples, led to a virtually uncontested belief in the all-invasive influence of religion on Indian life. This understanding of the dynamics
of religious belief in India is at the root of the understanding of sati
as a religious phenomenon. Much more so than at any previous point,
the sati is represented as the adherent of a religious doctrine that
outlines every aspect of her life. The Rev. William Tennant, in 1803,
expresses this idea when he says of sati:

Various causes have been assigned for this unexampled fortitude, which
perhaps is owing to the all-powerful effect of custom in this country, and
the immediate hope of entering on a state of exquisite enjoyment. An
Hindoo no more thinks of evading the customary rites of religion, than an
European thinks of evading the unerring stroke of death. Its dictates appear
to him the call of invincible necessity, to which he submits without reluctance, because unavoidable; and without choice, because ordered by the
Brahmins.[42]

The essentialist image of the Hindus, as dominated entirely by their
religion and as revealed to them through their priests, was reinforced
by a conception of their submission to the unerring force of tradition.
Asiatic society was repeatedly characterized throughout this period as
static and unchanging, a particularly poignant image when we consider
that European society at this time was thought to embody all that was
best about progress and change. The Indian climate, its political institutions, and the predominance of religion in ordering people's lives
were all deemed to contribute to a society that had changed very little
over the centuries and which still closely resembled its distant ante-
cedents. Many Europeans believed, as John Henry Grose did, that

'...none are more tenacious of old customs than the Gentoos'.[43]
Paradoxically sati was deemed to be both proof of and the consequence of a characteristic tendency of Hindus to follow unquestioningly the dictates of their religion. Adherence to the sati custom was
put forward as the most emphatic example proving this idea, whilst
at the same time sati itself was explained primarily in these terms. The
idea that Hindus are dominated by their religion was thus a self-
reinforcing one. They do this because they are religious, and they are
proved religious because they do this. The prevalent European view
of Indian society allowed this paradox to exist uncontested. Questions
of the chicken and the egg were largely irrelevant in the context of a
people who have supposedly not altered for millennia.

Reason and Religion: Sati, Superstition, and Suicide

The image of a sati acting out of religious conviction, whether falsely
imposed on her or not, created a context in which her sacrifice could
be incorporated into a wider debate about the nature of religion. The
new interpretation of pagan beliefs, as manifestations of coherent
religious systems, represented a considerable theoretical challenge to
the assumed superiority of the Christian faith. The *philosophes*, with
their rampant anti-clericalism and distaste for religious dogmatism,
were fascinated by the new religions of the East, primarily due to the
belief that if their antiquity and internal moral integrity could be
confirmed, it might be used to undermine the pretensions of the
Christian churches to represent the one true faith. Some deists even
went as far as to argue that God had revealed himself in many ways,
at many different times, and to many different people. A belief in
'natural religion' was not entirely incompatible with certain aspects
of Christianity, which allowed for the possibility of instinctive devotion. But the suggestion that this could be expanded to validate extensive and extremely ancient religious systems in other parts of the
world, represented a considerable threat to orthodox Christianity and
its worldview. Fortunately for the faithful, this threat could be coun-
tered by magnifying the discreditable aspects of popular practices
such as sati.

As was the case with earlier missionaries, those who sought to
defend Christianity at the expense of Hinduism first made sati a
religious issue and then used it to discredit that religion. In particular,
the sati's precipitation of her own death, as with other forms of

religious suicide, was used as an example of the dangers inherent in the doctrine of the transmigration, one aspect of Hindu theology which even the most 'enlightened' Europeans often found difficult to reconcile with their own beliefs. The Abbe de Guyon, who was for the most part relatively sympathetic to Indian society and culture, lamented:

Among all these customs there are few which do not resound to the praise of the Indians; but the sentiments some of them entertained to death cannot be excused. They looked upon it with such indifference as must be a shock to nature, if reason and religion teach not to hope for a better state....This practice is founded on their notions of the metempsychosis,[44] which passes among them as an undoubted truth.[45]

The horrors of sati and the implications for the widow's soul continued to be a powerful tool in support of missionary enterprise. Kate Teltscher includes a fascinating instance in *India Inscribed*, taken from the Jesuits' *Lettres Edifantes*, in which a sati, having listened to the discourses of her Christian serving woman, announces at the moment of her sacrifice, 'Alas! What does human happiness lead to? I am well aware that I am about to cast myself alive into hell!'[46] The widow then invokes the names of her gods and throws herself into the flames. The anomaly created by the pagan woman espousing a Christian frame of reference in her conception of suicide is striking, but the utility of such a story to the missionary cause is clear: that the teachings of the Bible can and do infiltrate the Hindu mind, and inspire it with right thought, even when conversion does not take place. Given the singular lack of success the missionaries experienced in converting meaning-ful numbers of high-caste Hindus to Christianity, such an image would be very useful in suggesting the beneficence of the labour even when concrete results were not forthcoming. Moreover, the widow provided a potent image of the battle of conversion, internally strug-gling between the 'truth' of Christianity and the inexorable weight of false custom and religion.

Interestingly, given the potential capital to be gained from it, it does not appear that those who used sati to denigrate Indian society placed as much emphasis as might be expected on the image of sati as suicide. Of course, the above example plays on the image of the sati's self-destruction, and it was not unknown in this period for churchmen to refer, as Jesuit Father Maudit did, to the sati as an 'unhappy victim of Satan'.[47] It is hardly surprising, of course, that men dedicated to saving the heathen soul should be concerned with the spiritual consequences of the sati's self-destruction. For the most part, however, the suggestion of the sinfulness of sati appears to have disappeared from the debate to a large extent. The iconography of the widow precipitating herself into the fiery pit is much rarer during this period and has been replaced with depictions of her progress towards the place of execution. Of course, artistic sensibilities must take some of the credit for this as the stately procession to the pyre fitted much more comfortably with the fashionable neo-classical style of the eighteenth century, but it also suggests that observers were less inclined to view the sacrifice as suicide, or to extend the Christian consequences of self-destruction to the pagan practitioner. Indeed, the artistic depiction of sati, particularly those by John Zoffany and Tilly Kettle (Fig. 6), suggest heroic sacrifice and martyrdom rather than suicide and damnation.[48]

This heroic treatment of sati may in part be explained by the general tendency towards the toleration of other religions, encouraged by the

Fig. 6. 'Suttee' by Tilly Kettle in G. Moorehouse, *India Britannica* (London: Harvill, 1983). By permission of the Random House Archive and Library.

Enlightenment thinkers. This emerging sense of cultural relativism created a situation in which the sati's death could be judged in its own terms rather than being forced into a Christian framework. For some intellectuals in this period, the exact nature of a person's faith was less important than that they followed it sincerely and without hypocrisy. Under these conditions, whatever their feelings about the sacrifice itself may have been, it would be inconsistent for them to condemn it solely because it transgressed Christian morality. This is not to suggest that the sati's action was accepted unproblematically as resulting from her faith, of course, but rather that an intellectual climate existed in which customs like sati could be judged in terms of 'rationality' rather than Christian morality. Voltaire, for example, attacked the custom of sati not because it transgressed Christian beliefs, but because it represented religious bigotry and dogmatism generally. In *Zadig*, published in 1747, the eponymous hero at one point prevents a widow from committing sati, persuading her instead to admit that she had detested her husband and that she was only intent on performing the rite from deference to others and to gratify her own vanity. He also manages to persuade the leaders of the tribe to abolish the custom. When his friend Setoc asks, 'For more than a thousand years women have had the right to burn themselves. Which of us shall dare to alter a law which time has consecrated? Is there anything more respectable than an ancient abuse?', Zadig, in typical Enlightenment fashion, replies, 'Reason is more ancient.' For Voltaire, the issue of sati could be used as a medium through which to attack superstition and religious dogmatism in general, and his satire of the rite in *Zadig* is directed as much, if not more, at the superstitions of the Christian Church as at Hinduism itself. As Dorothy Figueira comments, for Voltaire the sati 'represented the ideal victim of religious superstition'.[49]

Despite his great admiration for what he considered to be essence of Hinduism, Voltaire was violently opposed to sati. Others took a more sympathetic stance. The religious toleration that was an avowed principle of Enlightenment thought, allowed some to attempt to understand the subject of sati from the Hindu point of view. John Zephaniah Holwell, for example, goes to considerable lengths to place the rite in its Hindu context and shows an unusual willingness to grapple with the metaphysical principles that underpin belief in it. He asks his reader to:

...view it (as we should every other action) without prejudice, and without keeping always in sight our own tenets and customs, and prepossessions that too generally result there from, to the injury of others; if we view these women in a just light, we shall think more candidly of them, and confess they act upon heroic, as well as rational and pious principles.... Although these principles are in general so diametrically contrary to the prevailing spirit and genius of our fair countrywomen...yet we will depend on their natural goodness of heart, generosity and candour, that they will in future look on their Gentoo sisters of the creation in a more favourable and consistent light than probably they have hitherto done; and not deem that action an infatu- ation that results from principle.[50]

Holwell even goes so far as to openly conflate the sati's sacrifice with that of the Christian martyrs, reminding his reader that Europe's '...own history affords illustrious examples in both sexes of voluntary sacrifices by fire, because they would not subscribe even to a different mode of professing the same faith'.[51] Thus, Holwell approaches the subject from the view point of a cultural relativist, seeing sati as a rational choice when viewed within the framework of the widow's own religious belief.

If the religious toleration and cultural relativism of the Enlighten- ment created a space for sati to be judged within its own religious context, the almost total alienation of the stigma of self-destruction from sati in this period must also be understood in terms of changing attitudes towards suicide in Europe itself. As we have seen, suicide was generally held as innately sinful, a perception supported both by canon law and popular perception. By the eighteenth century, atti- tudes were beginning to change, however. On an intellectual level this was part and parcel of the general ferment of ideas that took place during the Enlightenment. Rationalists and deists who rejected reli- gious dogma as a prescription for right behaviour, were hardly likely to accept untested religious arguments for the sinfulness of suicide. This is not to suggest that there was a wholesale rejection of the immorality of suicide during this period—the majority still deplored it—but rather that the frame of reference was changed from a religious to a rationalistic one. The right of man to take his own life was increasingly to be judged not in terms of divine injunction, although some did argue that intolerable suffering should be viewed as imply- ing divine sanction for suicide, but in terms of natural law. The question of whether suicide was a natural impulse or an anathema to natural instincts, perplexed the intellectuals of the day. Some stoically argued that it was rational to attempt to escape suffering by whatever means, and championed the right of man to follow his reason, even to this fatal end. Others found that suicide contravened universal laws, man being the only creature capable of it.[52]

If the intellectual elite were debating the ideological nature of suicide, Michael MacDonald has shown that attitudes were also shifting on a popular level. He suggests that the increasing tendency of juries to return verdicts of *non compos mentis* in *felo-de-se* cases between 1680 and 1800 reflected a 'secularisation of suicide' in England in this period.[53] The use of madness to protect the families of suicides from forfeiture suggests not only sympathy with their plight (which could have been expressed in a variety of other ways), but also the rejection of religious interpretations of suicide that condemned it utterly in favour of medical interpretations that excused it.[54] Thus the shifting nature of both popular and intellectual attitudes to suicide created an environment in which a number of interpretations of the sati's action could be considered normative. Outright denunciations of her act as against God decreased significantly, but reference to it in relation to natural law increased. Pierre Sonnerat, for example, commented that

To dispose them for this heroic, or rather insane, action, the Brahmins make use of beverages mixed with opium; and it is thus they animate and inflame the unhappy victim of conjugal fidelity. The kind of furore with which they rush to this certain death, sufficiently proves that the head is disturbed by the fumes of this strong and intoxicating liquor. Fanaticism may induce the consent to such a sacrifice, but reason must be lost in the execution.[55]

For Sonnerat, the issue of suicide entered the discussion of sati not in terms of sinfulness, but in terms of a natural and rational reaction against it. Intoxicating substances are administered not as a coercive tool, but as a means of overcoming the natural antipathy to suicide. In the case of those who went to the pyre apparently in their senses, the sati's lack of instinctive horror at the flames is the cause of some consternation. Some Europeans praised her courage in tolerating the fire, while for others this stoicism was explicable only by an altered mental state verging on madness. Luke Scrafton, for example, commented that '...their minds raised to the utmost pitch by this strange commotion of love, grief and honour, they go through the terrible trial with amazing fortitude'.[56]

Not only did the debate about suicide alter the manner in which the sati's sacrifice was perceived, but conversely her action was itself incorporated into the debate on suicide in Europe. The Indian penchant for religious suicide was used as a cautionary tale to illustrate the dangers of immoral attitudes to self-destruction and a society's awareness of its sinfulness used as a measure of civilization. In a sermon denouncing both the growing tendency towards leniency in suicide cases and reformers' calls for an end to profane burial, English clergyman John Cockburn in 1713 asserted that '...all civilised nations, for expressing their just abhorrence of it, have ordered some indignity to the body of such as did make themselves away'.[57] He then goes on to conflate toleration of suicide with barbarism, using the example of sati.

Both Civil and Cannon law to severely inhibit the burying of any such person without ignominy, and some or other mark of indignation, which is observed everywhere throughout the Christian world; and 'twas always practised every other where, except in some places where there was a barbarous custom of giving leave for one to make away with himself. For at this day in some part of the pagan world, it is permitted some wives as desire it to burn themselves upon their husband's death, so it is done with great solemnity and pomp.[58]

For Cockburn, then, toleration of suicide and leniency to its practitioners reduces civilized man to the level of pagans and barbarians, as epitomized by the Indians in their reverence for sati. The tendency to incorporate the image of sati as an example of a certain type of suicide within the metropolitan debate on the subject would continue into the nineteenth century and is illustrative of the way in which images of India not only shaped a 'colonial discourse' but also impacted on currents of thought within Europe. Interpretations of sati were not only important in shaping the European conception of Hindus and Hinduism, but also played a role in Europe's own attitudes and identity.

Exquisite Tortures: Sati as Heroine and Victim

The disappearance of the hell-bound self-murderer from the eighteenth-century depiction of sati did not mean that the custom had been completely renovated in the eyes of Europeans, but the mideighteenth century did seem to provide many favourable interpretations of the rite. John Holwell was not alone in seeing the sacrifice of the sati as analogous to that of the Christian martyrs and there was a general tendency in both literature and art to view the sati as a heroic figure. For those who would not go so far as to conflate sati with martyrdom, there was still room for admiration of the bravery and conviction with which she underwent her fate. Even as late as 1803, Rev. William Tennant could comment that '...these Indian ladies exhibit on occasion the most magnanimous exertion of fortitude of which history records any example'[59] and there are repeated references to her courage throughout the period.

The conflation of sati with heroic action might seem somewhat out of place when one considers the European tendency to explain her devotion in terms of religious and social conditioning on a weak and malleable mind. Indeed, this very consideration would be used by later generations to strip away the remnants of the heroic ideal and replace it with the image of the sati as the miserable dupe of super-stition. In the eighteenth century, however, it seems that heroic action and indoctrination were not considered to be mutually exclusive. Rather, many observers seem to have recognized the influence of custom while still retaining the highest regard for the sati's heroism. Quentin Craufurd, for example, tells us that

Such is the influence of custom, and the sense of shame, that a woman of the highest birth, brought up with the care and delicacy suitable to her rank, and possessing that timidity and gentleness of manners natural to her sex, and for which the women of Hindustan are so eminently distinguished, will undergo this awful sacrifice with as much fortitude and composure as ever were exhibited by any hero or philosopher of antiquity.[60]

Similarly, Bernard Picart comments:

Whether this heroic courage proceeds from any artful preparation, or the force of a law, which fixes a mark of shame and disgrace on such women as cowardly survive their husbands, or from a preternatural tenderness and affection, we shall not determine; but 'tis unquestionably true, that there are incredible stories told of the constancy and resolution of these Indian women. The horror of the raging flames seems so contemptible in their eyes, that one might venture almost to say, they would gladly suffer even more exquisite tortures, if possible, for their husbands' sakes.[61]

The paradoxical understanding of sati as a combination of religious indoctrination and heroic action related to the prevalent view of sati as a deliberate action. It was also recognized that in some cases overt force was used to compel the widow to the pyre, but for the most part

Europeans writing on sati during the first three quarters of the eighteenth century viewed the sacrifice as a voluntary one. Some observers go as far as to stress the premeditated nature of the widow's choice. William Tennant for example tells us:

This resolution is formed with deliberation, and is declared to be voluntary and fixed, three several times [*sic*] in the presence of relations. This is done that no advantage may seem to have been taken of the transient ebullition of frantic grief, and that the person devoting herself might have full time to reflect on the important sacrifice she is about to make to her affections, or to the customs of her country.[62]

John Holwell also stresses that the act is premeditated and purely voluntary in nature. The power of persuasion is widely acknowledged, but the connection does not seem to be made between persuasion and the negation of the widow's will. This is not to suggest that the use of force is not recognized, but that it is seen as a means of enforcing a decision voluntarily made rather than compelling the sacrifice in the first instance.

The heroic treatment of the sati's sacrifice by many eighteenth-century observers undermines completely the common contemporary assumption that European reactions to sati have always been characterized by moral objection and outrage. Rather, they appear to have been composed of a complex mixture of admiration and disgust. This is all the more evident when we consider that this period of 'sympathetic' understanding also saw the genesis of modern interpretations of sati as victim. Despite the general tendency towards heroic, or at least sympathetic treatments of the widow's actions, not all observers of this period regarded the sati's sacrifice in a positive light. Indoctrination and heroic action were, for some, uneasy bedfellows and although the direct correlation had not yet been made between the force of religious superstition and the total subjugation of the widow's agency, the preconditions for a more negative interpretation of sati were beginning to emerge. Rather than being an autonomous agent in her own destruction, the widow is increasingly viewed as so dominated by her religion and her affections that she barely possesses the faculty to refuse her fate. Pierre Sonnerat, who had earlier expressed his belief that the sati went intoxicated to her death, presents an image of the ostensibly voluntary sati being murdered by her superstition:

While the woman is advancing to this fatal theatre (where her life is to end, often in the flower of age) and before she reaches this abode of horror, the Brahmins take great care to divert any regret that may remain, by songs in which are introduced eulogies of her heroism. This murderous concert sustains her courage in the midst of the forerunners of death; the band of superstition covers her eyes, and fatal moment approaches, when she is going to be devoted to the flames....[63]

Similarly John Henry Grose states that he '...attribute[s] it to the strength of passion, always the greatest in the weakest minds, from the greater power of all impressions on them, and of which the Bramins knew how to take advantage....'[64] Both he and Sonnerat utilize the stereotype that had become current in the eighteenth century, of the all-pervasive power of a corrupt priesthood over a devout society, and apply it to sati in a way which foreshadows later representations both of rapacious and self-serving Brahmins as the authors of the rite and of the widow as the helpless victim of religion. For some eighteenth-century observers, then, the widow's action was heroic and motivated by fine, if misguided, principles, but for others the logic of religious indoctrination provides another, more negative, interpretation and the sati begins to emerge as the voiceless, passive pawn, which interpretation would characterize her representation in the nineteenth century.

Private Influence: The Limits of European Intervention

The duality of the emerging eighteenth-century European representations of the sati as both heroine and victim is reflected in an ambivalent stance with regard to actual intervention in sati. Of course, the issue of forcibly preventing sati was one that had accompanied even the earliest accounts of the rite, as individual observers meditated on the possibility of intervention and in some cases actually rescued widows from the pyre. In the absence of any official position on the issue, approaches to preventing sati during the first three quarters of the eighteenth century followed a similar pattern, and interference in sati remained a question of individual conscience and capacity. For the most part, Europeans confined themselves to dissuasion in their efforts to prevent the sacrifice, but the image of the dashing European forcibly rescuing the widow from the flames remained a popular image in both fiction and travel accounts. *The Widow of Malabar* by Mariana Starke, which was performed in Covent Garden in 1791, concluded with the rescue of an unwilling sati by her European paramour,[65] while the now famous rescue of a

Hindu widow by Job Charnock, the founder of Calcutta, remained a popular tale. Indeed, Charnock's actions were immortalized in song, verses of which were found inscribed on the tombstone of Joseph Townsend, who died on 24 June 1738.

Shoulder to shoulder, Joe, my boy, into the crowd like a wedge!
Out with the hangers messmates, but do not strike with the edge!
Cries Charnock 'Scatter the faggots? Double that Brahmin in two!
The pale tall widow is mine Joe, the little brown girl's for you.[66]

Charnock did in fact marry his sati and lived a long and happy life with her, but as the above verse suggests, there was often a less salubrious subtext to the 'rescue fantasy' that juxtaposed the heroic rescue with the forcible abduction and rape of the widow. Certainly not all widows wished to be saved by Europeans and many refused their offers of aid and assistance. While the romantic image of the rescued sati saw her eternally grateful for her salvation, there was also the suggestion that in some cases the sati did not consider herself a damsel in distress and resented the interference that robbed her not only of the merit of the sacrifice, but of her caste and honour. Despite this, there is a general tendency for Europeans to assume that the widow must wish to be saved, and that any contrariness on her part in response to their good offices is merely the result of priestly pressure. Thomas Twining, for example, recounts in detail his attempts to dissuade a widow from her sacrifice in 1792:

Although she said nothing, I thought that her look seemed to express thankfulness for the proposition she had heard. I had not time to say more, the pressure of the Bramins, watchful lest their victim should escape, obliging her to move on. Having once more completed her round and come to where I stood, she herself turned to put some rice into my hand. I eagerly seized the last opportunity I should have of renewing my exhortations, promising her a pension for life and provision for her children. Though her head remained inclined towards the ground, she looked at me while I spoke, and her countenance impressed me with the assurance that if she had been free from the fatal influence that surrounded her, it would not have been difficult to turn her from her resolution.[67]

Despite the fact that the widow had not in any way attempted to avail herself of his assistance, Twining here conforms to Western assumptions about the widow's state of mind. By speaking for the widow, he removes not only her own voice but also any sense of her own autonomy, and so reinforces the image of the widow as the victim rather than the perpetrator of sati, an idea that would become normative in the next century.

The European's own self-image is closely bound up with their assumption that the widow is inclined to be rescued, for the salvation of the unwilling victim underpinned the popular image of the potent European and the pusillanimous Brahmin. A closer look at the rescue fantasy reveals that the European intervention might not have been as heroic or as selfless as the romantic image might suggest. In a period when Indian wives and mistresses were commonplace among the European community, the sexual aspects of the rescue fantasy were quite openly acknowledged, and it is not unusual to find a rescued sati remaining with the European who saved her. Although most accounts present this in romantic terms, there is certainly room to see a degree of coercion implicit in the situation. For once she has been defiled by European hands and dishonoured by not finishing the sacrifice, it would not be uncommon for the widow's family to disown her. In want of security and support, the widow might have little choice but to avail herself of European protection, whatever the quid pro quo of so doing. The potential benefits for the European rescuer are made clear in an account by the French traveller L. de Grandpre, who goes into some detail in his narrative about his intentions for an ultimately abortive rescue. Grandpre is made aware of the impending sacrifice by his servant, and

Having enquired into the circumstance, I learned that she was both young and handsome, and that she had already twice put off the ceremony, but that the day being a third time fixed, nothing could longer defer it. I conceived that a woman who had twice hesitated, would find at least no great pleasure in submitting, and conjecturing that she might not be sorry to escape altogether, I formed the resolution of endeavouring to save her.[68]

He here conforms to the prevalent European assumption that the widow would welcome intervention; indeed he expresses his belief that '...if left to themselves they would never consent to so cruel a sacrifice....'[69] He then goes into exhaustive detail about his preparations for the rescue. He enlists the help of his servant, his servant's friend, and twenty European sailors whom he '...encouraged...by offering them the sixth part of the value of whatever jewels the woman should have about her, intending to leave the remainder for herself, if she did not chose to stay with me….'[70] Grandpre here not only makes free with the woman's projected valuables, but gives a vital hint as to his motivation in attempting the rescue. The European sailors clearly were motivated less by moralistic outrage over sati than by the potential for loot, while Grandpre makes it clear that he hoped the sati would remain with him, in which case we can assume that the desired outcome of this 'benevolent' rescue was that the European gain both a concubine (one who is indebted to him for her life) and five-sixths of her valuables. Although he avers that, 'My intention was to leave the woman afterwards to her own disposal, that is to say, to give her the choice of either going with me, or of settling at Calcutta on the proceeds of her jewels, which I should of course have the precaution to bring away with her,'[71] it is clear from the tenor of the account that he expected to gain a beautiful mistress. Indeed, he admitted from the outset that it was her supposed youth and beauty that encouraged him to intervene. The denouement of this 'romantic' fantasy, so carefully constructed by the author, is an almost farcical anticlimax. Grandpre concludes his account:

My whole plan was prepared and ready, and I set out to execute it. I arrived at the place and alertly jumped ashore. The arrangements agreed upon were made with precision. I advanced and was astonished at the stillness and silence that prevailed. I came to the spot. Alas! The dreadful sacrifice had been completed the preceding evening. I had been misinformed of the day. The wall was still warm and the ashes were smoking. I returned with an oppression of heart that I could hardly express, and as much affected as if I had been witness to a barbarous execution. My regret for this woman was as great as the pleasure I should have felt in saving her, and the idea I had formed of her youth and beauty.[72]

Were it not for the fact that the woman actually died, Grandpre's dramatic posturing would make his final failure more comic than cathartic. Even to the end, however, we retain the sense that it was the loss of a beauty rather than a woman that he regretted.

Despite the sexual subtext of his attempted rescue, Grandpre maintained an unquestioning belief in the moral integrity of his project; his presumption in speaking for the intended victim and his assumption that she would be happy to be saved reflects the cultural arrogance inherent in the rescue fantasy. Not all European observers saw the issue so unproblematically, however. John Holwell, for example, questions the rectitude of interfering in sati, saying:

There have been instances known, when the victim has by Europeans been forcibly rescued from the pile; it is currently said and believed (how true we will not aver) that the wife of Mr Job Charnock was by him snatched from this sacrifice; be this as it may, the outrage is considered by the Gentoos as an atrocious and wicked violation of their sacred rites and privileges.[73]

The suggestion that any interference with sati was a violation of the Hindu's religious freedom would, of course, become central to the nineteenth-century debate on the rite's abolition and would be institutionalized in instructions forbidding authoritative intervention in the rite. Where previously intervention had been left to the conscience of the individual, increasingly men holding positions of authority in the new administration found that they had to balance personal reactions to sati with 'official' policy. The two did not always coincide. Although no official instructions on sati were issued to magistrates until 1813, it was generally understood that the government did not sanction interference. This was partly a pragmatic concern. Interference could cause unrest and inspire local resentment among the Hindu community, as is made clear by the following letter about the conduct of one Captain Tomyn in intervening in a sati in Madras in 1772.

…a Boutique merchant having died the 12th instant, his widow was desirous of being burned with the body, and everything was prepared accordingly, when the Captain at that place came and took the woman by the hand, and carried her to her late husband's house, and put a guard over it; and on this near 700 of the polygars, and other people, assembled and prepared for action, sending a letter writer advice of the imprudent conduct of the captain, and saying that they would all sacrifice their lives on the occasion; that the letter writer sent them a proper answer to this, but could not get them to desist, nor prevent them surrounding the captain's tent, at last however, by sending the commandant of the Nabob's sepoys to the leading men amongst the polygars' people, he got them to suspend everything until the next morning; that the consequence of the European's behaviour has been this, the hindering of the people from procuring either their rice or grain, every chittyman, shopkeeper, and merchant having fled to different places on account of the riot there; that he the letter writer begged to have an answer to this letter as soon as possible; and that he should send away the dealers in horses and their horses to Davelohenoos the next morning.[74]

Concern with the stability of their possessions led the Madras government to denounce such unauthorized intervention, despite the fact that the widow had been successfully rescued.

Concern about the desirability of forcible intervention rested on more than a fear of violent reprisal, though this was to be a recurrent theme in the discussion on sati. The East India Company had pledged itself to respect the religious beliefs and customs of the native population, as well as to govern them, as far as possible, by their own laws. Intervention in sati thus became a political issue for those in authority, one in which their own personal inclination to intervention might sit ill at ease with their expressed principles of government. In 1789 the collector of Shahabad in Bengal brought the inconsistency between personal inclination and official policy to the government's notice for the first time. He reported that the relatives of a widow had approached him requesting sanction for the sacrifice, which he had positively refused to grant. He opened by saying that '...cases sometimes occur in which the collector, having no specific orders for guidance of his conduct, is necessitated to act from his own sense of what is right'[75] and then went on to justify his decision to oppose the sati as follows: 'The rites and superstitions of the Hindoo religion should be allowed the most unqualified tolerance, but a practice at which human nature shudders I cannot permit within the limits of my jurisdiction, without particular instruction.'[76] Although ostensibly merely seeking approbation for his actions, the collector raised the question of the complete abolition of sati and his letter revealed the inherent contradiction between the emerging vilification of sati and the avowed principles of religious toleration. The reply that he received is indicative of the ideological stance of the government at the time. He was commended for withholding his consent, but was told that the East India Company Board of Directors:

...though they are desirous that he should exert all his private influence to dissuade the natives from a practice so repugnant to humanity and the first principles of religion, they do not deem it advisable to authorise him to prevent the observance of it by coercive measures or by any exertion of his official powers; as the public prohibition of a ceremony, authorised by the tenets of the religion of the Hindoos, and from which they have never yet been restricted by the ruling power, would in all probability tend rather to increase than to diminish their veneration for it; and prove the means of rendering it more prevalent than it is at present.[77]

Despite the government's inaction here and again in 1797, when the acting magistrate of Midnapur asked for approbation for preventing a child of nine performing the sacrifice, there was a general belief by the end of the century that the British were opposed to the rite and working for its discontinuance. The success of these endeavours was the subject of some controversy. Quentin Craufurd, writing in 1792, believed that 'In the territories belonging to the English it has everywhere been opposed, and rarely happens there unless it be done secretly, or before those who may have the authority to prevent it have been sufficiently appraised.'[78] East India Company civil servant Abraham Caldecott was more pessimistic, saying, '...the fact is so well established and so many instances of the like nature have occurred since writing my letter as leaves no doubt of the generality of the practice all over Bengal and notwithstanding the endeavours of the English to prevent it, their attempts have proved ineffectual'.[79] Despite their differing assessments of their success, the two men shared the assumption that the British were working to prevent the rite, although as we have seen, apart from individual attempts to dissuade the widow, there had in fact been very little done to stem the number of immolations. The practice was banned from the British part of Calcutta by Lord Anstruther in 1798 and it had for some time been discouraged on Bombay Island and in British Madras, but outside these British enclaves very little was done to prevent it before 1812.

Perhaps the protestations of British activity against the rite should be viewed as representative not of what was actually being done, but

Fig. 7. *The Burning System Illustrated* by Thomas Rowlandson. By permission of the British Library, P 2 687.

of a growing sense among the new British rulers that something should be done. As the flattering, heroic image of the sati gave way towards the end of the century to one that saw her as a passive victim, so too emerged a new construction that conflated British morality with the eradication of sati and set the terms of reference for the debate on sati in the nineteenth century.

The government's inaction on sati did not go unnoticed, or unsatirized. This illustration in Fig. 7 was produced in 1815, but its content is reflective of changing moral attitudes to the prevention of sati that had their roots in the late eighteenth century. The speech bubbles read, 'This custom, though shocking to humanity we still allow in consequence of the revenue it brings in, which is of importance! I also have private reasons for not suppressing the burning system immediately'; 'Why my Lord, with a view to economy under existing circumstances it might be imprudent to press the measure at present; besides I think I feel also the private motives which actuate your Lordship'.

The Exigencies of the Country: Changing Political Relationships and the British Encounter with Sati

The last quarter of the eighteenth century saw major shifts in both the political and the intellectual relationships between Europe and India. In a practical sense, it was the period in which the British consolidated their power in the Subcontinent, not as peripheral traders but as outright rulers. Their predominance in Bengal, which had been effectively sealed with the victory at Plassey in 1757, was formalized in 1765 when the British were granted the right to collect revenue. In 1772 the East India Company finally 'stood forth as diwani of Bengal' and took control of the local administration, ending a period of inequitable joint rule in which the Company held the power and the revenues, but the nawab remained responsible for civil and judicial administration. The priority of the first governor general, Warren Hastings, who arrived in India in 1772, was to stabilize the Company's possessions, for while the French threat had been effectively eliminated in 1760–1, threats to the British paramountcy in the region remained in the form of the Marathas and the rulers of Mysore. Partly as a result of this need for stability, Hastings sought to implement a system of rule that would allow the British to exert their influence through the existing structures and institutions of the territories they were now governing.

As he told the court of directors in 1772: 'We have endeavoured to adapt our regulations to the manners and understandings of the people, and the exigencies of the country, adhering as closely as we are able to their ancient uses and institutions.'[80] This principle of government was founded both on expediency and on Enlightenment ideas of cultural relativism and religious toleration. As Hastings himself put it: '...it would be a grievance to deprive the people of the protection of their own laws, but it would be a wanton tyranny to require their obedience to others of which they are wholly ignorant, and of which they have no possible means of acquiring knowledge'.[81] The decision to utilize native structures was qualified in several ways, however. The sway of Hindu and Islamic law was only to extend to religious and familial issues (such areas as marriage, inheritance, and religious observation, which would in Britain have fallen under the purview of the ecclesiastical courts). Moreover, noninterference in existing structures and practices was only observed as long as it did not interfere with the exigencies of British rule. Brahmins, for example, were not to be exempted from capital punishment solely because their religion forbade it. This decision to separate religious and 'lay' legal matters was to have considerable impact, especially in terms of the official attitude to sati, as it placed the government in the position of having to determine what constituted a religious issue, a central theme in the nineteenth-century debate on sati, as Lata Mani has illustrated in such detail.[82]

Concomitant to the decision to rule through native institutions was the development of a civil service that engaged itself actively with the study of Indian languages and society. The decision to use native laws and institutions as the basis for governing the country made it necessary for the British rulers to have a sound understanding of what these laws were and how these institutions worked. The impact of these developments on the study and understanding of Indian society cannot be overestimated. The knowledge of India produced by Europeans had always had its political facets, of course. The travellers' tales of the early modern and Enlightenment periods not only diverted and informed the reading public at home, but also helped shape their world view and their conception of their own identity. Indeed, the information contained in accounts and itineraries often had a material impact on the shape of Europe's world by informing decisions about trade and exploration and providing a body of literature that underpinned the expansionist tendencies of the West. The political importance that knowledge of India acquired in the last quarter of the eighteenth century went far beyond this, however. The expediencies of exercising power over the indigenous inhabitants made a detailed knowledge of this population an absolute necessity and implicated all sorts of previously 'apolitical' knowledge in the colonial project.

In particular, the study of Indian languages took on a fundamental political significance during this period, as it became necessary for the British to master the tongues in which much of their business would perforce be conducted. A scholar as well as an administrator, Hastings eagerly encouraged the study of Indian languages among his civil servants and was instrumental in the founding of the Asiatic Society in 1784. The work of the Asiatic Society extended well beyond linguistics, of course, and its breakthroughs in this field opened whole new areas of inquiry by making Sanskrit and other texts available for European study for the first time. This had a profound effect on the way in which knowledge on India was created. The Society's journal, the *Asiatick Researches*, was eagerly received in Europe and was the catalyst of what Raymond Schwab has referred to as 'the Oriental renaissance'.[83] Serious academic study on Indian themes became an acceptable pursuit, but it was now being carried out in a situation of colonial domination and on this basis has since been accused of being wholly implicated in expediencies of power.[84] The dynamics of the relationship between the production of knowledge and the imperatives of the colonial state were more complex than Said suggests, however. Though the vast majority of the contributors to the Asiatic Society were Company servants of some description and while many of the subjects dealt with had political applications, the Society also dealt with subjects of 'pure' academic interest (if such a thing can ever exist) such as literature and art, which had no political application. Rosaline Rocher explores the contradictions that allowed men like Sir William Jones to both serve the colonial state and to produce purely academic research, and in so doing creates a considerably more complex picture of the early creation of colonial knowledge than Said allows for.[85] The complexity of the relationship between power and knowledge is particularly relevant to the study of British reactions to sati because as the British took up their role as rulers and administrators, the custom of burning women alive necessarily shifted from a curiosity to a legislative dilemma, forcing the British to decide how far they should extend their principles of religious toleration.[86]

A Motley Dress of True and False Colours: Orientalist Scholarship and Textual Authority

As we have already seen, the assumption that sati was a Hindu religious rite was one which had only really come to the fore at the end of the seventeenth century, although at this stage it was premised not on accurate information but on the assumption of the all-pervasive power of religion in India. The breakthroughs in the study of the Sanskrit language at the end of the eighteenth century significantly altered the parameters of European knowledge on the subject, however, as religious authenticity could now be quantified by reference to textual authority. As the century progressed, and as Europeans gained increasing access to sources of information on Indian society and culture, the question of the exact religious status of sati became open for debate. In a work published in 1768, Alexander Dow broke with the previous European image of sati, saying, 'The extraordinary custom of the women burning themselves with their deceased husbands, has, for the most part fallen into desuetude in India; nor was it ever reckoned a religious duty, as has been very erroneously supposed in the West.'[87] Dow's textual sources are now widely believed to have been spurious, but his rejection of sati's religious significance was the opening salvo in a debate on the rite's religious authenticity that would underpin the nineteenth-century discourse on abolition. His comments prompted a direct response from Nathaniel Brassey Halhed in the preface of his *A Code of Gentoo Laws*, which was published in 1776. Halhed makes the religious rewards for sati explicit and asks: 'How then shall we reconcile so splendid and exalted a benediction pronounced upon this spontaneous martyrdom, with the assertion of an author, that the custom for the wives to burn themselves with their husband's bodies was never reckoned a religious duty in India?'[88] Later he comments that

The Bramins seem to look upon this sacrifice as one of the first principles of their religion, the cause of which it would hardly be orthodox to investigate...which they closely conceal from the eyes of the world, among the other mysteries of their faith: but we are convinced equally by information and experience, that the custom has not for the most part fallen into desuetude in India as a celebrated writer has supposed.[89]

Code of Gentoo Laws was the first concerted attempt by the British to codify the indigenous laws and customs through which they intended to rule the areas under their control. Halhed did not speak Sanskrit himself, although he was an excellent linguist who produced the first Bengali grammar in 1778. Because of this, it is impossible that he should have studied the Hindu religious and legal texts himself. Rather, his code was compiled with the aid of Indian pandits who collected the material and rendered the contents into Persian, which Halhed then translated. The code he produced was a major landmark, though William Jones' *Institutes of Hindu Law* soon superseded it in practical terms. For our purposes, Halhed's work is perhaps the more significant of the two, however, for in his lists of ordinances he includes one relating to sati and so institutionalizes the practice in the statutes of British law in India. The ordinance appears in chapter twenty of his code and is the only one of the twenty-five ordinances on women in that chapter to mention widow burning. It says:

It is proper for a woman, after her husband's death, to burn herself in the fire with his corpse; every woman who thus burns herself, shall remain in paradise with her husband three crore and fifty lakhs of years, by destiny; if she cannot burn, she must in that case preserve an inviolable chastity; if she remains always chaste, she goes to paradise; and if she does not preserve her chastity she goes to hell.[90]

Although the ordinance is very far from making sati an inviolable duty, its inclusion confirms both the legal and religious authenticity of sati as a Hindu rite and it is this assumption of sati's religious authenticity that underpins the debate over its abolition in the early nineteenth century.[91]

The acquisition of linguistic competency in Sanskrit, combined with the 'discovery' of complete Hindu texts, had an immense impact on the structure and method of European knowledge about India and Hinduism. Previously, knowledge of the country's religious doctrines and rites had been based primarily on personal observation and hearsay. Of course, attempts had been made as early as the fifteenth century to uncover the authentic source of the Hindu religion, and missionaries, particularly the Jesuits, had made attempts from the seventeenth century on to learn the language of the Hindu texts. It is believed that Roberto de Nobili may have composed prayers in Sanskrit, though none of his work on it appeared in Europe. For the most part, however, the early missionaries found themselves dealing with members of the lower castes, who imposed their vernacular between the Europeans and pure Sanskrit. It was not until the Hastings era that the Brahmins, who held the key to the sacred language, could be prevailed upon to share their knowledge with Europeans. The willingness of the pandits to collaborate with the government was carefully nurtured by Hastings, and coincided, perhaps not incidentally, with the acquisition of complete copies of various Hindu texts. The existence of a comprehensive body of Hindu scriptures had long been conjectured at, though doubts existed as to whether the majority of texts were still extant. As late as the 1780s, Charles Wilkins could express doubt that there were anything but unintelligible scraps remaining. Collaboration with Brahmin pandits increased the accessibility to various texts, however, and in 1789 Captain Polier announced that he had recovered a complete set of the Vedas and deposited them with the British Museum. Linguistic breakthrough and the availability of texts, combined with a favourable political climate in which the governor general actively encourage Orientalist study, allowed a much greater scope for the systematic study of Indian society and culture than had been possible at any point in the past.

In terms of the European understanding of sati, these breakthroughs meant that skilled European observers could go direct to 'source' for information on the rite, as the religious texts on which the rite was supposedly premised were now available for study. The first European to make a concerted inquiry into the textual authority for sati was Sir Henry Colebrooke. His article, 'On The Duties of a Faithful Hindu Widow', appeared in the fourth volume of the *Asiatic Researches* in 1794 and provided an inventory of the ordinances relating to sati and ascetic widowhood that he had uncovered. He justified his project in terms of the unreliable nature of previous material, saying:

Several late compilations in Europe betray a great want of judgement in the selection of authorities; and their motley dress of true and false colours tends to perpetuate error; for this reason it seems necessary on every topic to revert to original authorities for the purpose of recalling error or verifying facts already published; and this object will in no way be more readily attained than by the communication of detached essays on each topic, as it may present itself to the Orientalist in the Progress of his researches.[92]

He then proceeded to list Hindu ordinances that extol the virtue of sati and prescribe how it is to be performed, as taken from various religious texts. Colebrooke recognized that sati was not an absolute imperative as an alternative was provided, but he made clear the point that 'Though an alternative be allowed, the Hindu legislators have shown themselves disposed to encourage widows to burn themselves with their husband's corpse.'[93] He also elaborated the circumstances under which the widow was forbidden to burn, thus preempting the nineteenth-century concern with defining 'legal' and 'illegal' satis.

Colebrooke's essay on sati is not significant for breaking with former ideas—most informed opinion by this time accepted, as Colebrooke did, that sati was sanctioned as meritorious in the Hindu religion, but was not an imperative injunction on the widow, who might instead chose the course of ascetic widowhood. Rather, its importance lies in the fact that it represents the first occasion on which these ideas about sati had been put together, supported by direct quotations from the *shastras*. Colebrooke's essay is in effect the first attempt at codifying the Hindu position on sati and, while it was far from the definitive statement on the religious authenticity of the rite, its concentration on the textual authority as the source of the most authentic information on sati set a precedent in terms of the frame of reference for future debate.

Although not overtly political, and presented in a scholarly journal, the nature of Colebrooke's account illustrates the complex dynamics between power and knowledge in this period. His concentration on the scriptural authenticity of sati is indicative not only of his personal research interests, but also of the imperatives of a British government in India that would soon have to formulate policy on the subject. Colebrooke's article is sterile in terms of interpretive material, consisting primarily of direct quotations from the texts, suggesting that the issue he was addressing was not a broader understanding of the socio-cultural meaning of sati, but a codification of its scriptural status. By so doing Colebrooke privileged scriptural authority above the intricacies of local custom and assumed a homogeneity in religious observance in India that both reinforced earlier assumptions about the all-pervasive nature of Indian religion, and created a framework through which this religion could be studied without direct recourse to the people who actually practiced it. In doing so he set a precedent in regard to the terms of the nineteenth-century debate on the abolition of sati.

Emerging Evangelism

The serious academic study of Indian civilization did not automatically imply a sympathetic understanding of Hindus or their religion.

India's major glories were considered to lie in the very distant past and the supposed degradation of its contemporary society and culture deemed to be the result of millennia of degeneration. Even the great Orientalist Sir William Jones saw little to admire in India's present, stating '...we cannot doubt, how degenerate and abased so ever the Hindus may now appear, that in some earlier age they were splendid in arts and arms, happy in government, wise in legislation and eminent in various knowledge....'[94] The degeneration theory is somewhat paradoxical when one considers that Indian society was supposed to be immutable and unchanging, but perhaps it sprang from the need to bridge the ever-growing gap between the scholars' assessment of the Hindu past and the unflattering portrayal of India that was gaining increasing popularity in the present. The relatively sympathetic attitude of the Indianists was increasingly being challenged by a rising number of Anglicists who saw little of any worth in Indian civilization and favoured a policy of Westernization. Part of the catalyst for these changing attitudes was the rise of evangelicalism in Britain at the end of the eighteenth century. The cultural relativism and religious toleration of the Enlightenment was increasingly giving way to an energetic Christianity that supported social reform along Christian lines, both at home and abroad. The ethos of evangelicalism, as it emerged in the early nineteenth century, is epitomized by the key aims of the Clapham sect, whose famous members included Sir William Wilberforce and Sir Charles Grant and which worked, among other things, for the abolition of slave trade and opening up of India to missionary activity. Charles Grant himself had close associations with India and in 1792 he produced a tract called *Observations on the State of Society Among the Asiatic Subjects of Great Britain,* which he circulated in support of the missionary cause and which was published by the House of Commons in 1813. In it he presented an unflattering picture of Indians as steeped in iniquity, licentiousness, and corruption. His account of sati is situated within this framework of criticism and condemnation, and the rite itself was appropriated by the argument for missionary endeavour in India as a prime example of the backward and barbaric nature of the Hindus. Grant clearly situated sati within a religious context, saying of it that 'The strong recommendations and injunctions from a law giver believed to be divine is of course admitted to have the force of a religious obligation; and it is one of those institutions of which the Bramins are very tenacious.'[95] This is hardly surprising, of course, as to separate sati from the Hindu religion would remove a key weapon in the arsenal against Hinduism and weaken the case for immediate missionary activity. Unlike earlier observers who were prepared to separate an estimable pure Hinduism from the anathemas of popular practice, the new evangelical position relied heavily on the assumption that Hinduism, and all pagan religions, were inherently iniquitous.

Grant does not content himself with using sati as an example of the barbarity of Hindu religious practice. He goes on to link the rite with the very structure of Hindu society itself and places the blame for the growth of the custom on the caste system and the fact that women are under no circumstances permitted to marry beneath them. He states:

When a woman's husband therefore dies, she is reckoned a useless being, and what is worse, a dangerous one. The jealousy of the Eastern people has placed their honour in the conduct of their women, as being what touches them most. Not the husband himself only, but the whole family are stained by the misbehaviour of a wife; and if she degrades herself after his death, they are still affected by her dishonour. If she should bring other children by a man of inferior caste, she would introduce, more signally than any misconduct in a man could, that disorder and confusion into the society which would tend to break down the lines of separation between castes. But seeing the number of widows must always be great, and they have no effectual superintendent or protector, there must be a proportion danger of such irregularity as would at length make the exceptions bear down on the rule.... How then, might it be said, shall the evils to be apprehended from this source, notwithstanding prohibitions and disgrace, be prevented? Let an ordinance, professedly divine, recommend to widows a voluntary departure with their husbands to paradise, under an assurance of enjoying there a very long succession of felicity; honour shall stimulate them to embrace this choice, and lest the love of life should still prevail, the fear of infamy shall compel them to die. Nor would this expedient appear as shocking to the Hindu as it does to us. Admitting the separations of castes to be a sacred institution, whatever tended to subvert it might be obviated not only lawfully, but as a matter of duty.[96]

Grant thus uses sati to subvert not only the Hindu religion, but also the whole social structure, for how can a system that legitimizes the burning of women be anything but despicable? In his emphasis on the potential threat of the Hindu widow's sexuality, Grant resurrected concerns that had been common in the early modern period, but which had all but disappeared in an eighteenth-century construction of Indian women as sexually pure. In doing so he undermined the rationale for the 'heroic' sati, making the widow instead the victim of her own capricious sexuality. He does not go as far as to relate Strabo's account for sati's origins, but the logic is very similar and is indicative of an emerging trend to denigrate all aspects of Indian society as a means of justifying both the colonial presence and missionary enterprise.

Although the *Observations on the State of Society* had a specific agenda in its advocacy of proselytizing activity in India, the opinions about Indians and about sati that it expresses were ones that were beginning to gain currency more generally among the British in India and at home. The last years of the eighteenth century was a period of considerable ideological debate about the cultural policy that should be adopted in India. Warren Hastings' principle of non-intervention was under attack from both the evangelical and the utilitarian groups, both of which felt that Britain had a duty to intervene in the social and cultural affairs of India. The former in the interests of the propagation of the Gospel, the latter under the rhetoric of greater good. We shall return to these issues in more detail in the next chapters, but for the moment we shall conclude by looking at the way in which some of these ideas had become institutionalized by the end of the eighteenth century by looking at the attitudes to sati that were being inculcated in the students of Fort William College, Calcutta.

The College at Fort William was founded by Governor General Wellesley in 1800 in order to instruct new Company servants and '...fix and establish sound and correct principles of government in their minds at an early period of life' on the basis that this was '...the best security which could be provided for the British power in India.'[97] Unlike the Asiatic Society, Fort William College was almost entirely political in nature, for while it taught a wide range of Indian subjects, its ultimate purpose was to equip new recruits for their responsibilities as agents of the colonial state. A look at some of the ideas that were being expressed in prize-winning essays by the students of the college is a sobering indicator of the government's changing attitude towards Indians. As a place where new civil servants could become acclimatized to India and learn the languages and skills needed to fulfil their role in the colonial administration, the time that recruits spent there played a formative role in shaping their attitude to India and its society. By 1802, when the essays in question were written, it seems to have become as much a place of indoctrination, as of instruction. The essays in question were written primarily to demonstrate the author's command of a particular vernacular, but the titles given seem to be designed to provide an opportunity for the students to show that they have grasped the more implicit agenda being taught in the college. Titles included: 'On the Character and Capacity of the Asiaticks, and Particularly the Natives of Hindoostan', 'The Distribution of the Hindus into Castes Retards their Progress and Improvement', and 'The Natives of India Under the British Enjoy a Greater Degree of Tranquillity, Security and Happiness than Under Any Former Government.'[98] The answers given to these loaded questions, while differing slightly in structure and content, reveal a uniformity of attitudes that suggest that more than just language skills were being taught at the College.

On 29 March 1803 public disputations in oriental languages were held in presence of the guest of honour, the Marquis Wellesley. One of the propositions up for debate was that 'The Suicide of Hindu Widows by Burning Themselves with the Bodies of their Deceased Husbands is a Practice Revolting to Natural Feeling and Inconsistent with Moral Duty.' Defending this position was William Chaplin, who had previously won the first prize for an essay on the same subject. His arguments reflect the cultural superiority that would come to characterize the British responses to sati in the early nineteenth century. He opened by saying:

In a society of Christians, or even among civilised nations of any persuasion, one would imagine that no argument could be adduced against the position that I have laid down. To my mind, gentlemen, it presents the irresistible conviction of a self evident truth....I am perfectly convinced that when you have weighed all the pernicious consequences of the practice to which I allude, your ideas will perfectly coincide with mine regarding its injustice barbarity and immorality.[99]

He then went on to denounce sati on various grounds, including the reciprocity of mutual affection implied by marriage and a parent's duty to their offspring. For Chaplin, sati was proof positive of the barbarity of Indian society and the backward nature of its religion. He claimed:

It is in fact impossible to reconcile it with the idea of civilisation and humanity; we must therefore suppose that it originated in that state of barbarism when mankind were either strangers to all the nobler feelings of the soul, or allowed them to be perverted by sanguinary religion.... We may search animated creation in vain for an example of such depravity. I may surely be allowed to term that barbarous in the extreme which action would degrade even the nature of brutes. Shall man then, a rational animal to whom religion has taught benevolence and humanity, shall he I say, under the flimsy veil of religion, persist in the murder of a disconsolate widow....[100]

He then went on in the strongest terms to accuse the Brahmins who 'endeavour to cloak it under the sacred sanction of religion'[101] and the power of superstition for fostering such a custom. He concluded by suggesting that it would be to the glory of Britain to put an end to this custom, and expressed the opinion that the spread of Christian faith would have that effect, but added:

It would be equally unjust and impolitic to make use of power to deprive men of the enjoyment of their religious freedoms. Mildness and persuasion in such cases are the only powerful advocates with the mind that revolts against every species of violence in matters of faith and conscience, which are supposed to be connected with the eternal felicity of mankind.[102]

This essay is particularly interesting for the way in which it combines the rhetoric of cultural superiority with a conclusion of religious tolerance. In later years the growth of evangelicalism and anglicism, and the impact of these ideas on Indian policy would have allowed Chaplin to carry his rhetoric through to the logical conclusion of advocating abolition. In 1803, however, the contest between anglicist and orientalist ideas had not yet been conclusively settled and proclaimed principles of religious toleration remained juxtaposed against growing cultural arrogance. This is reinforced by the fact that two other scholars actually argued against the proposition. Unfortunately these counterpoints to Chaplin's argument were not printed and so have been lost, leaving us to conjecture at what they might have said. One finds it difficult to believe that by this stage they would have provided outright support for sati, but they might have harked back to the cultural relativism of the Enlightenment, or stressed the importance of religious toleration as a principle in government policy. The inclusion of the issue of sati as a specific topic for debate is indicative of the degree of prominence that the rite was achieving as an indicator of the status of Indian society, while the nature of Chaplin's response makes it clear that certain ideas about the rite were becoming institutionalized by this point. It is also clear from this and other essays that the British now saw sati as firmly embedded in the religious sphere and that religion was held to be the most prominent feature and dearest institution of Indian life. These ideas were not merely widely accepted but were actually being taught in college to the men who would later be responsible for governing India. It is no surprise then that these ideas should be deeply entrenched when the abolition of sati came to be debated.

By the time Governor General Lord Wellesley made the first tentative inquiries into the issue of legislation on sati in 1805, certain assumptions about the nature of the rite, and the manner in which the issue should be addressed, had thus become prominent. The religious status of sati had become an accepted fact and the precise nature of the scriptural authority for it a key area of debate. The widow's agency and the sociological motivations for sati, which had been so prominent in earlier accounts, had been effectively marginalized. Although after a while, there remained the scope to see the heroic as well as the horrific aspects of the rite, there was a growing tendency to stress the role of manipulative priests and religious indoctrination in forcing the passive figure of the widow onto the pyre. The increasing tendency to vilify all aspects of the rite meant that the admiration for the widow that had been such a notable feature of many earlier accounts could now find only subconscious expression. These trends, which were crystallizing by the end of the eighteenth century, were to form the basis of European conceptions of sati in the early nineteenth century, but just as they had taken form at a specific historical juncture as a result of various ongoing processes, so too would they be modified and transformed by an assortment of forces and imperatives in the future. Indeed, changing political imperatives, the rise of evangelism and utilitarianism at home, growing missionary activity in India, and the generally changing attitudes towards issues such as gender, suicide, and religion meant that nineteenth-century European attitudes to sati would be no more static or homogenous than those of the preceding centuries, but rather continued to shift and mutate to fit the changing needs of the time.

Notes

1. John Zephaniah Holwell, 'The Religious Tenets of the Gentoos', in P. J. Marshall, *The British Discovery of Hinduism in the Eighteenth Century* (Cambridge: Cambridge University Press, 1970), p. 96.
2. Two very important collections were issued in 1704 and 1705 respectively. Churchill's *Collection Of Voyages And Travels* used translations of previously little-known texts, while John Harris's less original *Itinerantium Bibliotheca* relied heavily on earlier collections by Purchas and Hakluyt.

See Marshall and Williams, *The Great Map of Mankind: British Perceptions of the World in the Age of Enlightenment* (London: Dent, 1982), p. 47.

3. P.G. Adams, *Travellers and Travel Liars, 1660–1800* (Berkeley: University of California Press, 1962).

4. Cited in ibid., p. 9.

5. Marshall and Williams, *The Great Map*, p. 61.

6. Abbe de Guyon, *A New History of The East Indies, Ancient And Modern* (London: R. Dodsley and J. Dodsley, 1757), p. 445.

7. Donald Campbell, *A Journey Overland To India* (Philadelphia: T. Dobson 1797), p. 391. It is interesting to note that the Brahmins in this case seem eager for the European to observe the rite, and even hasten their preparations to ensure his attendance. Obviously, European presence at a sati was not yet consistently linked with disapproval and intervention.

8. Ibid.

9. William Hodges, *Travels in India During the Years 1780, 1781, 1782 and 1783* (Delhi: Munishram Manoharlal, 1999), p. 83.

10. The liberalization of attitudes to corporal punishment and the impact this had on British reactions to the spectacle of sati are dealt with in greater detail in the next chapter.

11. Hodges, *Travels in India*, p. 84.

12. Letter from Abraham Caldecott to Miss Pettet of Dartford, Kent, 14 September 1783 (Oriental And India Office Collection, European Manuscripts [Henceforth OIO, Eur. Mss]).

13. For more on the early origins of anthropology, see M.T. Hodgen, *Early Anthropology in the Sixteenth and Seventeenth Centuries* (Philadelphia: University of Philadelphia Press, 1964).

14. I am not here suggesting that eighteenth-century European ideas about sati were either homogenous or static. As Lisa Lowe has demonstrated, they shifted considerably both between nationalities and over time (Lowe, *Critical Terrains*). There were some common characteristics in the European image of India, however, and as the forthcoming discussion of their interpretations of sati will show, there was a general trend towards attributing certain characteristics and 'essences' to Indian society that conditioned their reactions to individual aspects of it.

15. de Guyon, *A New History*, p. 58.

16. Dellon, *Voyage To The East Indies*, p. 47.

17. F.F. Catrou, *The General History of the Mogul Empire: Extracted from the Memoirs of N. Manouchi, a Venetian and Chief Physician to Orangzebe for Above 40 Years* (London: Jonah Bowyer, 1709), p. 66.

18. The term 'Hinduism' did not come into common use among Europeans until the nineteenth century, although the concept it represented emerged around this time. I will use the word here for simplicity's sake, though eighteenth-century observers would have referred instead to 'the religion of the Hindus' or of the 'Gentoos'.

19. Marshall and Williams, *The Great Map*, p. 98.
20. Holwell, 'Religious Tenets', p. 91.
21. Ibid., p. 92.
22. John Henry Grose, *Voyage To The East Indies With Observations On The Several Parts There* (London: Hooper and Morley, 1757), pp.144–5.
23. Pierre Sonnerat, *A Voyage To The East Indies And China Between The Years 1774 And 1781* (Calcutta: Stuart And Cooper, 1788), p. 118.
24. Luke Scrafton, *Reflections On The Government Of Indostan* (London: W. Richardson and S. Clark, 1763), p. 9.
25. Elizabeth Fox-Genovese, 'Women and the Enlightenment', in R. Bridenthal, C. Koonz, and S. Stuard (eds), *Becoming Visible: Women in European History* (Boston: Houghton Mifflin, 1987), p. 251.
26. T. Hitchcock, *English Sexualities, 1700–1800* (Basingstoke: Macmillan, 1997), p. 47.
27. Ibid., pp. 42–7.
28. Fox-Genovese, 'Women and the Enlightenment', p. 265.
29. Rev. William Tennant, *Indian Recreations: Consisting chiefly of strictures on the domestic and rural economy of the Mahametans and Hindoos* (Edinburgh: C. Stewart, 1803), pp. 190–1.
30. Grose, *Voyage To The East Indies*, p. 308.
31. Ibid., pp. 307–8.
32. Scrafton, *Reflections*, p. 9.
33. Bernard Picart, *The Ceremonies And Religious Customs Of The Idolatrous Nations* (London: W. Jackson, 1733), p. 26.
34. Abbe J.A. Dubois, *Hindu Manners, Customs and Ceremonies* (New Delhi: Book Faith India, 1999), p. 363.
35. Eliza Fay, 'Original Letters From India', Letter XX, 5 September 1781, in P. Thankappan Nair (ed.), *Calcutta in the Eighteenth Century* (Calcutta: Firmakum, 1984), pp. 200–1.
36. Ibid., p. 201.
37. Voltaire for example was a great admirer of what he deemed to be the 'essence' of Hinduism.
38. Holwell, 'Religious Tenets', p. 92.
39. Ibid.
40. Sonnerat, *Voyage To The East Indies*, p. 113.
41. Picart, *Ceremonies And Religious Customs*, pp. 27–8.
42. Tennant, *Indian Recreations*, p. 191.
43. Grose, *Voyage To The East Indies*, p. 143.
44. The doctrine of the transmigration of the soul.
45. De Guyon, *A New History*, pp. 57–8.
46. Cited in Teltscher, *India Inscribed*, p. 103.
47. Lockman (ed.), *Travels Of The Jesuits* (London: T. Piety, 1762), p. 425.
48. For 'Sacrifice of an Hindoo Widow upon the Funeral Pile of her husband' by John Zoffany, see C. Bayly, *The Raj: India and the British 1600–1947* (London: National Portrait Gallery, 1990).

49. Dorothy Figueira, 'Die Flambierte Frau: Sati in European Culture', in John Stratton Hawley, *Sati: The Blessing and the Curse* (New York: Oxford University Press, 1994), p. 58.
50. Holwell, 'Religious Tenets', pp. 95–6.
51. Ibid.
52. See S.E. Sprott, *The English Debate on Suicide from Donne to Hulme* (La Salle: Open Court Publishing, 1961), pp. 94–152.
53. MacDonald, 'The Secularization Of Suicide'.
54. Ibid., p. 76.
55. Sonnerat, *A Voyage To The East Indies*, pp. 113–14.
56. Scrafton, *Reflections*, p. 9.
57. Cockburn, *A Discourse on Self Murder*, p. 3.
58. Ibid., p. 23.
59. Tennant, *Indian Recreations*, p. 191.
60. Quentin Craufurd, *Sketches Relating to the History, Religion, Learning and Manners of the Hindoos* (London: T. Cadell, 1792), p. 16.
61. Picart, *Ceremonies And Religious Customs*, p. 26.
62. Tennant, *Indian Recreations*, pp. 190–1.
63. Sonnerat, *Voyage To The East Indies*, p. 114.
64. Grose, *Voyage To The East Indies*, pp. 144–5.
65. Marianne Starke, *The Widow Of Malabar* (London: William Lane, 1791).
66. In *Bengal Past and Present*, vol. 2:1, 1908, p. 84.
67. Thomas Twining, 'The Hindoo Widow' in H.K. Kaul (ed.), *Traveller's India* (New Delhi: Oxford University Press, 1979), p. 94.
68. L. de Grandpre, *A Voyage in the Indian Ocean to Bengal, Undertaken in the Years 1789 and 1790* (London: C.J. Robinson, 1803) p. 70.
69. Ibid., p. 68.
70. Ibid.
71. Ibid., p. 73.
72. Ibid.
73. Holwell, 'The Religious Tenets', p. 97.
74. *Parliamentary Papers: Papers Relating to East Indian Affairs*, vol. 18 [Henceforth *PP*, 18], Paper 749, Extract from Fort St George Military Consultations, 19 October 1772, p. 268.
75. *PP*, 18, Collector of Shahabad to Government of India, 4 February 1789, p. 22.
76. Ibid.
77. Ibid.
78. Craufurd, *Sketches*, p. 15.
79. Letter from Abraham Caldecott to Miss Petter (OIO, Eur. Mss).
80. Cited in Metcalfe, *Ideologies of the Raj*, p. 10.
81. Quoted in Rosalind Rocher, 'British Orientalism and the Eighteenth Century: The Dialectics of Knowledge and Government', in C.A. Breckenridge and P. van der Veer, *Orientalism and the Post Colonial*

Predicament (Philadelphia: University of Pennsylvania Press, 1993), p. 220.
82. Mani, *Contentious Traditions.*
83. Raymond Schwab, *The Oriental Renaissance Europe's Rediscovery of India and the East* (New York: Columbia University Press, 1984).
84. Said, *Orientalism.*
85. Cited in Rocher, 'British Orientalism', p. 218.
86. For more on the colonial formation of knowledge and its implication in the imperial project, see Bernard Cohn, *Colonialism and its Forms of Knowledge* (Oxford: Oxford University Press, 1996).
87. Alexander Dow, 'The History of Indostan', in P. J. Marshall, *The British Discovery of Hinduism* (Cambridge: Cambridge University Press, 1970), p. 96.
88. Nathaniel Brassey Halhed, *A Code of Gentoo Laws, or Ordinations of the Pundits,* (London: 1777), p. 164.
89. Halhed, *A Code of Gentoo Laws,* p. 179.
90. Ibid., p. 253.
91. No reference to sati is made in Jones' *Institutes.* Although it might be tempting to ascribe this to a desire to avoid legitimating a custom that the British found repugnant, the actual explanation would seem to be more mundane. Jones' work was based on the *Code of Manu,* which makes no reference to sati whatsoever.
92. Henry Colebrooke, 'On the Duties of a Faithful Hindu Widow', in *Asiatick Researches,* vol. 4, 1793–4, p. 205.
93. Ibid., p. 210.
94. Cited in David Kopf, *Orientalism and the Bengal Renaissance: The Dynamics of Indian Modernization, 1773–1835* (Berkeley: University of California Press, 1969), p. 45.
95. Charles Grant, *Observations on the State of Society Among the Asiatic Subjects of Great Britain* (London: House of Commons, 1813), p. 56.
96. Grant, *Observations,* pp. 56–7.
97. Kopf, *Orientalism and the Bengal Renaissance,* p. 47.
98. *Essays by the Students of Fort William,* vol. 1 (London: British Library Collections, 1802).
99. William Chaplin, 'The Suicide Of Hindu Widows By Burning Themselves With The Bodies Of Their Deceased Husbands Is A Practice Revolting To Natural Feeling And Inconsistent With Moral Duty', *Primitiae Orientalis* (Calcutta: Royal Asiatic Society Library Collections, 1803–4).
100. Ibid.
101. Ibid.
102. Ibid.

4

INFERNAL SCENES
Sati and the Spectacle of Suffering

CRSO

Had the deed been constantly perpetrated in the sight of all, as was formerly the case in Smithfield; had the helpless victim to superstition been bound at the stake in the open view of the multitude, as were formerly the victims to Romish bigotry—had the flames been suffered to kindle on her publicly—had the convulsions and agonies of the widow expiring in torments, often in the bloom of youth, been fully witnessed by the aged, the young, the neighbour, the near relative, humanity must have spoken out long ago....[1]

The first three decades of the nineteenth century saw an exponential rise in British interest in sati. There were several reasons for this. On a basic level there were now many more Europeans living and working in India who were witnessing and reporting on sati firsthand, as well as an increasingly diverse number of outlets for their accounts. In addition to the travel narratives and works of synthesis that had been the main source of information on foreign customs in the eighteenth century, information about India was reaching a wider audience than ever before through national newspapers and journals. *The Times* carried its first full-length account of a sati in 1808 and the *Edinburgh Review* reported on the custom in 1824. Moreover, as the generation of nabobs gave way to that of colonial rulers and the British community in India settled in for the long haul, colonial society began to develop its own organs of expression, both in terms of regional newspapers like *Bombay Gazette* or *Bengal Hukuru* and specialist journals such as the the *Asiatic Review*, *Oriental Observer*, and *Quarterly Oriental Magazine*. These media both disseminated knowledge about sati more widely and provided a forum in which it could be discussed. Whereas in the eighteenth century those who wrote about sati had done so primarily to supply their readers with (supposedly) objective information, by the nineteenth century much of the material produced on sati was far more personal and subjective, as authors and readers alike offered their own views and challenged the ideas and opinions of others.

The new political situation in India made the issue of sati more relevant and contentious than ever before. Previously, accounts of sati had been of interest as curiosities, one of the strange customs of a foreign land and religion that, whether admired or deplored, were outside the European sphere of action. The new role of the British as the rulers of a large part of India gave the issue new urgency. Sati was no longer solely of academic interest, but was to become a matter of politics. Rather than merely recount the spectacle of a sati, observers were increasingly likely to pass not only a moral judgement on the act, but also a political one about whether and how the rite should be prevented. This was especially the case after 1821 when the first volume of *Parliamentary Papers* on sati was published and several philanthropic societies adopted the issue.[2] Sati became something of a *cause célèbre*, both in India and at home, and was debated not only by the Government of India, but also by the East India Company Board of Directors and its proprietors and stockholders, the British Parliament, missionaries, philanthropists, and the regional and national press.

The opening of India to missionary activity indirectly helped to create one of the most copious sources of information and opinion on sati. Of course, foreign missionaries of various denominations had been working in India for centuries and had from the outset reported on the rite, but, financial sponsorship for the Lutheran missions by the Society for the Propagation of Christian Knowledge notwithstanding, British missionary involvement in India did not really take off until the nineteenth century. While sources such as the Jesuits' *Lettres Edifantes* or individual accounts by missionaries such as Abraham Roger were sometimes available in English editions prior to 1800, these were specialist items not readily available to the general public. It was not until 1793, when the first British Baptist missionary, William Carey, arrived in India that the British evangelical community had a direct link to contemporary conditions in India. Carey reported on his experiences in India in a series of letters to the society and his observations and accounts were regularly published in the various Baptist missionary journals. From the outset sati was a cause of concern; indeed, one of Carey's earliest letters, written in 1793, discussed sati in detail and was published in the *Periodic Accounts of the Baptist Missionary Society* in 1800. Carey was soon joined by other British missionaries; first by the other members of the famous Serampore trio, Joshua Marshman and William Ward, and then, particularly after 1813, by missionaries of other denominations. Their experiences and accounts were widely available as their letters home were published in the journals of their various societies.

Missionary accounts, as might be expected, tended to concentrate on the discreditable aspects of Hindu society. In many ways sati was only one of a catalogue of 'horrors' that could be used to denigrate Indian life. As in previous centuries, missionaries in particular were keen to stress the abhorrent aspects of Indian religion and culture in order to justify their own presence in the Subcontinent and to gather funds for their work at home. At the same time as the official debate on sati was going on in government circles, there was also a concerted campaign being waged by the various missionary groups and other philanthropic societies to bring the more shocking aspects of Indian life to the public attention, both for the purpose of bringing pressure on the government to act against practices such as sati and to validate the missionaries' own enterprise. In works such as the Reverend James Pegg's *India's Cries to British Humanity*,[3] or the anonymous pamphlet *Deplorable Effects of Heathen Superstitions, as Manifested by the Natives of Hindustan*,[4] the sacrifice of the Hindu widow was lined up alongside such 'atrocities' as infanticide, *ghat* murders (the exposing of the ill on the banks of the Ganges or other rivers), the drowning of lepers, human sacrifices (particularly before the cart at Jagannath Temple), hook swinging, self mortification, and religious suicide in a catalogue of horrors designed to shock and motivate the God-fearing British public. These sensational subjects reached a wider audience than ever before, as accounts of these atrocities were distilled down into pamphlets and cheap tracts that could be distributed among the poorer sections of the community, with the aim of raising awareness of conditions in India and garnering support for the missionary enterprise.

While all of these 'barbaric practices' had their own intrinsic appeal to the charitable impulses of the evangelical community, it does seem that sati in particular caught the population's attention, and concern with the rite extended far beyond the immediate sphere of missionary activity. A look at the articles on India carried by *The Times* in the nineteenth century will show that sati was by far the most extensively reported of these 'humanitarian' issues in India. In the thirty-three years between 1800 and 1833 (when the last article relating to its abolition appeared) *The Times* carried eighteen separate articles on the subject, some of considerable length. In the whole of the nineteenth century, forty-one articles on the subject appeared. Compare this to the seven articles on thuggee (all of which appeared between 1841 and 1883), four articles on human sacrifice in India (between 1864 and 1901), or the total of sixteen articles relating to infanticide in India and it becomes clear that sati received some of the most extensive coverage over the longest duration.[5] Indeed, the only subject to receive greater attention was the question of child marriage, which was had forty-seven references in the nineteenth century. Forty-three of these, however, appeared in the period around 1891, when the Age of Consent Bill sparked controversy both in India and at home. Obviously it would be dangerous to read too much into these figures; *The Times* was only one of many newspapers available at the time, but given its circulation and prestige in the nineteenth century, it is possible to use it as an indicator of public interest, particularly as the figures are supported by the extent of concern with sati as recorded elsewhere.

The expansion in media coverage of sati was accompanied by a marked change in attitudes towards the rite and the early nineteenth century was characterized by the almost universal vilification of it by all sections of the British public. As we have seen, accounts of previous centuries displayed a significant ambivalence towards sati, with distress at the physical suffering of the widow being counterbalanced by a regard for her chastity and bravery, producing a judgement on sati that was far from entirely negative. By the early nineteenth century, however, almost all positive aspects of the sacrifice had been purged from the European understanding of it. Reactions to the rite, instead of being characterized by heterogeneity and personal subjectivity, become homogenized into a collective expression of horror. The image of the widow, once lauded for her bravery, loyalty, and conviction even to the point of being compared to the Christian martyrs, is recreated as a passive, agencyless victim, to be pitied rather than admired. The possibility for a culturally sympathetic understanding of sati is removed and where some eighteenth-century writers had asked for an understanding of sati in its Hindu context, by the nineteenth century most observers were ready to condemn it outright. Indeed, it became almost mandatory for any discussion of sati to be prefaced with an authorial expression of disapprobation. Eyewitness accounts pre-empt the moral judgement of the reader by referring to the rite from the outset as 'shocking', 'barbarous', or 'infernal' and most of the authors of the early nineteenth century conformed, outwardly at least, not only to a widely accepted intellectual assessment of the rite, but also to a preconditioned emotional response. The suggestion of admiration for the widow still existed to some extent, particularly in the romanticized rendering of sati in fiction, but increasingly this was being purged, on a superficial level at least, from the popular portrayal of the rite. Instead, eyewitnesses and editors alike sought to emphasize their moral outrage over sati and we increasingly find that accounts of sati are prefaced with comments like that of the editor of the *Quarterly Oriental Magazine* in 1825, who states that 'We have so often expressed the absolute abhorrence with which we record these abominable acts, that we can only repeat in the same terms, the sense we entertain of their atrocious wickedness.'[6]

There were several reasons for this consolidation in the moral judgment against sati. Christopher Bayly has suggested, and it has been widely accepted, that it was indicative of a wider change in attitudes towards Hinduism itself that underpinned the shift from Orientalist to Anglicist policies in the 1820s.[7] While, in the eighteenth century, Enlightenment ideas about religious toleration and cultural relativism allowed space for a sympathetic approach to understanding Hinduism, the growing evangelicalism of the nineteenth century was accompanied by an impulse to denigrate rather than celebrate non-Christian religions. Increasingly, Hinduism and it accretions were seen as a malign influence on Indian society. The Baptist missionary journal, *Friend of India,* for example, claimed that 'The infelicity of [India's] inhabitants arises not from ungenerous soil, but from an unnatural system of morals; and from rites and customs, which though deemed to be sacred, are inimical to human happiness.'[8] These customs were seen to be 'hostile to reason and humanity'[9] and were used to emphasize India's lack of civilization, and to characterize her society as backward and barbaric.

Closely connected to this shifting attitude towards Hinduism was the change in the popular conception of Britain's role in India—what P. J. Marshall refers to as the 'moral swing to the East'.[10] Increasingly by the early nineteenth century, public opinion demanded that the imperial presence in India be justified not in terms of economic gain but in terms of the benefits it brought to the indigenous population.

Public support for the empire in India, which had waned somewhat in the late eighteenth century amid damaging revelations about the East India Company's behaviour there, gave way to tacit support as the role of the British was increasingly portrayed in utilitarian or humanitarian terms. This was especially the case after 1813, when the renewal of the East India Company's charter included the lifting of the ban on proselytizing activities. This increased emphasis on the beneficence as well as the profitability of colonial rule placed issues such as sati firmly within the remit of the 'civilizing mission.' As the *Friend of India* put it in relation to sati:

That the British Government has in a great degree fulfilled the high trust committed to it by the Almighty Disposer of events, by endeavouring to render its subjects happy is unquestionable—and it is equally unquestionable that while misery continues to exist, the energy of benevolence can never be consistently relaxed.[11]

The existence of a custom such as sati in a land under British control could be considered to undermine the benevolence of colonial rule—humanitarian Fowell Buxton even went as far as to call the toleration for sati a 'disgrace to Britain'[12]—at a time when British presence in India was increasingly being rationalized in humanitarian terms.

While both these factors certainly had a huge impact on the way in which sati was represented and understood, they are not sufficient in themselves to explain Britain's obsession with it in years before 1829. As we have already mentioned, numerous other rites and customs elicited British criticism, but none received the same level of fascination and vilification accorded to sati. The unprecedented level of interest in it suggests that the popular obsession was about more than just Britain's changing relationship with India, or the imperatives of justifying colonial rule, although these certainly both played a part. Rather, I would argue that sati intrigued the British in this period because it embodied certain issues that were of particular relevance in Britain itself at the time. The sati debate coalesced with concerns in Britain over religious toleration, penal reform, suicide, and changing gender ideology; and all of these played a part in firing British interest in and forming British opinion of sati. Moreover, sati itself played a significant role in defining British ideas about these and other issues. Far from being a monolithic and unidirectional process tied solely to the relationship of power between Britain and India, as Edward Said might have us believe, the debate on sati was both multifaceted and multidirectional, and reflected and affected Britain's own internal preoccupations as much as her relationship with India. Exactly how this occurred will be discussed over the course of this and the next two chapters.

The Incredulity Natural to Men: Reasons for Attending Sati

The large number of eyewitness accounts of sati produced in this period makes it clear that righteous horror at the spectacle of immolation did not necessarily translate into an avoidance of it. Of course, the burning of widows was to some extent viewed as a public nuisance by the British, and rules relating to it reflect this. Lord Ansthruther for example, banned it from the British-dominated centre of Calcutta in 1798 (a fact which may, to some extent, account for the relatively high incidence of sati in adjoining districts) and it was not permitted in British parts of Bombay or Madras. As Radhika Singha has pointed out, moral indignation about the practice of sati was exacerbated by the proximity that the sacrifices often had to what was considered British public space.[13] Sati was distasteful in all circumstances, but it was even more so when it encroached upon the European view. The famous philanthropist and anti-sati campaigner John Poynder cites a report made by a British lieutenant of two satis which took place in June 1826, saying that they were performed 'under circumstances of particular audacity, in the immediate front of the Government House and College'.[14] Indeed, he quotes the lieutenant as saying that 'from the spot where the scene occurred, one would imagine it had been chosen just out of triumph'.[15]

The desire to purge 'British' space of the offensive ritual did not prevent Europeans seeking out sati in large numbers, although it does appear that by doing so they were in most cases entering 'Indian' space. When William Carey upbraided the family of a potential sati for their actions, they told him, '…it was an act of great holiness, and added in a very surly manner that if I did not like to see it I might go further off, and desired me to go'.[16] Carey at first insisted on staying, but left shortly after the fire was kindled, claiming he 'could not bear to see more'.[17] Many Europeans, however, stayed to witness the whole of the immolation and their collective fascination with the rite belies the suggestion that that sati was offensive because it imposed physical suffering on their view. Rather, there is a more complex dynamic at work here that sees the voyeuristic attraction of the rite counterbalanced by emerging sensibilities that condition the nature of their professed response to it—they go to see it, but it is no longer appropriate to 'enjoy' it.

For the most part, the overt 'tourist attraction' attitude that had prevailed in the sixteenth and seventeenth centuries was no longer acceptable, although we do still find stray references to sati that refer to it in this manner. One eyewitness observer, for example, commented, on being handed a flower by a sati, that he wished it had been something more durable so that he might have kept it as a souvenir, adding that his wife had expressed the same regret when he recounted the day's events to her. In another fascinating incident, Fanny Parks recounts:

> Several of our friends requested me, in case another suttee occurred, to send them timely notice. Five days afterwards I was informed that a ranee was to be burned. Accordingly I sent word to all my friends. Eight thousand people were assembled on the suttee ground, who waited from mid-day to sunset: then a cry arose—The mem sahiba sent us here! The mem sahiba said it was to take place today! See, the sun has set, there can now be no suttee! The people dispersed. My informant told me what he himself believed, and I mystified some 8000 people most unintentionally.[18]

It is not clear from Parks' account whether the friends she refers to were British or Indian, but it is interesting to note that, while she herself was never witness to a sati and professed herself adverse to the 'grilling' of women, she shows little compunction in facilitating others to witness the event, even allowing her own servants the day off to go and see the *'tamarsha'*.[19]

Clearly some observers still saw the sati as one of the unmissable spectacles of the East, either simply stating that they went to witness a sati, or referring to curiosity as the motivating factor in their presence. Such voyeuristic motivations were largely becoming unacceptable, however, and for the most part eyewitnesses felt it necessary to offer a more convincing justification for their presence. For some, it was enough to stress that they were taking an accurate account of events, a conceit common in the eighteenth century when scientific investigation had replaced pure voyeurism as a justification for attending immolations. This was particularly the case in the early part of the nineteenth century when some observers apparently felt the need to counterbalance the relatively positive and heroic image of sati that had predominated in the eighteenth century. An anonymous correspondent to *The Times*, for example, claimed in 1810 that he attended a sati out of:

...a strong and natural curiosity, to observe narrowly the deportment of a human being about to take a voluntary and public leave of existence, and believing from what we had read of similar cases, that our feelings would not be shocked by any open exhibition of the actual pains of dissolution. I do not recollect to have seen any account of a Suttee, which did not, upon the whole, tell rather favourably for the humanity of those whom an imperious ordinance of religion calls upon, to preside or officiate at such ceremonials. I think it therefore a duty I owe to the cause of truth, to record at least one instance on the other side of the question.[20]

Another anonymous eyewitness commented: 'I was last September an eye-witness to a Gentoo burning with her husband; and as I stood by all the time, and took notes of all that passed, you may depend upon the following narration to be strictly true.'[21] For the most part, however, sati was, by this point, so well reported that there was little validity in the suggestion that the observer was there out of public spirit, to provide his compatriots with an accurate account. As Maria Sykes put it in her journal, '...these ceremonies...have been so often described that it would be time thrown away to enter into the horrible details of this inhuman custom....'[22]

A key exception to this trend away from justifying presence in terms of scientific observation came in the form of those officers who took an interest in the nature of sati in order to allow them to participate authoritatively in the discussion over its abolition. E. Molony, the magistrate of Burdwan, for example, commented in 1819 that he had 'attended several suttees myself, for the purpose of gaining as much information as possible on the subject.'[23] For magistrates such as Molony and other government servants, it was possible to rationalize their presence at satis as part of their official duties. One English officer reported to *The Times* in 1823 that

In my present situation it falls to my lot to preside over the execution of criminals, and also over those horrible exhibitions peculiar to this country, of a widow burning herself on the funeral pile of her dead husband; and as the authentic account of such a scene may be interesting, I send you a short description of a suttee at which I was lately present in my new character as presiding officer.[24]

In actual fact, the government regulations on sati did not make it obligatory for the magistrate, or any other British official to be present at a sati, and the responsibility for ensuring the sacrifice was 'legal', could be and often was, delegated to Indian subordinates. That said, many British officials did choose to superintend satis themselves. There were several reasons put forward for this, most prominent of which was the apprehension that Indian, and particularly Hindu, officials could not be trusted to do all that was necessary either to dissuade the widow or ensure the legality of the sacrifice. J. Sage, magistrate for the Lower Provinces of Bengal, for example, referred to the need to 'prevent the police officers from making the power vested in them a source of oppression and emolument, by undue exactions, either for their acquiescence or forbearance to interfere in all applications that might be made to them in cases of suttee'[25]. Others feared that religious belief would make them more likely to wink at irregularities. Even the Nizamat Adalat was of the opinion that 'the reports of the police *darogahs*, in such matters, are not much to be trusted'.[26] Under these circumstances some British officials felt it their moral duty to superintend satis themselves, even though there was a general concern that by attending themselves British officers somehow legitimized the sacrifice in the eyes of the local population.

It is in the accounts of those who did not have an official reason for being present at the sacrifice that we find the most telling tension. For those who attend out of curiosity or morbid fascination in the rite, there was a need to balance their professed horror—at the thought of witnessing it—with an underlying desire to do so. In some cases curiosity was considered enough to explain attendance, at least at your first sati. William Johns referred to the 'incredulity natural to men on this extraordinary subject'[27] as a motivation for attendance, while the Baptist missionary Amos Sutton could comment, 'I…felt a desire to witness the horrid work that I might speak from experience…'.[28] For others there is a suggestion that, distasteful as it is, the witnessing of a sati is a cathartic event. Missionary Anne Chaffin in 1814 reported that

I was asked if I had any objection to be a witness. I replied shocking as it is [*sic*] the idea of a person blindly devoting herself to the flames, I felt the wish to see for once the immolation of a widow—Since my arrival in India, tho many such unhappy had suffered near Serampore yet I never had opportunity of being a spectator. Certainly a missionary cannot view such a scene without retiring with more compassion for perishing souls and under a deeper conviction that the gospel is a blessing to India, notwithstanding this opposing sentiment of modern men.[29]

Another missionary commented that he had gone to see a sati because, '…no representations of this diabolical ceremony are calculated so powerfully to impress the mind as the sight….'[30]

The most common explanation given for European presence at a sati, for missionaries, officers, and civilians alike, was the professed desire to prevent the sacrifice by reasoning with the widow. Of course, the government instructions about the acceptable limits of European intervention meant that the unilateral armed interventions of men like Niccolao Manucci and Job Charnock were no longer acceptable. Despite this, however, many eyewitnesses attended sati with the avowed intention of reasoning with the widow, or at least providing her with an alternative option and ensuring that she received 'fair play'. In particular, the missionaries would often use the occasion of a sati to expostulate with both the widow and onlookers about the futility of the deed and the fallacy of their belief.[31] On rare occasions this restricted intervention was successful. Fanny Parks, for example, recounts events at a sati attended by her husband in which the widow leapt from the pile, only to be prevented from remounting by the magistrate. In another case, the Baptist missionary Amos Sutton recounts his intervention to prevent the burning of a visibly intoxicated woman. Despite these isolated incidents, however, government restrictions on intervention rendered most European observers impotent. The missionary John Edmonds, for example, commented that 'I have not been present at the burning of a widow, only because my heart has sickened at the idea of witnessing such a scene of woe without having it in my power to prevent the murder that is then perpetrated',[32] while just prior to his successful intervention, Amos Sutton had reported that 'Brother B., having seen one suttee, and being so disgusted at the horrid scene, declined going. Feeling persuaded from what he then saw, and did, that it was vain to attempt to save the wretched victim, he despaired of doing any good.'[33]

The impotence felt by the European observers is to some extent displaced in their accounts onto the widow herself. Despite the fact that it is actually the observer who is restricted in his capacity to act, the eyewitness accounts that exist for the most part represent the observer as the active participant of the scene and the widow as the passive one. As Lata Mani has quite correctly pointed out, European accounts contain little appreciation of the courage and agency displayed by the widow in quitting the pyre, or changing her mind, seeing these women as '...objects to be saved—never as subjects who act....'[34]

Tortured Bodies: The Spectacle of Pain

Whatever the reason put forward for attending the rite, the very fact that so many eyewitness observers felt it necessary to justify their presence in terms more worthy than voyeuristic curiosity and were so vitriolic in expressing their horror at what they witnessed, is representative of changing attitudes to more than just sati itself. It is surely not coincidental that the zenith of both fascination with and horror at sati occurred at a time when existing attitudes towards the nature of individualism and the treatment of the human body were being challenged and renegotiated in Europe. In particular, the debate on sati coincided with a discussion in Britain about the nature of crime and punishment, with men like Samuel Romilly and William Eden leading a campaign for reform of the penal code and the reduction of capital offences that finally culminated in Robert Peel's rationalization of the criminal code in the 1820s and 1830s. A brief consideration of the themes and ideologies of this movement reveals significant correlations between emerging ideas about the public infliction of pain as punishment and reactions to the public spectacle of sati.

There are several reasons for the increased 'squeamishness' of early nineteenth-century observers of sati. On a basic level, Europeans would certainly be less conditioned by frequent exposure to sights of human suffering than they were in preceding centuries. Executions were still public in the early nineteenth century, but they were now almost exclusively carried out by methods designed for their efficiency rather than the infliction of pain.[35] While early modern observers would have been used to seeing executions by burning, particularly during the height of the witch-craze,[36] or during periods of religious turmoil when heretics were burnt at the stake; the Enlightenment reaction against barbaric justice and the liberalization of punishments in the eighteenth century meant that such spectacles regained their power to shock a society that was no longer desensitized by familiarity. As Michael Foucault puts it, the eighteenth century 'saw the disappearance of the tortured, dismembered, amputated body, symbolically branded on the face, on the shoulder, exposed alive or dead to public view'.[37] On a fundamental level, then, the liberalization of public opinion as regards torture and execution meant that the sights, sounds, and smells of burning flesh were rendered all the more shocking in themselves.

It does appear that the method of the widow's death added to the sense of European revulsion at the sacrifice of female life. Victorian sensibility meant that many authors refrained from a detailed description of the final moments of the sati's life, depicting it instead as being submerged in noise and smoke and leaving it to the reader to imagine the tortures inflicted. A contributor to the *Calcutta Journal*, for example, commented that he had witnessed 'a catastrophe that in fictitious tragedy would have been performed behind the curtain'.[38] Some, however, do give candid accounts of the widow's dying moments, which make it clear that the eyewitness would often have experienced all the horrors that they did not like to dwell on in print. A correspondent for *The Times* in 1810 reported:

I scarcely know how to paint in colours that will not disgust and shock our readers, the horrible close of that scene. Suffice to say, that soon after the fire took effect, the wretched woman within, in her torment, stretched forth her leg, which now protruded from the knee, beyond the scanty pile; and by the quickness with which she attempted to withdraw it, on its touching a burning brand, it was evident that she was still too sensible of the tortures she must then have been enduring. Owing to the brushwood being scattered only at the extremities of the pile, the fire there was fiercest. In a minute or two more the scorched and mutilated limb was again thrust out, and slowly consumed before our outraged eyes, while the tremendous and convulsive motion which it exhibited to the last (for many minutes), plainly showed that sensation and life yet existed in the miserable wretch within.[39]

Similarly, John Poynder cites this account from the *Bombay Courier* of a sati who escaped from the pile:

I cannot describe to you the horror I felt on seeing the mangled condition she was in: almost every inch of skin on her body had been burned off; her legs and thighs, her arms and back, were completely raw; her breasts were dreadfully torn; and the skin hanging from them in threads; the skin and nails of her fingers had peeled wholly off, and were hanging to the back of her hands. In fact, I never saw, and never read of, so entire a picture of misery as this poor woman displayed.[40]

The horrified reaction of the European observer was more than just the result of increased sensitivity, however. The shift from torturous to 'utilitarian' punishment was accompanied by a renegotiation of the role of the state in everyday life. As Christopher Bayly points out in *Imperial Meridian*, after the Napoleonic Wars, 'The old legitimacies...were fortified with new systems of economic and political management, and began to promote a much greater degree of state intrusion into society.'[41] This new interventionist polity was in evidence both at home and in the colonies, and manifested itself in a variety of ways. As Uday Singh Mehta points out, the emerging liberalism was 'committed to securing individual liberty and human dignity through a political cast that typically involved democratic and representative institutions'.[42] Where before it had been the Church and religion that had acted as the arbiter of morality, increasingly the 'liberal' state was taking on the role of guarantor of social 'humanity'. In particular, the state sought to reserve for itself what Radhika Singha refers to as 'the privilege of taking life'.[43] Thus, at the same time as punishments were 'sanitized' they were also bought more closely under state control. In India, as imperial power grew, the colonial state increasingly sought to reserve to itself the authority over life and death. This process can be seen at work in the rejection of Brahminic impunity from capital punishment and in the progressive curtailing of the Indian princes' right to inflict the death penalty. The sati's precipitation of her own death and the complicity of friends, family, and Brahmins not only offended sensibilities about the visual experience of suffering, but also affronted the colonial state's claim to sovereignty over the widow's life and raised a number of interrelated issues about the social meaning of pain and punishment.

The understanding of the symbolic meaning of corporal punishment and the infliction of pain was changing rapidly in the late eighteenth and early nineteenth century, and it is likely that the educated observer of sati would have been influenced by an emerging moral and ideological climate that saw public displays of torture as brutalizing both the spectator and society in general. The impact of ideas of humanitarianism and utilitarianism allowed nineteenth-century reformers to represent the transition from corporal to custodial punishment as an appropriate corollary to the development of both humanitarian society and effective government. Torturous punishments were viewed as the instruments of weak governments who needed to demonstrate their power through the example of physical suffering—instruments that an effective government ruling a civilized society no longer needed. Thus judicial reform was represented as the humanitarian impulse of a more refined and well-ordered age. The seminal work of Michel Foucault has shattered this comfortable assumption about the progress of 'humanity', which he sees as a 'respectable name' for a new economy of power aimed at the manipulation of the individual. For Foucault, the rationalization of punishments had less to do with humanitarian impulses than the measured and effective exercise of state control. Foucault rejects the professed motives of the reformers as irrelevant and instead represents the change in the nature of punishments as contingent on the independent dynamics of power.[44] Foucault's work has thrown open the field of criminal history and cleared a path for the revaluation of penal reform. That said, it would be wrong on the basis of Foucault's analysis to suggest that the 'humanitarian' ideology of the reformers did not have a significant impact on national thinking, even if we can no longer see it as the driving force for change. Indeed, several historians are now using Foucault's work as a starting point for a revaluation of changing attitudes to reform, and so reinserting human motivation into the equation.[45]

For Randall McGowan, the ideology that underpinned the move away from barbaric punishments revolved around the symbolic treatment of the human body. He tells us: 'The treatment of the body during punishment offered a condensed image that was meant to convey a message to society.'[46] During the period of reform the nature of that message changed. Whereas in an earlier period the body of the criminal was used as a metaphor for the body politic with the criminal being amputated before the contagion spread, by the second half of the eighteenth century concern was increasingly focusing on the individual body itself, which came to be seen as the locus of human rights and autonomy. Both life and the human body were viewed as having an innate value that society had no right to treat lightly.[47] Thus, while British opposition to sati was based to a large extent on the fact that it challenged the British assumption about state control over the lives of its subjects,[48] this was exacerbated by the fact that the nature of even the state's right to kill was being challenged at this time.

In the light of this increased emphasis on the importance of individual life, it is hardly surprising that the destruction of innocent life embodied by the sati should be seen as emblematic of what William Johns referred to as a 'monstrous propensity for the destruction of human life'[49] and indicative of the fate of a society that did not respect the individual. The disproportionate amount of attention the subject received in liberal circles might thus be considered reflective of the concerns of an educated elite who were in the process of purging the remnants of a barbaric justice system from their own society. Under these circumstances, abhorrence of sati can be seen as being as much about defining European society as civilized, as being about condemning Indian society. A consideration of the rhetoric of penal reform will help to elucidate this connection.

Like those who opposed the toleration of sati, the penal reformers tended to characterize themselves as 'friends of humanity'. The Whig radical Josiah Darnford, for example, claimed that 'humanity for my fellow creatures and jealousy for the honour of my country'[50] motivated his involvement in the penal reform movement. A custodial rather than corporeal penal code was seen by the reformers as an indicator of progress, a sign that society was becoming ever more refined and polite. As Samuel Romilly put it, 'in proportion as men have reflected and reasoned on this subject, the absurd and barbarous notions of justice, which have prevailed for ages, have been exploded and humane and rational principles have been adopted in their stead',[51] while William Eden commented: 'when the rights of human nature are not respected, those of the citizen are gradually disregarded. Those areas are in history found fatal to liberty, in which cruel punishments predominate.'[52] For the reformers and those who ascribed to their views, the existence of capital punishment for crimes such as petty theft was at odds with British claims to be a progressive and civilized society.

Another key argument of the penal reform movement was that the frequent spectacle of public execution was debasing to human nature. Samuel Romilly, for example, claimed that, 'In proportion as these spectacles are frequent, the impression which they make upon the public is faint, the effect of example is lost, and the blood of many citizens spilt, without any benefit to mankind.'[53] Similarly, William Eden complained that, 'The sensibility of the people, under so extravagant an execution of power, degenerates into despondency, baseness and stupidity....'[54] Rather than instilling the watching crowd with the moral knowledge of the futility of crime, frequent exposure to corporal punishments simply degraded their humanity. This concern is mirrored in British accounts of sati from the same period. In 1822, for example, correspondent to the *Asiatic Journal* asked:

And is the brutalizing influence of the horrid scene, on the minds of thousands of spectators, a matter of no moment in such an estimate? Picture to your mind, Sir, this multitude returning to the concerns of social life—extensively returning to their respective circles. With what feelings do they thus return? With a combination of passions which it must be difficult to conceive, or an apathy yet more debasing.[55]

He was not alone in his concern. Indeed one of the key causes of indignation among European observers of sati was the behaviour of the Indian spectators, who were vilified for not showing more compassion. In the early modern period, and even in the eighteenth century, accounts of sati display little surprise or alarm at the large numbers attending immolations—they are simply portrayed spectators at a religious rite. By the nineteenth century, however, the nature of the gathered crowd has changed significantly in British representations and they are more often than not represented as a baying mob intent on witnessing the pain and suffering of another human being.

There are a number of reasons for this demonization of the Hindu crowd. Those who wished to facilitate government intervention in sati by undermining its religious status used the actions of the Hindu spectators to prove that the rite was popular as an entertainment rather than a sacred ceremony. John Poynder, for example, points out that 'all of the deceased's family came as to an entertainment'[56] while Mr Bird in 1817 refers to sati as being 'a spectacle to the assembled multitude, who, with barbarous cries, demand the sacrifice'.[57] The behaviour of the mob is thus used to counter the suggestion that sati is a sanctified event, and to reinforce the perception of it as the result of a degraded and desensitized humanity. In an account that is in many ways reminiscent of those reporting the behaviour of crowds at public executions in Britain, a correspondent for the *Calcutta Journal* tells us that

Amidst this scene of sorrow and misery it may not be amiss to glance a moment at the behaviour of the surrounding mob. Here nothing but merriment, laughter, noise, and obscenity abounded in all directions. Not a man or woman amongst them seemed to have heart to pity or understanding to judge. One sally of wit set the whole audience at laughing for half an hour, and gave occasion for many more good jokes. 'Come on' cried a wag 'ye women of Sulkeah, as many as are fond of fire and husbands, now is your

time to hug and burn'—another on the importunity of the poor wretch, who
was the subject of their merriment, to be put out of misery as quickly as
possible, tauntingly replied, 'Don't be so impatient my dear, you will be
among the faggots soon enough.' Indeed, so far was any religious solemnity
from being attached to the occasion, that no levity, confusion, and indecency
could have been greater, than were exhibited in the conduct of both Hindoo
and Mussulman spectators.[58]

Similarly, the Baptist missionary Joshua Marshman reported that

The most shocking indifference and levity appeared among those who were
present. I think I never saw any more shockingly brutal than their behaviour.
The dreadful scene had not even the least appearance of being a religious
ceremony. The rabble, for such it literally was, presented the appearance of
an abandoned rabble of boys in England collected for the purpose of worrying
to death a cat or dog. Such was the confusion, the levity, the bursts of brutal
merriment while this poor creature was burning alive before their eyes....[59]

Compare these accounts with that of William Dawes, who complained of a British justice system that executed criminals 'before a
surrounding multitude who make the useful spectacle a holiday rather
than a scene of solemnity and sorrow'[60] and we will see that concern
with the nature of human behaviour when faced with the spectacle of
pain was not confined to India. Indeed, it appears the behaviour of the
Hindu 'mob' was not as alien as British protestations of horror at it
might suggest. I would argue that in light of the debate about the
impact of spectacles of pain in Britain, the extreme emphasis placed
by most European observers on their own disgust at sati may be as
much about defining themselves as civilized as it is about condemning
the surrounding Indians as barbaric.

The aspect of self-definition in European reactions to sati is made
explicit in several accounts that suggest that horror is the only possible
reaction of a 'civilized' person. Joshua Marshman, for example, complained of the above-mentioned sati that the spectacle 'must have
moved the compassion of the most insensible European...',[61] by implication suggesting that the European is possessed of a greater humanity than the uncompassionate Hindu. It was not only eyewitnesses
of sati that felt the need to delineate their own reactions to the rite
from that of the surrounding mob. Responses to written accounts of
sati also display a tendency to emphasize the moral outrage of the
reader. Thus, a correspondent to the *Calcutta Journal* claimed, 'The

perusal of the account of a suttee at Chitpore...created in me those feelings of horror which it must excite in every being of human form, and possessing the common sentiments of our nature...'[62] while another commented: 'The following dreadful circumstance...needs no comment: to the humane and reflecting mind, it must present images of horror, more impressive than the most laboured description could give.'[63]

The implications of this sort of commentary are twofold. Not only does the author make his own sentiments on the subject clear, he also implicitly asserts his superiority over the Hindu who is not horrified by sati. By so doing, the European observer defines both himself and the Hindu observer who, united in their desire to witness the spectacle, are then separated by their responses to it. Expressions of horror at sati are also part of a wider agenda that sees the need not only to differentiate between the 'civilized' European and the 'barbaric' Hindu, but also between the modern humanitarian and his own not so distant ancestor. Thus, 'a subscriber' to the *Asiatic Mirror* could muse:

Some four or five centuries back, when mankind was less civilised, the dreadful penalty of fire we find to have been awarded to offenders as a punishment, in expiation of heinous crimes. But how much more shocking is it to behold in these days of civilisation the prevalence of the horrible practice of human immolation: not for the purpose of punishing offenders, to deter others from the commission of crime; but as a free will offering of the soul and body, on the part of the devotee, whose caste demands the sacrifice for the support of religious principles.[64]

In actual fact, this past was closer than most cared to admit—the burning of heretics had been common in Britain not 250 years previously, and the last witch was burnt in Europe as late as 1780.

In addition to the desire to delineate his reaction from a brutal European past, the protestations of horror that characterized 'liberal' accounts of sati may also have represented a desire on the part of the observer to distance himself from his contemporary lower-class compatriots. In a period when members of the working classes still gathered in their numbers to witness public executions, and cheap tracts detailing the last moments of Newgate felons were circulated for popular titillation (thinly disguised as moral instruction), it is hardly surprising that the professed liberal humanitarian would wish to assert his moral superiority over those who found voyeuristic enjoyment in such events, whatever their nationality.

If the behaviour of the Hindu spectators at a sati (See Fig. 8) made a useful cautionary tale as to the effects of such spectacles on society, there was also concern over the impact that continued exposure to them might have on Europeans in India. The Archdeacon of Calcutta, for example, lamented that: The scenes around me are becoming horribly familiar...,'[65] while John Poynder complained of the 'hardening tendency and demoralising influence of these sacrifices'[66] on those who lived and worked in India. For Poynder this influence was illustrated as much by judges who claimed to 'have the pleasure' to transmit the annual sati returns[67] as by the more general refusal of the government to intervene on the matter. The Baptist newspaper the *Friend of India* also lamented that

We are struck on our arrival with the barbarous rites practiced in India—rites from which every feeling of humanity revolts. In the process of time we become familiarised with them, and the sharp edge of abhorrence is worn dull. We see no prospect of reform, and are led, for the sake perhaps of our own comfort, to behold them with diminished indignation, till the feelings of humanity become unwelcome and eventually retire to rest.[68]

Fig. 8. 'A Suttee', anonymous watercolour, *c*.1800. By permission of the British Library, WD 248.

Compare this with William Eden's comment about public executions that:

We leave each other to rot like scarecrows in the hedges; and our gibbets are crowded with human carcasses. May it not be doubted, whether a forced familiarity with such objects can have any other effect, than to blunt the sentiments and to destroy the benevolent prejudices of the people?[69]

And it appears clear that the moral concern over the impact of sati on the observer was not simply restricted to a denigration of Hinduism, but was closely related to a more general debate about what was acceptable as public spectacle and how a 'civilized' society should deal with 'uncivilized' sights. I would argue therefore that the horror expressed at sati was not only about denigrating Hinduism, but was also about redefining the limits of acceptable behaviour by 'modern man.' The juxtaposition between the unprecedented level of fascination with sati and the almost universal expression of disgust with it is reflective of the internal struggle of a society that is trying to reinvent itself as progressive and humane and of individuals who are trying to conform to the expectations of what constitutes 'civilized' behaviour. Of course, the difficulty that was faced in the context of sati was that new sensibilities about the innate value of human life and brutalizing effect of spectacles of public execution that would have seen sati condemned outright are counterbalanced by equally dearly cherished ideals about religious toleration, which are the subject of Chapter 6.

Notes

1. Extract from the *Friend of India*, in the Nicolls Collection (OIO Eur. Mss).
2. Governmental interest and debate on the subject had in fact been going on since 1805, but the publication of the *Parliamentary Papers* was the first opportunity for the general public, and philanthropic societies, to get full access to the material.
3. James Pegg, *India's Cries to British Humanity* (London: Seely and Son, 1827).
4. Anon., *Deplorable Effects of Heathen Superstitions, as Manifested by the Natives Of Hindustan* (Dunfermline: John Miller Cheap Tracts, 1828).
5. This information was gathered from the entries in *Palmer's Index To The Times* (British Newspaper Library, Colindale).

6. *Quarterly Oriental Magazine*, vol. 3, 1825, p. 10.
7. Christopher Bayly, 'From Ritual to Ceremony: Death Ritual in Hindu North India', in J. Whaley (ed.), *Mirrors Of Mortality: Studies in the Social History of Death* (New York: St Martin's Press, 1981).
8. *Friend of India*, vol. 1:3, (Serampore: Mission Press, 1821), p. 636.
9. Ibid.
10. P. J. Marshall, 'The Moral Swing to the East: British Humanitarianism, India and the West Indies', in K. Ballhatchet and J. Harrison (eds), *East India Company Studies: Papers Presented to Prof. Sir Cyril Phillips* (Hong Kong: Asian Research Service, 1986), p. 69.
11. *Friend of India*, vol. 1:3, p. 636.
12. Fowell Buxton's comment is cited by E.A. Kendall in a letter to the *Asiatic Journal*, vol. 13, 1822, p. 447.
13. See Radhika Singha, *A Despotism of Law: Crime and Justice in Early Colonial India* (New Delhi: Oxford University Press, 2000), p. 118.
14. John Poynder, *Human Sacrifices In India: A Speech To The Court Of Proprietors Of East India Company Stock* (London: J. Matchard and Son, 1827), p. 113.
15. Ibid.
16. William Johns, *A collection of facts and opinions relative to the burning of widows with the dead bodies of their husbands: and to other destructive customs prevalent in British India: respectfully submitted to the consideration of government, as soliciting a further extension of their humane interference* (London: W.H. Pearce, 1816).
17. Ibid.
18. Fanny Parks, *Wanderings of a Pilgrim in Search of the Picturesque* (Karachi: Oxford University Press, 1975), p. 94.
19. Ibid., p. 93.
20. *The Times*, 11 June 1810.
21. Anon., *Deplorable Effects Of Heathen Superstition*, p. 16.
22. Extract from Memoirs of Maria Sykes 1781–1865 (OIO Eur. Mss.)
23. E. Malony, magistrate burdwan, to W. Ewer, acting superintendent of police in the Lower Provinces, 11 January 1819, *PP*, 18, p. 231.
24. *The Times*, 12 May 1823.
25. Extract from Bengal Judicial Consultations, 21 March 1817, *PP*, 18, p. 49.
26. E. Watson, forth judge, to M.H. Turnbull, Register of the Nizamat Adalat, Fort William, 16 April 1818, PP, 18, p. 99.
27. Johns, *Facts and Opinions*, p. 1.
28. Amos Sutton (ed.), *A Narrative Of The Mission To Orissa: The Site Of The Temple Of Jugurnath* (Boston: David Marks for the Free Will Baptist Connexion, 1833), p. 185.
29. Anne Chaffin to J. James Smith Snr, 27 November 1814 (Baptist Missionary Society Archives, Angus Library, Regent's Park College, Oxford [Henceforth BMSA]).

30. H. Towney to Rev. G. Burden, Chinsurah, 15 April 1822 (London Missionary Society Papers, Council for World Mission Archive, SOAS, London [Henceforth LMSP]).
31. For more on the tactics employed by the missionaries on these occasions see, Chapter 5.
32. John Edmonds to Rev. Dr Bogue, Chinsurah, 28 June 1825, LMSP.
33. Sutton, *A Narrative Of The Mission To Orissa*, p. 185.
34. Mani, *Contentious Traditions*, p. 162. Anne Chaffin provides a rare example of the mutual impotence of widow and observer when she laments, 'Then she was so near our boat that I could have touched her with a walking stick. She gazed several times full into my face an I being almost bewildered at the scene I thought within myself what if this poor woman should have some little hopes that I should at length be her deliverer. But alas I had no authority to do it.' Anne Chaffin to J. James Smith Snr, 27 November 1814, BMSA.
35. By hanging in Britain or by guillotine in France.
36. England actually viewed witchcraft as a felony and as such punishable by hanging, but in Scotland and on the Continent it was viewed as a heresy and punishable by burning.
37. Cited in Randall McGowan, 'The Body and Punishment in Eighteenth Century England', in *Journal of Modern History*, vol. 59, 1987, p. 652.
38. *Calcutta Journal*, 5 December 1820.
39. *The Times*, 11 June 1810.
40. Poynder, *Human Sacrifices*, p. 123.
41. Christopher Bayly, *Imperial Meridian* (London: Longman, 1989), p. 165.
42. Uday Singh Mehta, *Liberalism and Empire: India in British Liberal Thought* (New Delhi: Oxford University Press, 1999), p. 3.
43. Singha, *A Despotism of Law*, p. 80.
44. M. Foucault, *Discipline and Punish* (New York: Vintage, 1979).
45. McGowan, 'The Body and Punishment', pp. 651–3.
46. Ibid., p. 653.
47. Ibid., p. 669.
48. See Singha, *A Despotism of Law*, p. 118.
49. Johns, *Some Facts and Opinions*, p. 1.
50. McGowan, 'The Body and Punishment', p. 668.
51. Ibid.
52. Ibid., p. 669.
53. Ibid., p. 671.
54. Ibid.
55. *Asiatic Journal*, vol. 13, 1822, p. 556.
56. Poynder, *Human Sacrifices*, p. 10.
57. Ibid.
58. *Calcutta Journal*, 5 December 1820.

59. Joshua Marshman to J. Ryland, 29 January 1807, BMSA.

60. McGowan, 'The Body and Punishment', p. 672.

61. Joshua Marshman to J. Ryland, 29 January 1807, BMSA.

62. *Calcutta Journal*, 8 October 1819.

63. Ibid., 17 May 1820.

64. Johns, *Some Facts and Opinions*, p. 34.

65. Poynder, *Human Sacrifices*, p. 126.

66. Ibid.

67. Ibid., p. 125.

68. *Friend of India*, vol. 6:14, (Serampore: Mission Press, 1826), p. 455.

69. McGowan, 'The Body and Punishment', p. 672.

5

INFATUATED CREATURES
Women, Suicide, and Madness

ॐ

It is urged that these are voluntary immolations; if it is meant that no outward brutal force is used, I allow that in this sense they are voluntary. But in what other country under heaven would they be allowed to burn? Where are men, except in India, to be found who would not use force to prevent these immolations? But has not all knowledge been denied to the Hindoo female; and have not their minds been shockingly perverted by superstition? Can a child in the same sense as an adult be called a free agent?[1]

By declaring that sati, whether performed freely or not, was an act of criminal violence, Bentinck's Regulation of 1829 theoretically made the question of the widow's volition in sati irrelevant. Despite this, the issue of the widow's will remains one of the most prominent aspects of the debate on sati to this day. This is in part because of the degree of emphasis placed on the issue by the British in the years before abolition, when the widow's volition, or lack thereof, was seen as the defining feature of a sati. If a widow was proved to have been an unwilling participant in the sacrifice it was relatively unproblematic, theoretically at least, to designate the rite as murder.[2] In the case of an ostensibly voluntary sati the position was more complex and the supposedly freely chosen sati was the cause of moral, legal, and ideological debate. Not only was there an ongoing debate about the precise nature of the scriptural sanction for voluntary sati, but there was also considerable disagreement about the nature of the widow's agency and the degree to which she could, under the circumstances, be deemed capable of exercising free will and rational judgement. Such issues were the central paradox of a discourse on sati which, while at one level trying to differentiate between 'legal' voluntary satis and 'illegal' coerced ones, was simultaneously epistemologically undermining the widows' potential to exert any agency at all.

Despite the fact that numerous examples exist, throughout the early nineteenth century of women insisting on their right to burn, and while colonial legislation on the subject before 1829 was premised on the very idea that it was possible for a 'voluntary' sati to take place, these realities were often superseded by a theoretical discussion about the nature of the widow's agency that concluded that she was incapable of exerting it. Increasingly, the self-devoted heroine of the eighteenth century was replaced in the British imagination by a passive victim, who was to be pitied rather than admired. Almost all the aspects of the sati's behaviour previously considered praiseworthy or heroic were undermined in this period by a construction that saw her as incapable of any free will. Even widows who exhibited an apparently lucid and rational resolve to burn were often referred to in terms that undermined their self-determination. In 1827, for example, a correspondent for the *Quarterly Oriental Magazine* reported on a sati in which the wealthy widow behaved with perfect composure throughout, even making a will and answering attempts to dissuade her 'fully, calmly and steadily'.[3] Despite the fact that the widow herself scorned the idea that she might be acting under compulsion, the correspondent repeatedly refers to her as 'poor miserable object' and 'poor infatuated creature'.[4] Such descriptions were far from uncommon in this period, as the reality of individual satis was replaced with a preconceived stereotype of her that saw her as an eternal victim, even in the face of direct evidence to the contrary.[5]

This new construction of the sati as a passive victim was the result of a number of forces that coalesced at this time to create this specific image. On a practical level it is deeply implicated in a political debate about abolition, which made it imperative for the anti-sati lobby to present the rite as an act of violence against women. By undermining the possibility of the widow's agency, anti-sati campaigners could discredit the governmental construction of 'voluntary' sati, on which toleration of the rite was based. In addition to this, the new construction of sati was deeply embedded in changing social ideologies in Britain, in particular those relating to gender and suicide. These ideas affected the thinking of missionaries, administrators, and officers alike and permeated both the official and the popular discourse on sati, with the result that the early nineteenth-century image of sati was based as much on a subconscious assumption of certain universal characteristics as on the deliberate construction of a politically viable image of difference.

Amiable Creatures: Sati and the Nature of Woman

At all stages of the European encounter with it, the image of the sati has been closely tied to the prevailing understanding of the nature of woman. In the early modern period, ambivalence with regard to the moral status of women was reflected in a construction of the sati that lauded her capacity for virtue while fearing her potential for sexuality. The eighteenth century witnessed the resolution of the 'woman question' in favour of her virtue rather than her vice and, consequently, unflattering interpretations of the sati's the behaviour were purged from the popular image of her. The suggestion that sati was a punishment for husband-murdering was rejected and motivation for the rite represented almost entirely in terms of the widow's conjugal devotion and religious conviction; features of feminine behaviour that resonated with emerging patriarchal constructions of the ideal woman in

Fig. 9. 'The Suttee' from Rev. James Pegg, *India's Cries to British Humanity*,[6] (London: Seely and Son, 1830). By permission of the Edinburgh University Library.

Europe. By the nineteenth century, as Victorian gender ideology began to solidify, a new understanding of femininity and female capacity emerged, and with a new ideological order that redefined the relationship between the sexes. While the debate on the nature and position of women in nineteenth-century Britain is too well known to require extensive treatment here, a brief overview of the main themes of the period will help us elucidate the impact of this new ideology on attitudes to sati.

The late eighteenth and early nineteenth centuries saw a significant shift in the way in which gender roles were understood in Britain. In particular, the development of the doctrine of 'separate spheres' and the 'cult of domesticity' saw women and their interests increasingly being confined to the private arena of home and family, leaving the public space of politics and economics to men. This was in part a consequence of the Industrial Revolution, which saw a relocation of centre of production from the home to the factory or office. Also, the growth in the power and status of the middle class motivated them to attempt to cement their respectability by differentiating themselves from the lower orders, a feat in part achieved by 'protecting' their women from contamination by the public sphere. In poorer families, of course, such a luxury was not feasible and the working-class woman often bore the double burden of home and work. The separation of spheres was thus in part a means of emphasizing the economic and social status of the middle class—the same class, significantly, that was the most involved in evangelical and missionary activities. The result was that the image of an 'angel in the house' came to represent the ideal of respectable, Victorian womanhood. The ideal woman was content within the domestic sphere and possessed the qualities of passivity, serenity, and spirituality. She was cast as the guardian of moral virtue and a calming influence on her husband's more manly passions, being sexually restrained and passive, if not passionless. As Carol Groneman points out, scientific and pseudo-scientific advances in the nineteenth century also contributed to the image of women as being weak and unfit for life in the public sphere.[7] The medicalization of the female body justified her seclusion in terms of her physical frailty, monthly 'illness', delicate nervous system, and smaller brain[8]. She was a creature to be protected and cherished and should not be contaminated by base thought or violent or disrespectful treatment.

It is in the context of this emerging interpretation of the nature of femininity that we must consider the new emphasis on horror and

condemnation in the European reaction to sati, for while the immolations offended European sensibilities on several different levels, the
whole was rendered even more reprehensible by being visited on the
'weaker sex' by men who were supposed to protect and cherish it.
Thus in 1816 William Johns could lament:

That the most delicate and tender part of our species should be kept in
degraded and servile circumstances through life, as are Hindu women, is
truly afflictive; but that custom should require them to grace their husband's
funeral in a manner so dreadful, and thus, if possible to perpetuate their
servitude in a future state, carries the cruelty of oppression to its furthest
extent. The feeble and affectionate are the victims of this superstition; and
those who by nature and right should be their protectors and saviours, are
their cruel and unrelenting destroyers![9]

Similarly the *Friend of India* could comment:

...let us consider for a moment who those are, doomed to undergo those
agonies, unpitied, because never beheld. They are *the most amiable part of the
Hindoo race!* In the most case they are females, possessing some degree of
wealth, for the very poor seldom thus devote themselves to death: they are
not worth the labour required to work up their minds to a sufficient pitch
of delusion. If the term be applicable to any female in the present state of
Hindoo society, they are in general persons of *education*; and whatever be the
degree of polish and delicacy which accompany opulence, whatever the ideas
included in the superior mode of living; they are in general possessed by those
whom this dreadful custom marks as its victims. It follows therefore, as a
matter of course, that if among the higher ranks of society in this country
there be any *delicacy of feeling*, it is possessed by these who may be said almost
from their birth to be devoted to the flames.—And if there be anything to
be found of conjugal fidelity, it resides among these, since an extraordinary
degree of conjugal affection, either real or ascribed, is made the lure by which
these unhappy victims are betrayed to death, the enjoyment for numerous
ages of the highest felicity with their deceased husbands being held out as
the bait to draw them on till they make the irrevocable declaration that they
will commit themselves to the flames. It is probable, therefore that those who
are thus cruelly murdered year by year, are in most cases the best educated,
the most amiable and the most virtuous of the Hindoo race.[10]

The Hindu widow is thus represented as conforming to a universal
pattern of womanhood that sees her as more moral and spiritual than
man, but also as weaker and more dependent. It is hardly surprising

that the widow should be portrayed as passive when women in Britain were similarly being confined in terms of their autonomy and sphere of influence. Women were expected to defer on all important matters to their husbands (the rationale for not giving women a vote was the assumption that her opinion would, of course, be the same as that of her husband) and had little scope for autonomous decision making outside the confines of the home and family. Of course, the extreme passivity perceived in the Hindu woman was of a different magnitude to that assigned to European women, but it sprang from the same assumptions about her inherent nature. While European women were represented as achieving a certain degree of authority through a benign and civilized society that nurtured and protected their interests (provided they remained confined to the appropriate sphere), Hindu women were represented as having what little autonomy they possessed by nature crushed by an oppressive society, a domineering religion, and an unfeeling family. Thus the differentiation between British and Hindu women was more one of environment than of nature; both were seen as inherently passive, but the conditions of their life determined the degree to which they were oppressed.

For the Victorian observer, one of the most shocking aspects of sati was the fact that it broke the natural bond between families, which by this time was viewed in Britain as the fundamental social unit and the foundation stone of social stability and propriety. The supposed tendency of the Hindu family to coerce the widow to the flames was seen as an outrage against the natural duty of men to protect women and of the family to provide a safe haven for its members. As William Johns complained:

In this violation of the laws of nature there is no parallel in the history of any other nation. Instead of the friends and relatives commiserating the distress of a disconsolate widow, they combine together to force her destruction; and in opposition to the best and strongest feelings of our nature, the offspring of her own body becomes the perpetrator of this most horrid outrage.[11]

The lack of family feeling, either filial piety or maternal instinct, apparent in the practice of sati was repeatedly used by missionaries and others to denigrate Hindu society[12] and the failure of the family to support the widow was viewed as undermining any potential she might have for agency in escaping the flames. As the *Friend of India* put it:

From these even the slightest hint that *they wish her to die* must operate on
a widow of delicacy and sensibility like a sentence of death pronounced by
a judge. With what feelings could she commit herself for life to the mercy
of those who had discovered this wish in the slightest degree, and felt in the
least disappointed by her refusing to precipitate herself into the flames,
particularly when the laws of the country provide her with so little relief
against any unkindness or barbarity she might hereafter experience from
them?[13]

The failure of the Hindu family to live up to what in Britain would
have been viewed as its most fundamental duty, the protection of its
weakest members, was one of the key charges levelled against Indian
society. It is viewed as the natural outcome of a social system that sent
a child bride into a strange and unfeeling family[14] and of a religion that
has little respect for human life. Indeed, sati was a major tool in the
missionary and imperial discourse precisely because it emphasized
Hinduism's degrading influence even over emotive bonds.

Mothers Become Monsters: Immolation and the Maternal Bond

The importance of emerging Victorian gender ideology in informing
the British reaction to sati is particularly well illustrated by the emphasis that was increasingly being placed upon an issue that had previously received scant attention—that of the children orphaned by the
rite. Indeed, the abandoned child became such a potent image in the
nineteenth century that it permeated all the strands of the discourse
on sati and increasingly both official and popular attention was being
focused not only on the widow herself, but also on the infants she left
behind. This was a significant break with the practice of previous
centuries, when the offspring of the widow had been conspicuously
absent from accounts. Occasionally a son appeared to light the pyre or
a daughter was chastised for failing to do more to prevent the sacrifice,
but for the most part they merge with the faceless crowd of friends
and relatives who attend the immolation. In the early nineteenth
century, however, the infants orphaned by sati became almost as much
an icon of the practice as the widow herself, with the image of the
deserted child being repeatedly invoked to highlight the iniquity of
the custom. Mrs Phelps, for example, who wrote an extended and
highly romantic account of sati for an Oxford poetry competition in
1831, included the following verses:

But what arrests her steps with that dread start,
What sudden anguish rends her broken heart?
....She feels a little hand within her own,
And hears her tender infant's plaintive moan;
'Tis more than human nature can withstand,
The tender pressure of that little hand;
And the poor baby's weak and mournful cry,
Awakes the mother's bitterest agony.
She wildly turns, and on each cherub face
Imprints, in frenzy, one farewell embrace;
While the stern Priests her kind attendance chide,
And bid them take the babes and quickly hide
Them from her gaze; as none may dare to stay
The wretched suttee on her destined way....[15]

For Mrs Phelps, as for many others, the breaking of maternal bonds is but another source of anguish for the widow who is pressurized into acceding to the demand to perform sati. That the child is portrayed as being almost ripped from her breast reinforces the image of the sati as a passive victim of a custom that she does not have the power to resist. It was a powerful image and one that was utilized to great effect by anti-sati campaigners. John Poynder, for example, in his speech on the subject to the proprietors of East India Company stock, supplemented his moral and political arguments for the rite's abolition with an emotive appeal on behalf of the orphaned children. In a detailed analysis of the yearly sati returns, he repeatedly estimated for each year the number of children left without what he referred to as 'their only remaining, perhaps most valuable, parent'.[16] The utility of such an approach is evident. Despite an increasing tendency to portray the sati as a passive victim, there was still a question mark over the nature of her complicity in the rite. The infant, on the other hand was an entirely innocent victim. Thus while, the representation of sati as a crime against the widow could be problematic, the representation of it as a crime against her children was relatively clearcut.

The new emphasis on the child, and the nature of the maternal bond when discussing sati, was reflective of an emerging gender ideology in Britain that privileged woman's role as mother, above all else in its construction of femininity. Barbara Caine points out that, in the emerging ideology of 'separate spheres', woman's role in the care and nurturing of children was stressed, with a new emphasis being placed on breast feeding and direct and close maternal involvement with her children.[17] In particular, the ideas of Jean Jacques Rousseau, which had by the end of the eighteenth century become very influential in Britain, represented women as being defined by their natural procreative function. Rousseau emphasized the importance of women's domestic role, and in particular her responsibility for the spiritual, moral, and educational welfare of their children, to the socio-political order. Indeed, throughout Europe childless women were encourage to find employment caring for the children of others, as governesses or nursery maids, in compensation for their failure to fulfil their natural role. For some, the importance of woman's function as mother was a route to recognition of her individual rights. Mary Wollstonecraft, for example, argued that the responsibility entailed by motherhood should automatically confer citizenship. For others, however, the emphasis on motherhood could be used to reinforce woman's domesticity. Raising children was a social duty and a full-time job, which was incompatible with economic activity outside the home. The new 'maternalism' was instrumental in reinforcing the ideology of separate spheres both for men and for upper and middle-class women, who used their experience of motherhood to transform both their self-understanding and their world-view.[18]

Under these circumstances it is hardly surprising that women such as Mrs Phelps should emphasize the mother's pain in parting with her child. Many British observers seem to have considered the maternal bond between mother and child to be the most effective deterrent to sati, and attempts to dissuade a widow from her course in this period almost always involve appeals to the widow's maternal instinct. In some cases they were successful. The magistrate for Tipperah in 1815 reported that

During the year specified…two women have, agreeably to their own free will and consent, been saved from destruction…the change of determination of one…proceeded from motives of compassion for her child, a female of ten years of age, who, at the time of final parting from her, when the latter was on the eve of submitting to undergo the ceremony of being buried alive with her deceased husband, set up the most bitter lamentations, which eventually had the effect of inducing the parent to forego the resolution which she had previously taken of sacrificing herself in the manner above described.[19]

In some cases proponents of the sacrifice appear to have been aware that the maternal instinct might undermine the impetus to perform sati. A contributor to *The Times*, for example, informed readers that in the case of a sati that occurred in December 1823, the widow's '...last wish to see her child was refused, perhaps it was feared that her maternal feelings would have destroyed her fatal resolution, and thus have deprived the Hindoos of the enjoyment of witnessing her being burnt alive'.[20]

The implications of sati for the maternal bond were not always understood sympathetically; for many, the infant was not torn from the mother's breast, but deliberately deserted. A correspondent for the *Calcutta Journal* reported of a sati in 1820 that, 'The devotee...on this occasion, as on many others, regardless of maternal feeling, had left an infant child at home to come to the awful pile.'[21] Indeed, the sati's willingness to abandon her child, in common with the supposed prevalence of infanticide of various types, was seen to be indicative of the degraded nature of Hinduism and Hindu women. An anonymous missionary pamphlet of 1828, for example, declared that

Instigated by the demon of superstition, mothers have been seen casting their offspring amongst a number of alligators, and standing to gaze at these monsters quarreling for their prey.... Yes; while we see the cow butting with her horns, and threatening the person who dare approach her young, we see WOMAN in India throwing her living child to the outstretched jaws of the alligator...[22]

While William Ward enquires of his female readership:

And does no mother interpose her tender entreaties to spare her daughter? 'Can a woman forget her sucking child, that she should not have compassion on the infant of her womb?' Oh what need of the softening and enlightening influences of the gospel, where mothers have become monsters—have sunk below the wolf and the tiger. Through what unknown, unheard of process must the female heart have passed, thus to have lost all its wonted tenderness; thus to have laid hold of a nature not found anywhere else upon the earth....[23]

The concentration of missionaries on the orphans of sati and on forms of religious infanticide reflected an understanding of femininity that privileged motherhood beyond all else. Hinduism was represented as being so perverted and unnatural that it could even break the most innate of bonds—that between mother and child. As a reporter for *The Times* put it in 1811, 'I endeavoured to awaken the maternal affections, conceiving them to be the strongest that rise in the human mind; but superstition had extinguished even them.'[24]

The tensions between the image of the widow who deserts her child and the one who has that child torn from her, created an ambivalence that underpinned the common depictions of the widow as struggling between the 'natural' bond of maternal affection and the 'false' weight of superstition. A correspondent for the *Calcutta Journal* reported of a sati in 1820 that

Yet when a Gentleman present observed to her that by giving her life to be destroyed she was not only acting contrary to the will of God, but also doing an injury to society by leaving her child unprotected, she evinced the most poignant anguish that can be conceived. With a look of wild and pitiable distraction she said 'Speak not of my child—Why do you wound my bosom with the idea?' Then relapsing into superstitious ravings she added 'But that child no longer belongs to me—I am not its mother...'—so powerful is bigotry over the nobler emotions of nature.[25]

Here the widow is depicted as torn between natural affection and religious indoctrination, between her instinctive reactions and her moral degradation. The willingness of the sati to be separated from her child was often put forward as proof that she was not a rational agent in the sacrifice for, had she been lucid, how could she have abandoned her infant? The bond between mother and child was viewed as one of the holiest and purest of earthly ties and the destruction of it repeatedly portrayed as a perversion of nature.

If concentration on the widow's willingness to desert her child was a useful tool in emphasizing the degrading nature of Hinduism, and the distortion of the widow's reason in choosing sati, the level of public concern with the fate of the orphaned child was also indicative of social concerns in Britain. The emerging emphasis on woman's reproductive role was accompanied by a backlash against traditional practices such as wet-nursing, which were increasingly deemed to be both unnatural and immoral. It was also accompanied by the vilification of both working-class mothers who neglected or even destroyed their own children, and delinquent middle-class mothers who refused to nourish their babies as nature intended—a 'habitual neglect of the maternal duty' that formed a 'foul blot on the moral escutcheon of the mothers of England'.[26] In particular, infanticide among a deviant working class was considered a significant social problem, the more disturbing because it did not seem that poverty could be offered in defence. The Poor Law Commissioner's Report of 1834 found that '…in no civilized country, and scarcely in any barbarous country, has such a thing ever been heard of as a mother killing her child in order to save the expense of feeding it'.[27] The fascination with the sati's willingness to abandon her child, and more especially with religious infanticide in India, can thus be seen as a displacement of concerns about the reality of motherhood in Britain, Rousseau notwithstanding.

Concern with the fate of those orphaned by sati was not confined to an emotional response to the severing of maternal ties, however. As the above extract reveals, motherhood was also considered a social duty and the widow who deserted her offspring was 'doing an injury to society by leaving her child unprotected'.[28] In Britain the industrial Revolution had given rise to considerable concern over the social implications of the number of 'latch-key' children left to roam the streets while their mothers worked in the factories.[29] These 'multitudes of children' were considered at risk from disease, idleness, moral depravity, and criminal experience because of the lack of parental supervision.[30] Similarly in India, the creation of orphans by sati was seen as a social as well as a moral evil and it is in this respect that the question of orphaned children entered the official discourse on sati. From their inception, the sati returns stated not only the number of immolations, but whether the widows had any children, their age, and whether a relative had agreed to take care of them, thus providing a record of the social cost of sati, both in terms of the number of widows who were immolated and of the number of orphans created.

The issue of the fate of sati orphans was first raised with the government by the magistrate of Burdwan, who, having received the 1813 instructions about legal and illegal sati, had prevented four women from burning on the sole grounds of their having infant children. In a fifth case he had been unable to prevent the sacrifice and had arrested those who had abetted it on the grounds that the woman had a two-and-a-half years old child.[31] He received a severe rebuke from the Nizamat Adalat, on the grounds that their instructions had not authorized such an intervention, but his letter did instigate a detailed discussion of the rules relating to widows with young children. As with all other aspects of legislation on sati, the touchstone of legitimacy was to be found in Hindu law and the pundits of the Nizamat Adalat were asked to elucidate the scriptural position on this issue. The response came that 'a Hindoo woman having a child within three years of age should not be allowed to burn herself with the body of her deceased

husband, unless some person will undertake to provide a suitable
maintenance for the child'.[32] The result was that the instructions to
magistrates were modified on the grounds that 'justice and humanity
forbid that a practice attended with the destruction of human life, and
often productive of calamitous consequences for the children of the
deceased, should be promoted or permitted beyond the extent of the
rules prescribed for it in Hindoo law'.[33] From 1815 on, it was thus
made mandatory that any widow with infant children should be prevented from burning unless someone was willing to provide a 'written
engagement in duplicate on stamped paper'[34] to the effect that they
would support her children. In this way the social and financial cost
to the state was mitigated, and the sati's abandonment of her child was
legitimized in legal if not in moral terms.

Sound States of Mind: Sati, Suicide, and Insanity

As we have seen, the willingness of the sati to break the maternal bond
could be used to suggest that the widow was non compos mentis when
she went to the pyre, the more so because a woman's abandonment of
her child was an acknowledged indicator of insanity in a period before
the diagnosis of post-natal depression. In this respect, this idea was
intimately connected with another debate that helped to form the
early nineteenth-century image of the sati, that about suicide and its
corollary: insanity. The debate about the prohibition of sati and the
hiatus of public interest in the custom that accompanied it, coincided
with a debate in Britain that sought to redefine the legal and social
position of self-destruction as 'Religious and magical ideas which had
justified savage punishments for self murder were gradually eclipsed
by medical and philosophical ideas that exculpated it.'[35] In the medieval and early modern periods both a Christian and civil abhorrence
of suicide combined to impose the punishments of profane burial and
forfeiture of the suicide's property. The only mitigation for suicide
was the suggestion that the perpetrator had died non compos mentis
and was therefore not responsible for his or her actions. While there
were obviously numerous specific local considerations that might
sway a jury to return a verdict of non compos mentis at any period, a
marked increase in the number of cases resulting in such an acquittal
in the years following 1680 may have signaled what Michael MacDonald
refers to as a 'fundamental change in the cultural significance of suicide'.[36] While a verdict of non compos mentis fulfilled a growing

social need to alleviate the position of a felo-de-se's family by circum-venting the laws of forfeiture, MacDonald believes that it also reflects a new tendency to excuse suicide in medical terms. In the eighteenth century, Enlightenment rationalism increasingly rejected diabolical explanations for suicide, which were replaced with an understanding of it based on natural morality and modern medical practice. A rational analysis of a suicide saw it as an unnatural act that could only be perpetrated by someone not in control of his or her senses. Thus, rather than needing evidence that an individual was non compos mentis, the very act of suicide was increasingly being viewed as proof of the perpetrator's insanity and the felo-de-se was increasingly being portrayed as a lunatic to be pitied rather than a sinner to be punished.

This liberalizing of public opinion on suicide did not go uncon-tested, of course, and pamphlets, often of a religious nature, appeared throughout the eighteenth century warning people against the sin of suicide and against the dangers of too great a leniency towards the felo-de-se. For the most part, however, a combination of reaction against the harshness of anti-suicide laws and a shifting awareness of the medical causes of suicide led to a mitigation of the crime in the public imagination. MacDonald comments that by 1760, juries had all but ceased punishing suicide itself, reserving the felo-de-se verdict in-stead for those who would otherwise have escaped censure for other crimes.[37] Thus, while the laws of profane burial and forfeiture re-mained on the statutes until 1823 and 1870 respectively, they were increasingly being circumvented by shifting popular opinion.

The anomalous situation created by this disparity between the law and liberal opinion on the matter of suicide, combined with the return to religious values heralded by the rise of the evangelical movement in the early nineteenth century, created the circumstances for a heated debate on the subject of suicide. From the liberal side, calls for the abolition of forfeiture—which was seen as unfairly punishing the innocent family of the deceased—gathered pace in the nineteenth century as Sir James Mackintosh, a leading figure of the reform move-ment, took up the case in parliament. The result was a flood of pamphlets in the years leading up to 1823, as proponents of more lenient laws on suicide confronted those who wished to reinforce suicide's status as a crime and a sin. Ministers in particular were keen to reinforce the religious connotations of suicide as a mortal sin in the face of the new medical and philosophical understanding of it and to deter their flock from a adopting a tolerant attitude towards it. On the secular front, many moralists, including religious figures, were concerned that increased leniency would remove the existing deterrent to suicide, which was already seen to be a growing social problem. Indeed, many went as far as to call for more severe punishments for precisely this reason.[38] Of course this call for harsh punishments as a deterrent presupposed volition on the part of the suicide, something that had been cast into doubt by the new concentration on the mental state of the perpetrator and the assumption that suicide itself was a symptom of madness. While many of those who spoke out strenuously against a change in the suicide laws accepted that it could be the result of insanity, they were eager to stress that this was not necessarily the case and to warn against too great an alacrity in ascribing suicide to lunacy rather than to the vices of arrogance or despair.

Clearly the considerations of this debate have extremely important connotations for our understanding of the British position on sati. Indeed, the debate on sati was closely interlinked with the debate on suicide and each played a role in informing and defining the other. Not only did assumptions about sati's inherent 'unnaturalness' lend weight to an understanding of her sacrifice that replaced heroic action with (temporary) insanity and uncontrolled action—an idea that was to be central in stripping the last vestiges of agency from the widow—but the example of the sati as representing a certain type of suicide was also incorporated into the broader debate about the nature of self-destruction at home. Indeed, it is possible to correlate the unprecedented level of attention given to sati during this period with a growing fascination, particularly in artistic and literary circles, with the taboo subject of suicide more generally. There was a very real concern in the early nineteenth century that suicide in Britain had '...of late increased an alarming degree'.[39] It may be possible, then, to understand the early nineteenth-century obsession with sati as reflecting a desire to both debate and displace the delicate issue of suicide, as fascination with sati mirrored preoccupation with the self-destruction of British men and (more particularly) women at home.

A good example of the way in which ideas about gender and suicide were bought into the debate on sati is the statement about the widow's volition made by William Ewer, the acting superintendent of police for the Lower Provinces of Bengal, in a letter to the Government of India in 1818. In this letter he attacks the suggestion that the sati performed the sacrifice of her own free will, claiming, 'there are many reasons for thinking that such an event as voluntary suttee very rarely occurs'.[40] He then goes on to explain at some length why he believes this to be the case. His arguments combine an assessment of the specific Indian context with contemporary British assumptions about women and suicide, and because of this are worth considering in detail. He states:

...very few widows would think of sacrificing themselves, unless overpowered by force or persuasion, very little of either being sufficient to overcome the physical or mental powers of the majority of Hindu females; and a widow who would turn with natural instinctive horror from the first hint of sharing her husband's pile, will be at length gradually brought to pronounce a reluctant consent; because, distracted by grief at the event, without one friend to advise or protect her, she is little prepared to oppose the surrounding crowd of hungry Brahmins and interested relations, either by argument or by force....In this state of confusion a few hours quickly pass, and the widow is burnt before she has time even to think on the subject.[41]

Ewer here follows the prevailing view of suicide as unnatural and irrational, an act that simply could not be entered into with a clear mind. To explain the apparently voluntary sati there must be other factors influencing the widow's decision. For Ewer, the frailty of the female intellect allows her to be turned from the 'natural' path (surviving) to the 'unnatural' one (suicide) by interested male protagonists. This essentialist view of Hindu women's frailty is, of course, at odds with the numerous accounts of widows resisting even the most determined endeavours to dissuade them. It does, however, fit neatly with contemporary European constructions of both the capacities of the weaker sex and the preconditions for suicide. While in Britain suicide was viewed as an indicator of possible insanity, in the Indian context Ewer suggests that the fragility of the Hindu widow's mental state created for her a temporary 'insanity' comprising grief, confusion, and outside pressure, which she was incapable of resisting.

Ewer's conclusion is that the widow has no agency. Both the conditions of her former life and the specific circumstances under which the decision to commit sati is reached, rob her of the power of rational cognisance. Under these circumstances, while Ewer is prepared to acknowledge the theoretical legitimacy of a truly voluntary sati, he claims that such an event is so rare as to make it negligible and that even should the widow appear determined this must be weighed against her state of mind. His opinion is supported by that of E. Lee

Warner, magistrate of the 24 Pergunnahs, who, in communication with Ewer, comments:

> ...the free consent alleged in palliation of the sacrifice appears to me to be inadmissible; that is, no fair judgment can be passed on a person *non compos mentis*, assenting to the performance of this act; for can a person be called actually in a sound state of reason and mind, under the agitation of grief?[42]

In an interesting inversion of existing ideas, Warner uses a verdict of non compos mentis not to excuse suicide, as was the case in Britain at the time, but to condemn the toleration of it. Although both Warner and Ewer draw on external factors (familial and priestly pressure, lack of education, indoctrination, grief) to stress the coercive nature of the circumstances under which the widow makes the supposedly voluntary decision to commit sati, in their concentration on the widow's mental state they are essentially buying into the new medical rhetoric on suicide that sees it as a symptom of insanity. The connection is even clearer when we consider that nineteenth-century medical thought saw madness not so much as a discreet internal illness, but as a state of mind that could be triggered by various external pressures. Women, like Ophelia, might go mad as a result of disappointment in love, and men as the result of intolerable dishonour or financial ruin. The parallels between Ewer's depiction of the sati's state of mind and the contemporary understanding of insanity, deserve further analysis as through this we can see the ways in which the debate on sati was intimately connected with the wider debates about femininity, madness, and suicide, that were going on in the metropole at this time.

Jarring Emotions: Sati and the Image of Female Insanity

The scientific advances of the eighteenth and nineteenth centuries saw a shift in the way in which insanity was understood both by the medical community and by popular culture. As Elaine Showalter points out, 'Where previously lunatics had been characterized as unfeeling brutes, ferocious animals that needed to be kept in check with chains, whips, straight-waistcoats, barred windows and locked cells, they were now seen instead as sick human beings, objects of pity whose sanity could be restored by kindly care.'[43] Concomitant to this, however, was a shift in understanding that saw insanity increasingly being characterized as 'female', even when experienced by men, and the development of a rhetoric that connected madness with the female characteristics of irrationality, frailty, and dependence. By the nineteenth century the repulsive male lunatic had been replaced by the appealing madwoman as the cultural icon of insanity.[44] Indeed, it was the suggestion of 'delicate' females being abused in lunatic asylums that provided the impetus for debate and the reform of the system.

It was widely believed in the nineteenth century that insanity was a predominantly 'female malady',[45] and there was indeed some statistical evidence to support this popular conception. As early as the seventeenth century, the files of doctor Richard Napier showed nearly twice as many cases of mental disorder among women as among men, and by the middle of the nineteenth century women made up the majority of patients in public lunatic asylums.[46] Indeed, in 1829 *The Times* reported that a recent French survey had found insanity one-third higher among women than men.[47] A number of explanations have been put forward, both for the statistical predominance of mental disorder in women during this period and for the prevailing popular typology of madness as female. It has been suggested that the constraints of patriarchal society and the sheer boredom experienced by the 'angel in the house' were enough to produce an 'unbalanced' response, which was exacerbated by the ministrations of a misogynistic medical profession. Some feminists, such as Helene Cixous and Xaviere Gauthier, have taken this further and suggest that the 'admirable hysterics' of the nineteenth century were a reaction by women against the constraints of patriarchy—a form of unconscious protest by the powerless against their oppressors. Shoshana Feldman, on the other hand, sees madness as the inverse of protest, the final resort of those whose cultural conditioning has denied all other forms of self-expression.[48] Diverging from these interpretations, Elaine Showalter has argued that madness was not in fact primarily found in women during this period, but that the structure of society meant that it was more common for the disorder to be diagnosed in women than in men. A woman who showed signs of mental disorder was more likely to be consigned to the madhouse than her male counterpart, who might be privileged to more discreet medical attention within the home. Thus it is possible that madness in women in the nineteenth century was not only misunderstood, but also misrepresented.

Whether it was more prevalent in women or not, nineteenth-century concern over the nature of madness was heightened by the fact that insanity generally, and suicide in particular, was widely conceived at the time to be a peculiarly English problem. References to the 'English malady' (madness) and the 'English vice' (suicide) appear repeatedly in contemporary texts on the subject. For many, this supposed tendency towards 'nervous disorder' was the result of the great intellectual and economic pressures felt by a highly civilized and successful race. This form of 'noble' madness was confined to men, however. The insanity suffered by women was represented in a very different way. In a woman, madness was seen as being closely associated with sexuality and to the essentially irrational nature of femininity. The pressures that drove the female mind to insanity were not the public masculine pursuits, but were often closely connected to her relationships with men. The three archetypes of female insanity in the nineteenth century—the jilted Ophelia, who is sent mad by Hamlet's 'mixed signals'; Crazy Jane, the serving girl who wanders aimlessly looking for her lost lover; and Lucia, whose madness takes the form of a violent rage against men—can all be seen as differing responses to male influence and control. Under these circumstances, with female madness so closely linked in the popular imagination to female sexuality and sexual-romantic interaction with men, it is hardly surprising that a sati's reaction on the death of her husband could be explained in terms of temporary insanity caused by a combination of religious fervour and grief at the death of her husband. Thus, a subscriber to the *Calcutta Journal* in 1819 could comment that the sati's state of mind was '…impaired, unnaturally perhaps, by intoxicating drugs; naturally by the immediate previous loss of one of the dearest ties upon the earth',[49] while Magistrate C. Brown could argue that, 'It is the usual custom to ask the woman's assent, a custom not a little absurd, as a person frantic with grief will naturally desire death, and is no more fit to be argued with than one under the influence of fever and delirium.'[50]

If the death of the husband was viewed as the immediate catalyst for the widow's mental disorder, then her religious 'fanaticism' whipped up at this moment by the priests and intensified by her grief, was viewed as the root cause. In Britain, religious conviction was believed to have a palliative effect on the mind of the lunatic, but in the case of the sati the reverse was deemed to be true, as her religious beliefs were depicted as contributing to her delirium. Thus the *Calcutta Journal* could report of a sati in 1826 that

...her mind appeared already so fortified with religious bigotry, so bewildered and occupied with the phantoms of a terrified and disordered imagination, that no persuasion could prevail, because no persuasion, no matter how forcible, could be understood. The jarring emotions of her soul had created such a degree of frenzy or madness that she already seemed to belong to another world.[51]

The all-pervasive power of religion, which had been seen in the eighteenth century to structure every aspect of Hindu life, is here depicted as determining the widow's very sanity. The concern with the inexorable force of religion in undermining the widow's rational agency appears repeatedly. A reporter for *The Times* in 1823, for example, commented that he had endeavoured to ensure that the widow 'went to her death in her senses, or at least as much so as she could be under the influence of such extraordinary fanaticism',[52] while the *Asiatic Mirror* reported in relation to a sati in 1811 that it '...exhibits the striking power of religious fanaticism to control the strongest laws of nature, to stifle the instinctive feeling and triumph over the closest ties of kindred and social affection'.[53]

The image of the widow driven mad by grief at the loss of her husband is often reinforced by the way in which her appearance is described. In some cases the imagery is explicit. In the following extract from the *Bombay Gazette*, the widow is described as

...absolutely insane from the effects of drugs administered to her. To describe the loathsome and yet pitiable state of that poor creature, her starting and bloodshot eyes, her slavering lips, her outrageous behaviour, mad gesticulations and yet madder cries, would be here useless.[54]

In other cases the widow's insanity was implied by an emphasis on aspects of her appearance that would have borne unmistakable connotations for European observers. It was conventional for stage productions of *Hamlet* to depict Ophelia with her hair unbound and dishevelled and decked with wild flowers and garlands as she sang and prattled nonsense. Similarly, Crazy Jane was said to 'dress her head with willow straw, and wild flowers, disposed of in a fanciful style'.[55] If we compare these images to descriptions of the sati, we find the same details stressed as the British observers emphasize the outward manifestations of the widow's state of mind as well as conjecturing at the internal ones. As early as 1787, Sir Charles Mallet had reported of a sati:

In the solemn moment in which alone I saw her, these beauties were conspicuous, not withstanding her face was discoloured with tumeric, her hair disheveled and wildly adorned with flowers; and her looks...like those of one whose senses wandered.[56]

Such romanticized depictions of the widow as a beautiful, young madwoman were to become commonplace in the nineteenth century as the iconographies of the sati and the madwoman helped to reinforced each other. In 1817, for example, a Baptist missionary in Orissa reported of a sati: 'She gave a few flowers to Jaya-huri-ghosa and began to sing *Vrinda-vuna vasee, kuribe leela rashee* (the dwellers of Vrinda-vuna will have heaps of pleasure) which she continued to repeat until she was like a madwoman; and her cruel relations persuaded her to embrace the flames',[57] while another missionary in 1825 described a sati as:

...under twenty years of age, and of an interesting appearance. Round her person was wrapped a white cloth smeared with turmeric.... Her jet black hair was smeared with ghee and other greasy substances, and decorated with flowers and other gaudy ornamented paper: round her neck was a large rope nearly as thick as my wrist, and one or two smaller ones: thus attired she looked like a picture of all that is degraded and wretched.[58]

Of course, not all widows appeared crazed. In 1823 a reporter for *The Times* could comment of a sati that she, 'heard me with calmness, and thanked me for my intentions, which she admitted were good, but again repeated her intention so decidedly as to preclude any hope of saving her. I felt her pulse, and it was far calmer than my own at the moment I am writing.'[59] Even in cases where the widow showed no outward sign of madness, she was often still depicted within a convention that allows the reader to make assumptions about her state of mind, however. Indeed, the tensions between the widow's presumed insanity and the outward display of her rationality abound, as officials and missionaries alike continued to argue that it was almost impossible under the circumstances for the widow to be deemed compos mentis. The following account from *The Times*, for example, both emphasizes the physical appearance of the widow and acknowledges her composure.

The widow was dressed in a robe, or sheet of bright red silk, and had her hair hanging loose and dishevelled, and stuck through with many wooden combs; her forehead was painted with yellow ochra, or orpiment, and she had no other dress or ornament whatever…. During all this dreadful note of preparation from first to last, the widow preserved the utmost, the most *entire* fortitude and composure, or rather apathy…we at first concluded her to be intoxicated, but were afterwards convinced of our mistake, by seeing the steadiness of nerve, and perfect composure with which she sprinkled the corpse of her husband, and mounted the funeral pile entirely unassisted and alone. We stood within six or seven feet of the pile and could not be mistaken.[60]

The implication that the widow is rational and sane when she commits this deed is too much for this observer and he rationalizes her apparent composure as apathy, a condition associated with madness. Similarly, Magistrate C. Brown reported in 1829 of a sati in Cumbum: 'As is usual on such occasions, the widow's behaviour was apparently calm and cool, but I was well aware that this cheerfulness was not real, but induced by despair.'[61] Brown is certain that he can speak for the widow's state of mind, despite outward appearances. For others the difficulty in ascertaining the widow's state of mind at the moment of her sacrifice was recognized, but for the most part the British were prepared to assume that it was disturbed unless evidence to the contrary could be provided. Thus, when 'a subscriber' to the *Calcutta Journal* posed the question, 'I know it can be urged…that the utmost freedom of action shall be allowed to the poor votary…who are to be the judges of her wish at that moment?',[62] he is referring to the difficulty in judging her sane, rather than finding her insane. That the British should follow this construction of the widow's action—as normatively undertaken while not in a 'sound state of reason and mind'[63]—is hardly surprising given their own understanding of suicide.

The correlation between the sati's suicide and her insanity is reflective of a popular assumption that women's supposed susceptibility to madness made them more prone to self-destruction than men. In actual fact, nineteenth-century records clearly showed that suicide rates for women were consistently lower than for men, but as these hard facts did not fit comfortably with popular preconceptions about women, many Victorians continued to believe in women's suicidal nature—a fact reflected in popular fiction of the time, especially in the genre of domestic melodrama in which dozens of jilted women were rescued from the jaws of suicide.[64] For those who accepted, or were aware of the statistical evidence, the low female suicide rate posed something of a conundrum. As Barbara Gates points out: 'Unless the weaker sex were to be credited with unwanted strength, the fact that women killed themselves less frequently than men needed some explaining.'[65] For a society that structured its gender relations around the assumption of mental and physical superiority of men, the suggestion that women's disinclination to suicide reflected her greater moral courage was clearly unacceptable. Instead, a woman's disinclination to suicide was explained in terms of her natural timidity and weakness, which, it was suggested, made her incapable of carrying through the suicidal impulse.[66] This idea was reinforced by the fact that when women did commit suicide it tended to be by the less bloody means of poisoning or drowning. Thus, women's dispropensity to suicide was explained not in terms of their will power, but of their will-lessness.[67] She was not better at conquering suicidal thoughts, but merely lacked the physical courage for suicidal action. Of course, this construction was challenged to its very core by the voluntary sati, who not only often overcame considerable male intervention to commit suicide, but did so in one of the most painful ways possible, often displaying unexampled mental and physical courage in the process. Thus, while the widow's determination toward suicide could easily be understood in terms of her temporary insanity, her physical courage in carrying through her design posed a more difficult problem, for if Indian women were capable of such bravery and endurance, what did that say about the inherent nature of women generally?

For some, a widow's bravery in the face of the flames could be explained in terms of her religious fanaticism. As we have already seen, religious indoctrination was seen by many as contributing to the imbalance of her mind on the death of her husband. Some went further to suggest that her fanaticism was whipped up to such frenzy that it carried her through her ordeal by fire. But, whereas, in the eighteenth century the religious component of the widow's determination had led to flattering comparisons with the Christian martyrs, in the early nineteenth century it was simply used to underline the tyranny of the Hindu religion over malleable minds. A correspondent to the *Asiatic Journal* summed up the prevailing opinion when he commented: 'When martyrdom is mentioned, it could not for a moment be intended to compare that sacred cause to the heartless and senseless superstition of misguided Hindoo widows....'[68]

For the most part, British observers preferred to deny the sati's physical courage altogether. This is not to suggest that accounts of satis sitting calmly amid the flames did not still exist, but they were increasingly considered the exception rather than the rule.[69] 'A subscriber' to the *Asiatic Mirror* expressed surprise that the sati he witnessed 'far from evincing any distrust or feminine weakness, displayed the utmost magnanimity'.[70] Whereas eighteenth-century commentators could refer to the 'unexampled fortitude' displayed by satis generally, in the early nineteenth century this construction had given way to the image of the widow who either went intoxicated and insensible to her death, or who was confined by various means to the pyre. The image of the widow being bound to the pyre became increasingly prominent and observers often stressed the fact that the widow could not have escaped even if she had wanted to. This was in part the result of anti-sati rhetoric that sought to present the rite as an act of violence visited on innocent women, but it can also be seen as reflective of concern about the natural capacity of women to endure suffering. Representations of the widow as forcibly constrained to the pyre undermined the suggestion that women might be more courageous than men gave them credit for, by removing the aspect of choice from her ordeal. Although examples did still occur of women sitting unbound in the midst of the flames, increasingly the normative image was one of a sati who, though she might have mounted the pyre of her own volition, only underwent the tortures of dissolution because she could not escape. Indeed, by the 1820s it was even suggested that if the widow were forced to mount an already blazing pyre (as was believed to be the scripturally prescribed mode for performing sati), rather than being tied to one which was subsequently set alight, then very few would have the courage to go through with the ceremony. As John MacDonald, who raised the issue in the *Asiatic Journal* in 1821, suggested:

...every miserable female deluded to self destruction, shall, unintoxicated and unstupefied by drugs, mount the funeral pile in full previous inflammation. It is safe to presume that few in their sober senses will agree to perish in this manner...few, if any, who will dare death in so dreadful a form, to precipitate themselves in to the fire burning fiercely and ready to consume them in agonies.[71]

MacDonald, like many others, believed that if the widow was confronted with the mode of her destruction before she committed herself to the pyre, she would naturally shrink back. Another correspondent to the same journal, writing under the pseudonym 'An Old Indian', commented, 'I have made experimental references to female feelings.... After explaining the general subject to a sensible woman, I concluded by putting the case as follows...die by either of these modes you must, which would you choose? The answer has invariable been for the uninflamed pyre.'[72] The supposition here is that the 'increased horror' of the burning pile would reawaken women's natural fearfulness, and that they are only capable of performing the sacrifice through passive means.

The probable efficacy of MacDonald's suggestion is to some extent supported by the number of women who either escaped the pyre when the pain became too much, or were seen contorted with agony, unable to escape. Perhaps many women would indeed have retracted at the sight of the flames had such a facility been open to them. That said, it seems slightly paradoxical that MacDonald considers the blazing pyre to be the greater horror, particularly when one considers the tales of widows enduring death by burning on pyres scarce big enough to consume the corpse alone. A correspondent for *The Times,* writing in 1812, for example, reported of a sati: 'They were very poor, and did not provide sufficient wood and oil: horrid to relate, the poor creature was repeatedly heard to cry out "more fire! more fire!" and shriek with agony until the noise of the instruments drowned out her cries.'[73] Similarly, John Poynder in his speech to the East India Company Board of Directors, cites the following account from the *Bombay Courier:*

The unfortunate Brahmin of her own accord ascended the funeral pile...but finding the torture of the fire more than she could bear, by a violent struggle she threw herself from the flames, and tottering a short distance, fell down....She retained her senses completely and complained of the badness of the pile, which she said consumed her so slowly, that she could not bear it, but expressed her willingness again to try it, if they would improve it.[74]

In the above instances, it is not so much the ferocity of the blaze that adds to the horror of the widow's ordeal, but the insufficiency of it. The sight of the preignited pile might have deterred some, but for those who would not, or could not retract, it also would have provided the swiftest dispatch. Whatever the nature of the widow's demise, eyewitness accounts clearly attest to the fact that many of the women certainly did not display the feminine timidity ascribed to them, a fact emphasized by the oft-reported incident of two widows in Calcutta, who when informed (supposedly by Raja Rammohan Roy) that they would in fact have to mount an already blazing pyre, rebuked the gentleman for doubting their resolution and cast themselves into the flames. In the face of such examples of fortitude, it seems hard to resist the supposition that the prevailing British tendency to represent the voluntary sati as a passive victim was more reflective of their own beliefs about women's physical and mental capacity for suicide, than their actual experience.

Barbarous Examples: Sati and the British Discourse on Suicide

The prevailing British conception of suicide thus played an important part in informing ideas about sati, but it would be wrong to assume that the relationship between the two was unidirectional, as the issues raised by sati were also incorporated into the debate on suicide in Britain. Sati could be used by those who opposed any alleviation of the punishments for suicide to illustrate the barbarous state of affairs that could result when self-destruction was not held with the appropriate abhorrence. Many of the numerous tracts on suicide that appeared in Britain in the late eighteenth and early nineteenth centuries used the Hindu widow's fiery death as a cautionary tale to impress upon the reader the importance of the correct moral attitude towards self-destruction. Any laxity on the issue would, it was suggested, lower British society to the level of the heathen. This argument was particularly common among Christian writers who sought to oppose reform of the suicide laws on religious grounds. The anonymous author of a sermon on suicide published in 1799 asked the reader to consider that 'Suicide is now no less creditable in China and India, than it was formerly at Rome or in Greece.... How different at all times, has been the state of those who live under divine revelation, from that of the heathen world!'[75] The intention here was to impress upon the reader the duty imposed by Christian enlightenment—suicide might be acceptable to the pagan who lacked God's guidance, but is inexcusable in a Christian. Failure to condemn it utterly would undermine Western claims to civilization.

This message is made even more forcefully in Harriot Cope's poem *Suicide*, published in 1815. After several verses dealing with the different causes of suicide in Britain (unrequited love, dishonour, abandonment, etc.) she tells the reader:

The hapless widow of Malabar's coast—
Makes it her pride, her duty and her boast,
Of her dead lord t'ascend the funeral pyre,
And self-devoted in the flames expire;[76]

And asks, 'Shall we then imitate the savage creed? No, rather pity,
and aghast recede…',[77] concluding:

But long has truth's benignant lucid ray,
Chased oracles and sibyls far away;
The pagan's doubts and empty fears dispersed,
And on the mind with bright refulgence burst,
Before the Christian faith dark error fled,
And revelation raised its beauteous head…[78]

The sati herself may be the object of pity rather than condemnation,
even when self-devoted,[79] but this pity is only an appropriate response
because of her ignorance of proper morality; it cannot be extended to
the suicide in Britain without a dangerous fall in standards. Thus,
Richard Hey, in a pamphlet chronicling the evils of gaming, duelling,
and suicide, stresses that we should not look for our morals to the
'heathen nations':

And, certainly, we are not to be guided in our customs by the
barbarous…Indians…if even the tender sex among the Indian nations have
demonstrated their conjugal fidelity by throwing themselves with alacrity
upon the funeral piles of their deceased husbands…are we, from these
barbarous Examples, to deduce a right over our own Lives? Upon such
grounds any action whatsoever might be justified.[80]

Similarly, Samuel Piggott, in his 1831 tract *Antidotes to the Follies, Vices
and Crimes of Youth*, blames the legality of suicide on 'The influence of
ignorant superstition and priestly craft over the minds of the Gentoos'.[81]
For Piggot, there is nothing to be admired in the sati's sacrifice.

How different is this from that voluntary sacrifice of life to achieve durable
benefits to our country, for the world, for our own souls and for God; where
heroic virtue excites the true patriot to daring deeds of valour and the
imminent risk of personal safety, or where the love of God and our Saviour
animates the Christian to the endurance of the greatest privations, and to
embrace the burning stake. Such sacrifices are applauded by all good men,
and well pleasing to God; and he will one day manifest his acceptance by
avenging them on their enemies.[82]

While he acknowledges some exceptional instances in which deliberately laying down life can be noble, he fails to see the parallel with the Hindu understanding of sati. Thus, while the 'forlorn hope' or the Christian martyrs are examples worthy of emulation, the sati is held up as a warning of the depth to which humanity can sink to if not guided by the right principles.

Nineteenth-century fascination with sati was thus deeply implicated with concerns and fears about the nature of self-destruction in Britain. As Barbara Gates tells us of the Victorians: 'If their culture condemned suicide and prevented full discussion of its contemporary insidiousness, it never the less encouraged a close look at self-destruction in other times and in other cultures.'[83] For Gates, 'Increased attention to *suttee* paralleled not just anti-Hinduism but an ensuing interest in and fear of self destruction that came with altered suicide laws after 1823.'[84] Thus in the same way as poets such as Matthew Arnold, Thomas Cooper, and Alfred Lord Tennyson used classical figures like Cato, Empedocles, and Lucretius to explore the philosophical and emotional issues of suicide, so too could increased interest in sati reflect a need to displace a controversial discussion about the nature of self-destruction in general. The result is that, far from being determined solely by attitudes to India, the image of the sati as it emerged in the early nineteenth century was influenced by a myriad of different concerns, preoccupations, and imperatives and reflected both a conscious assertion of Hindu difference and a subconscious assumption of universal similarities.

The Zeal and Influences of the Ladies: Sati and Missionary Enterprise

The importance of the issue of suicide to the British understanding of sati can be seen not only through the theoretical debate about the nature of the widow's agency, but also through the way in which Westerners, and in particular missionaries, interacted with potential satis. On one level, of course, the relationship between widow and Briton was carried out through the framework set by the terms of the government regulation of 1813, which set the limits of acceptable intervention at dissuasion and ensuring that the sati was 'legal'. Within these limits, however, there was considerable scope for interaction. Some officials confined themselves to the government line, or failed to attend at all, while others would make more personal appeals to the widow to give up her resolution. For the most part, however, officials confined themselves to secular arguments (assuring the widow of her safety, her future support, etc). The missionaries, who often attended satis with the avowed intention of dissuading the widow, took a more philosophical (or theological) approach to the matter and often raised the issue of suicide as a mortal sin. The London Missionary Society, for example, reported of a sati that

Brother Townley first strongly expostulated with this wretched devotee upon the inhuman sacrifice she was about to make and added 'consider that you are now about to plunge into eternity to appear before God who will visit you for this sin, have mercy upon your own soul I beseech you'.[85]

In his diary, William Ward reports of William Carey that

Bro. C. addressed them and her in the most tender manner. He entreated, he threatened, he declaimed. He told the widow she was about to commit a very great sin and that she was going to fall into hell. Her only response was 'Oh Ganga! Ganga! Ganga!' calling to the river to save, or wash or take her, or something else.[86]

The contradiction inherent in such arguments would seem clear to most. If the widow had not been converted to Christianity during her lifetime, its precepts were hardly likely to have an effect on her at this the moment of her own religious consummation. Indeed, in some cases even the widow herself seems well aware of the paradox, as William Campbell reports.

Stepping in amongst the crowd we took this early opportunity of warning her of the danger, and of entreating her to abandon her shocking design. In plain language we told her that she was about to murder herself, that this was the only light in which her conduct would be regarded by the God of heaven and earth and that enslaving misery was the only reward that could be given to such a crime. She laughed and wondered how we could object to an action that everyone besides seemed to laud and admire.[87]

Under these circumstances the repeated use by the missionaries of the image of suicide as a mortal sin in their attempts to prevent sati requires some discussion, especially as it seems, rather unsurprisingly, to have been the least effective of all the arguments, yet is, rather more surprisingly, the one which is most widely and repeatedly used.

As time goes on, it seems that the missionaries who attend satis, whatever their protestations, do so not so much with the hope of preventing the sacrifice, as of acquiring a captive audience. The Baptist missionary Amos Sutton, for example, reported that the long-serving William Bampton had by 1825 given up all hopes of dissuading potential satis, saying that '…persuaded…that it was vain to attempt to save the wretched victim; he despaired of doing any good'.[88] This is not to suggest that those who attended did not entertain a sincere desire to see the sacrifice prevented, but that under the existing rules on intervention many of the more experienced missionaries had become disillusioned with their chances of success. That said, the sacrifice of a Hindu widow ensured a large crowd and anyone speaking to the widow was bound to be the centre of attention. Thus we find attempts to dissuade the widow often couched in religious terms that concentrate on moral issues such as suicide, rather than the practical ones that might have been more effective. One Baptist missionary reported to the society in 1817:

I said again to her 'Tremble for yourself; think what you are doing; repent; I am a servant of the true God. If you go into this fire you will go from it into unquenchable fire. God forbids you, through my lips. I added, believe the words that I say, Jesus Christ is the only Saviour[89]

and that

I opened to Acts, xvi 28. I warned her that to die in this way would be an unpardonable sin in her, and that she ought to wait with patience until God removed her. For two hours I stood and exhorted her, frequently repeating the words of the Apostle 'do thyself no harm'; if you die in this manner you will forever perish. I am a servant of God; I entreat you to return home. I spoke also to her sons and daughter, but it had no effect…. Alas! What could I do? I left her, but stopped among the crowd and preached from Galatians v. 19, and returned home.[90]

It appears that the missionary here recognized an opportunity not only to try and save a widow's life, but also to preach a sermon. The argument about suicide may well have been intended less for the benefit of the widow than for those onlookers who overheard.

The concentration of the missionaries on the issue of suicide cannot only be understood at a local level, but must be seen as contributing to the wider debate on suicide in the metropole. Their reports, letters, and diaries were usually published by the societies to which they belonged and then circulated among their particular church community. Moreover, these societies might often have been affiliated with the ministers and other religious leaders who were at the forefront of opposing the relaxation of suicide laws and who were concerned with inculcating a proper abhorrence of self-murder among their flock. Under these circumstances, it seems reasonable to see the missionaries report of their encounters with sati as contributing to this wider debate. Certainly the image of heathen women ignoring the missionary's protestations against suicide and casting themselves into the flames would be a powerful cautionary tale, a living representation of the consequences of self-destruction. The missionary concentration on the suicidal aspect of sati in their accounts can be understood in two ways. It was an extremely useful tool in gathering support and funding for the missionary cause, providing as it did the perfect illustration of the destructive influence of Hinduism, not only on the lives of the inhabitants of India but also on their souls. The Reverend T. Lessey, for example, could declaim at a meeting of the Methodist Missionary Society in 1821:

...when they [Christian ladies] hear the account of...widows walking, or rather dragged, to the funeral pyre of their husbands, and connect each of these perishing victims with an eternal world (for it is ETERNITY that impresses upon all our missionary pursuits the importance they possess) they go first in silence and mourn over them, their tenderest feelings are touched; and then they go about on an errand of mercy, and collect the silver and gold, so our funds are replenished....[91]

On the other hand, however, it is possible to read these missionary extracts in terms of the implicit message that they give, which is the same as that made explicitly in the tracts on suicide, namely: the Hindu's predilection to self-destruction debases him/her, and that any stance on suicide other than downright abhorrence would reduce good Christians to the level of heathens.

Sati, then, was particularly valuable to the missionary cause, not only because it represented one of the worst excesses of Hindu iniquity but also because it embodied the negation of a series of Victorian ideas and values that were particularly prominent at the time. It was an act of violence by men against women at a time when emerging gender ideology posited man's duty to protect the weaker sex. It perverted familial bonds, orphaned children, and undermined filial piety. It represented the oppressive power of religious dogmatism and corrupt priesthood and, perhaps most damningly, condemned the victim to eternal damnation as a suicide. As a cause, sati had all the ingredients to make it the ideal subject of a moral crusade and the degree of attention that it received among the population in general reflects the fact that it touched a chord with contemporary concerns at home. The breadth of its appeal was widened still further by the fact that it was an issue that affected women, and as such was a suitable subject for endeavour by this newest constituency of evangelists.

Philanthropic and charitable societies, such as those set up to support the work of missionaries in India, provided a rare instance of the merging of public and private space. Thus, while women were for the most part debarred from public activity, the association of charity and religion with the work of these societies made female involvement with them respectable—a natural outgrowth of women's domestic role as nurturer and moral guardian. This is not to suggest that these societies represented an opportunity to circumvent patriarchal control, of course, and women's activity even in this sphere was confined within carefully defined limits. The causes that women were encouraged to get involved in were usually those with suitable themes such as morality or family, or which involved the uplift of other women. Even within this limited sphere, women's action was curtailed and they were only permitted to perform certain functions. As Hall and Davidoff point out, while involvement in these societies gave women an outlet for their organizational skills, their contributions were for the most part legitimized through their subordination to male members of the societies. Even this limited involvement in the public sphere caused controversy, however, as can be seen by the furore over their participation in door-to-door collections.[92] As Davidoff and Hall put it: 'Spiritual equality between the sexes had wrenched open a space for women in the extended activities of church and chapel but the extent of that space was constantly under discussion.'[93]

It is in the context of this contested involvement with philanthropic activity that we must consider the missionary call to the women of Britain to involve themselves in the anti-sati campaign. Sati provided an ideal cause for the zeal of evangelical women, concerning as it did the fate of her less fortunate counterparts in India. The stress on the orphaning of children and the immorality of violence against the softer sex made it a legitimate area of interest and one which could be considered particularly poignant given women's supposed natural instincts. Thus we find missionary tracts and pamphlets, of which William Ward's *Farewell Letters* is perhaps the most famous, appealing directly to women to help extinguish the burning piles, and improve Hindu women's lot generally. In an open letter to Miss Hope of Liverpool, Ward asks,

Shall I not hear, after my return to India, that the females of Britain and America have united to make the case of their sex in India a common cause— the cause of woman—but especially the cause of every Christian widow— of every Christian mother—of every Christian female? Will you not, females of Britain and America…deliver these females, doomed to a horrible death by usages that have been long devoted to endless execration? Will you not become the guardians of these Ten Thousand orphans surrounding these funeral piles, and endeavouring to put out these fires with their tears?[94]

Women were thus encouraged to take up the cause of the Hindu female in a manner that was designed to appeal to female sentiment and that made assumptions about the nature of Western women. Female involvement was acceptable because the reaction that was dictated for women was one that fitted in with a male ideal about the characteristics of respectable femininity. William Ward, for example, goes on to ask, 'Say how long, ye who never saw a tear, but ye wiped it away—a wound, but ye attempted to heal it—a human sufferer, but you poured consolation into his heart—how long shall these fires burn, these graves be opened?'[95] In doing so he attempts to mobilize female support not by creating a greater space for women's action, but by appealing to patriarchally prescribed characteristics.

Stress on the worst aspects of Hindu women's condition was of course designed to elicit a reaction from the female reader and maximize her endeavours, but there was also a more sinister subtext to these appeals. Not only is the condition of Hindu women represented as in need of amelioration, but a direct comparison is often made between her lot and that of the Christian ladies to whom the appeal is addressed. Thus, William Ward, after a long and detailed diatribe against the treatment of women in India, concludes:

…these infants must be saved; these fires must be put out; these graves must be closed forever. By such an interposition, so worthy of the sex in these countries, the females in India will be blessed with all that profusion of privileges that women in Christian countries enjoy; and, being thus blessed, will become the light, the shade, and the ornament of India.[96]

An anonymous missionary tract of 1828 similarly declared:

But if Christianity has greatly conduced to raise the moral character of man—it has in very great degree retrieved that of woman from the degraded state in which heathenism placed her; and in no country is their situation more debased than in Hindoostan.... Ye Christian women! What has the benign influence of the Gospel done for you! It calls upon you, in a special manner, to exert all your sympathies in behalf of your sisterhood in heathen lands. Many Societies exist who will be the means of conveying your bounty to those who are labouring in this good work.[97]

The comparison is, on a superficial level, designed to remind women of the need to help those less fortunate than themselves, but at the same time it also serves to impress upon Western women the benefits of her own position at a time and in an arena where some were beginning to contest the limits that circumscribed their own action. Thus, these tracts aimed at women serve two purposes—they mobilize Christian women within 'legitimate' spheres of action, and at the same time discourage dissatisfaction with their socially prescribed limitations by emphasizing the comparative advantages of their position. Thus the evangelical rhetoric on sati is not only involved in the assertion of difference between East and West, but also in a gendered discussion about the nature and place of women. By explicitly highlighting the disparity between the treatment of Christian and Hindu women, the Western observer sought to emphasize the superiority of his civilization and to play down the resonances that existed between these two patriarchal societies' conception and treatment of women.

Notes

1. Rev. William Ward, Letter to Miss Hope of Liverpool, 31 March 1821, in *Farewell Letters to a Few Friends in Britain and America on Returning to Bengal in 1821* (London: Black, Kingsbury, Parbury and Allan, 1821), p. 79.
2. I say relatively unproblematic because even when the sacrifice was blatantly involuntary the courts often found it difficult to make the label of murder stick and the perpetrators often escaped with only cursory punishments on the basis that they had acted out of mistaken religious conviction. These and other related issues will be dealt with more fully elsewhere.
3. *Quarterly Oriental Magazine*, vol. 8, 1827, p. cxcviii.
4. Ibid.

5. It is not my intention here to suggest that the volition of the widow in any way makes the sacrifice acceptable, but merely to critique the British assumption of the widow's lack of agency.
6. Pegg, *India's Cries*, p. 11. By the early nineteenth century the heroic representations of the widow's stately progression to the pyre had been replaced with far less flattering images. In these scenes, typical of there time, the crowds are depicted in the throes of savage merriment, with music being played and swords waved. Such images (Figs 8 and 9) reflect growing concerns about the impact of scenes of physical suffering on the 'humanity' of those who witnessed them. Indeed, in Fig. 9, we even see 'civilized' Britons turning their faces away with horror as the Indian crowd rejoices at the sati.
7. Carol Groneman, 'Nymphomania: The Historical Construction of Female Sexuality', *Signs*, vol. 19:2 (1993–4), pp. 341–6.
8. Ibid.
9. Johns, *Some Facts and Opinions*, p. v.
10. Extract from the *Friend of India*, reproduced in the Nicolls Collection (OIO, Eur. Mss).
11. Johns, *Some Facts and Opinions*, p. vi.
12. See below.
13. Extract from the *Friend of India*, reproduced in the Nicolls Collection (OIO, Eur. Mss).
14. *Friend of India*, for example, recounts the story of a man who left two young widows. On his death, both expressed their desire to burn with him in the most determined terms. One was accordingly burnt with the body, but the other, being pregnant, was persuaded to delay her immolation until a month after her confinement. In the intervening time she returned to her own natal family, who made her so welcome that when the in-laws arrived to complete the sati she refused point blank to consider it—a parable which the author uses to show that it is fear of treatment by the husband's family rather than religious conviction that motivates the sacrifice. Extract from the *Friend of India*, reproduced in the Nicolls Collection (OIO, Eur. Mss).
15. Mrs Phelps, *The Suttee* (Oxford: H. Bradford, 1831).
16. Poynder, *Human Sacrifices*, p. 71.
17. Barbara Caine, *English Feminism, 1780–1980* (New York: Oxford University Press, 1997), pp. 11–19.
18. Ibid.
19. Statement of suttees for 1815 and 1816, *PP*, 18, p. 74.
20. *The Times*, 24 December 1823.
21. *Calcutta Journal*, 5 December 1820.
22. Anon., *Deplorable Effects Of Heathen Superstition*, pp. 3–4.
23. Ward, *Farewell Letters*, p. 82.
24. *The Times*, 3 September 1811.

25. *Calcutta Journal*, 5 December 1820. Missionaries often used references to her children when attempting to dissuade a widow from the pyre. In drawing the sati's attention to the potential or actual suffering of her offspring, they attempted to overcome the 'unnatural' impulse to suicide by invoking the 'natural' one of motherly love.
26. Jill Matus, *Unstable Bodies* (Manchester: Manchester University Press, 1995), p. 163.
27. Cited in ibid.
28. *Calcutta Journal*, 5 December 1820.
29. Indeed, a number of charitable organizations, like the one founded in Birmingham in 1825, were set up to provide schooling for these infants to keep them off the streets. L. Davidoff and C. Hall, *Family Fortunes* (London: Hutchison, 1987), p. 421.
30. Ibid.
31. Nizamat Adalat to the vice president in council, Fort William, 4 October 1814, *PP*, 18, p. 36.
32. Ibid.
33. Draft of instructions to magistrates, 21 March 1815 *PP*, 18, p. 42.
34. Ibid.
35. MacDonald, 'The Secularization of Suicide', p. 52.
36. Ibid., p. 75.
37. Ibid., p. 91.
38. A popular proposal was to replace profane burial with dissection, though the Methodist leader John Wesley went as far as to suggest that suicides should be gibbeted and left to rot. See Michael MacDonald and T.R. Murphy, *Sleepless Souls: Suicide in Early Modern England* (Oxford: Clarendon Press 1990), pp. 50–1.
39. *The Times*, 31 December 1818.
40. William Ewer, Lower Provinces, to Government of India, 18 November 1818, *PP*, 18, p. 227.
41. Ibid.
42. E. Lee Warner, 24 Pergunnahs, to W. Ewer, Lower Provinces, 18 December 1818, *PP*, 18, p. 239.
43. Elaine Showalter, *The Female Malady: Women, Madness and English Culture 1830–1980* (London: Virago, 1987), p. 8.
44. Ibid.
45. Ibid., p. 3.
46. Ibid.
47. *The Times*, 22 June 1829.
48. Showalter, *The Female Malady*, p. 5.
49. *Calcutta Journal*, 8 October 1819.
50. Government Bombay to Court of Directors, 12 February, 1830, C.P. Brown, Trichinopoly, 3 June 1829 Board's Collections [henceforth BC], vol. 1506, col. 59097.

51. *Calcutta Journal*, 5 December 1820.
52. *The Times*, 12 May 1823.
53. Johns, *Some Facts and Opinions*, p. 32.
54. *Bombay Gazette*, 6 September 1834.
55. Showalter, *The Female Malady*, p. 11.
56. Cited in Poynder, *Human Sacrifices*, p. 7.
57. *Circular Letters of the Baptist Missionary Society*, vol. 10 (Serampore: Mission Press, 1817), p. 30.
58. Sutton, *Narrative Of The Mission To Orissa*, p. 186.
59. *The Times*, 12 May 1823.
60. Ibid., 11 June 1810.
61. Judicial letter from Government Bombay to court of directors, 12 February 1830, C.P. Brown, Trichinopoly, 3 June 1829 BC, vol. 1506, col. 59097.
62. *Calcutta Journal*, 8 October 1819.
63. E. Lee Warner, magistrate 24 Pergunnahs, to W. Ewer, acting superintendent of police in the Lower Provinces, 18 December 1818, *PP*, 18, p. 239.
64. B. Gates, *Victorian Suicide* (Princeton: Princeton University Press, 1988), p. 131.
65. Ibid., p. 128.
66. For a summary of the more detailed psychoanalytical explanations put forward after the improvement of data collection on means of death in 1858 made the low female suicide rate inescapable; see ibid., pp. 125–31.
67. Ibid., p. 128.
68. *Asiatic Journal*, vol. 14, 1822, p. 127.
69. A correspondent to the *Oriental Quarterly Magazine* reporting a sati in Howrah in 1828 could comment that the outward signs of agony '...came not from the flaming altar, unshackled by one cord, one straw, the victims hand was seen waving as before, and her voice (had it been possible amidst the yell of the worshipping multitude) might still have been heard as before calling upon the name of her God'. Despite this testimony to her bravery, the author continually refers to her in terms such as 'poor infatuated creature'. He also feels it necessary to insert some momentary reassertion of her natural feminine frailty, saying, '...I thought some momentary pangs heaved her bosom as she saw the frightful reality of the condition before her, her lips for a moment quivered, but she speedily rallied....' *Quarterly Oriental Magazine*, vol. 8, 1828, p. cxcix.
70. Johns, *Some Facts and Opinions*, p. 35.
71. *Asiatic Journal*, vol. 13, 1822, p. 122.
72. Ibid., vol. 14, 1822, p. 127.
73. *The Times*, 16 November 1812.
74. Poynder, *Human Sacrifices in India*, p. 122.

75. Anon., 'On Suicide', *Religious Tracts*, no. 154 (London: Religious Tracts Society, 1799), p. 4.
76. Harriet Cope, *Suicide: A Poem In Four Parts* (London: H. Bryer, 1815), pp. 48–9.
77. Ibid., p. 48.
78. Ibid., pp. 48–9.
79. Rev. Samuel Piggot, for example, comments, 'But if any emotions can excite the strongest emotions of pity for a suicide that can stir and agitate the human bosom, it is that of the Gentoo suicide—the poor deluded widow, who, allured by ignorant superstitions, and frightened by barbarous customs, family pride and priestly terrors, suffers herself to be bound to the dead body of her husband, and placed on the funeral pile to be burnt alive with him, in the feeble hope of living happily with him in Paradise for upwards of three thousand years.' Samuel Piggot, *Antidote To The Follies, Vices And Crimes Of Youth, To Gambling, Melancholy And Suicide In A Series Of Anecdotes And Actual Narratives* (London: J. Robins, 1831), pp. 146–7.
80. R. Hey, *Three Dissertations On The Pernicious Effects Of Gaming, On Duelling And On Suicide* (Cambridge: J. Smith 1812 (1st edn, 1783).
81. Piggott, *Antidote*, p. 146.
82. Ibid., pp. 146–7.
83. Gates, *Victorian Suicide*, p. 82.
84. Ibid.
85. Letter from H. Towney to Rev. G. Burden, Chinsurah, 15 April 1822, LMSP.
86. Ward, *Missionary Journal*, 10 August 1800.
87. Letter from W. Campbell to G. Burden, L.M.S., Bangalore, 26 March 1825, LMSP.
88. Sutton, *Narrative Of The Mission To Orissa*, p. 185.
89. *Circular Letters*, vol. 10, p. 31.
90. Ibid., p. 30.
91. *Missionary Notices of the Wesleyan Missionary Society*, vol. 3:62 (London: Mills, Jowett & Mills, July 1821), p. 99.
92. One Birmingham publication went as far as to suggest that women who went door to door did so primarily in the hopes of catching a husband! Davidoff and Hall, *Family Fortunes*, (Hutchison: London, 1987), p. 430.
93. Ibid.
94. Ward, 'To The Ladies Of Liverpool', in *Missionary Notices*, vol. 3:61, 1821, p. 3.
95. Ibid., pp. 3–4
96. Ward, *Farewell Letters*, pp. 82–4.
97. Anon., *Deplorable Effects Of Heathen Superstition*, p. 6.

6

INVETERATE PREJUDICES
Sati and Religion

CRSO

It is vain to hope that this detestable rite of the Hindu religion will be
extirpated; for as the bigotry attached to the one will always sanction the
other with the names of piety and devotion, the precept and the practice will
be coeval with the religion.[1]

As we have already seen, the eighteenth century saw the emergence of
a European construction of sati that understood it almost solely as a
religious rite. Indeed, by the beginning of the nineteenth century a
combination of Enlightenment reductionism and emerging anti-Hinduism had seen sati firmly situated in the religious sphere. The sati's
sacrifice was represented as the ultimate example of the influence of
religious belief on the Hindu mind. So deeply implicated was it in the
European understanding of Hinduism that it was difficult, even in the
face of scriptural evidence, to separate the two in the popular imagination. This interpretation of sati retained its prominence throughout
the first thirty years of the nineteenth century, despite an increasing
effort by anti-sati groups to facilitate abolition by attempting to alien-
ate sati from religion. Lata Mani points out that during this period 'All
colonial officials share to a greater or lesser degree three interdepen-
dent ideas: the centrality of religion, the submission of the indigenous
population to its dictates, and the religious basis of sati'.[2] This is
overstating the point somewhat; several officials, such as William
Ewer, argued strongly that sati did not in fact have religious sanction
and that it was carried out from secular rather than religious motives.[3]

Despite their arguments, however, and those of men like Raja Rammohan Roy, the idea of sati as a sanctioned religious rite remained the overriding trope of the official discourse on sati throughout the period. The decision of 1812, which was based both on declarations from the pandits and on the surviving eighteenth-century preconceptions to tolerate sati on religious grounds, set a precedent for the treatment of the rite and, as a result, many agreed with Judge W. Leycester that 'We could with no consistency declare to be murder today, that which we yesterday declared to be justifiable.'[4]

In order to abolish sati in 1829, the British Government in India was thus forced to challenge a construction of their own making in order to reconcile the demands of humanitarian reform with their own declared policy of religious toleration. Lord William Bentinck's declaration in the preamble to Regulation XVII, that sati was 'nowhere enjoined by the religion of the Hindus as an imperative duty',[5] represented the culmination of three decades of back-pedalling on the implications of sati's supposed religious status. While the scriptural position put forward in Regulation XVII of 1829 was fundamentally the same as that put forward by Sir Henry Colebrooke in 1794—that sati was sanctioned but not demanded by the Hindu scriptures[6]—the implications of this had changed. Whereas at the start of the nineteenth century any scriptural sanction for widow immolation was seen as proof positive that sati was embedded within the religious sphere and so entitled to toleration, by 1829 the lack of an actual injunction was being used to suggest a tenuous connection between sati and Hinduism that allowed plenty of space for intervention. The reasons for this shift in interpretation were, of course, not entirely to do with sati itself.

The 'official' debate on the abolition of sati that took place between 1805 and 1830 revolved primarily around the question of whether its prohibition could be justified theoretically and implemented practically. For Lata Mani, the concentration of the government in Bengal on the issue of feasibility was representative of a debate in which the nature and extent of colonial control was being contested. Rather than being about burning women, Mani sees the debate as an arena for the redefinition of Indian tradition and a renegotiation of the parameters of colonial control. Mani's arguments have been hugely influential and *Contentious Traditions* has been hailed as a 'landmark publication'[7] for its critique of the colonial discourse on sati. In terms of the official discourse in Bengal, her arguments are indeed insightful and go a long way towards deconstructing the image of the abolition of sati as the crowning glory of the so-called Era of Reform. That said, I feel that by isolating the 'official discourse' on sati in Bengal from the wider contemporary debate on the subject, including even the 'official discourses' in Bombay and Madras, Mani's analysis does not always take into account the myriad images and pressures that came to make up the subjectivity of the colonial official during this period, let alone the wider British perception of sati that led to the increasing public interest in the issue. Indeed, by choosing to deal with the various discourses about sati—official, indigenous, missionary—individually, she obscures the very real interaction between them in the run-up to abolition. Her reading of the official discourse, however insightful, is flawed by the very fact that she fails to fully acknowledge this wider picture, and the reader is left with the impression that the official renegotiation of the legal and religious status of sati occurred in a vacuum. Mani recognizes, for example, that the reawakening of government interest in the issue in 1812 might have been influenced by the impending renewal of the East India Company's charter in 1813, yet fails to develop this idea of interconnectedness between colony and metropole, popular opinion and official action. It is the intention of this chapter to attempt to redress the balance a little by looking thematically at the question of sati's perceived religious status and issues that it raised across the various colonial 'discourses' on sati, in order to analyse some of the ways in which they interacted with, reinforced, or contradicted each other.[8]

Indiscreet Zeal: The Practical and Ideological Basis for Non-intervention

As Lata Mani has demonstrated, the official discourse surrounding the abolition of sati concentrated not so much on the desirability of putting an end to the immolations, which was generally accepted, but on the practicality of doing so. She notes that the official debate 'revolved primarily around the question of the political feasibility of abolition rather than the ethics of its toleration'.[9] In doing so she makes two inter-related assumptions: that the officials involved in the production of this discourse were somehow isolated from the vocal moral debate about sati going on all around them, and that the issue of religious toleration, around which much of the debate circled, was a pragmatic rather than an ideological stance. On the first issue, I would argue that the very volume of the debate on sati suggests that officials were aware that its toleration was ethically questionable. Indeed, I would suggest that it is this very awareness that fuelled the ongoing debate about the feasibility of abolition through the permutations of two-and-a-half decades, for if they had not been conscious of the immorality of tolerating sati, the debate surely would not have been either so protracted or so virulent. Far from being absent from the debate, questions relating to the ethics of toleration and the tensions that emerged between these and the more pragmatic imperatives of colonial rule were at its heart and explain its longevity, especially as popular opinion on the subject solidified. Early enquiries into the possibility of abolition make the sense of moral unease with the continuing immolations clear. Governor General Cornwallis stated in 1805 '…it to be an indispensable duty to ascertain whether this unnatural and inhuman custom can be abolished altogether…',[10] while the governor of Bombay in 1813 considered it '…an object of the highest importance to the cause of humanity and good morals, if the practice [of suttee] were suppressed….'[11]

This awareness of the immorality of tolerating sati was a major change from previous attitudes, which had failed to totally condemn the rite, let alone consider it a duty to try to prevent it. The almost universal assumption of the 'desirability' of abolishing sati was the result of a changed interpretation of the rite that purged what had previously been seen as the heroic and praiseworthy aspects of the act. Far from being a moral constant, the British desire to abolish sati sprang not just from their new political situation, but also from changed ideological interpretations of sati that designated it as 'wrong'. The problem they faced was that while they had by this time constructed a moral argument against sati, they also perceived not only practical, but also moral impediments to interfering with it. This brings us to the second issue raised by Mani's contention that the debate on sati was not an ethical one.

For Lata Mani the government of Bengal's repeated use of the principle of religious toleration as an excuse for inaction on sati can be understood primarily in terms of pragmatic concerns about the stability of their Indian dominions. She tells us:

Official fear of the consequences of prohibiting sati was tied to their analysis of it as a religious practice and to their view of religion as the fundamental and structuring principle of Indian society. A third component was the official conception of the indigenous people. They were believed to be unreflective practitioners of their faith, but nonetheless jealous of it and prone to rebellion at the threat of its infringement.[12]

For Mani the original decision to adopt a non-interventionist stance with relation to Indian religion was a practical measure designed to minimize disruption to trade and commerce, while later adherence to it was primarily based on a paranoiac fear of the consequences of any intervention in religious matters. There is great deal of truth in this interpretation. It was widely believed at the time, for example, that 'It was chiefly owing to the indiscreet zeal, in what was considered the cause of humanity, that the Portuguese lost Basseen.'[13] The British understanding of the impact of religion on the Hindu mind led them to fear the consequences of interference with a religiously sanctioned custom, believing that '...inveterate religious prejudices are liable to be warmed into enthusiasm by the attempt to suppress them, or even by the apprehension of it....'[14]

It is demonstrable from the outset of the sati debate that the official commitment to religious non-intervention had a pragmatic aspect and was only as strong as the suspected consequences of interference. In 1812, for example, the Nizamat Adalat, after declaring sati a religious rite, commented that as some practices enjoined by Hindu law and formerly prevalent had since fallen into disuse or had been prohibited by Hindu princes, they had inquired into whether sati, despite its religious status, could be immediately abolished without greatly offending the people, concluding:

From these inquiries, conducted with caution lest any alarm should be excited, the court has reason to believe that the prejudices in favour of this custom are at present so strongly impressed upon the minds of the inhabitants in most parts of these provinces, that all castes of Hindoos would be extremely tenacious of its continuance.[15]

From this it would appear that it was not the scriptural status of sati that determined whether it could be interfered with, but the level of popular attachment to it. Thus, while the principle of religious toleration might be infringed to counter customs if there was little perceived danger, in the case of sati the principle combined with pragmatic concerns, was enough to keep the pyres alight.

Despite the obvious importance of political pragmatism in informing British policy, it is incomplete to characterize the government's commitment to religious toleration as a purely cynical stance based only on the need to maintain stability. The question of the safety of abolition of sati was certainly central throughout the debate, but there does also appears to be a sense that the policy of religious toleration was one of the hallmarks of a just and enlightened colonial rule in India and that violating that principle would not only be dangerous, but also unethical. R.B. Gardiner, the magistrate for Behar, sums up this duality when he comments in 1818:

> Much as I would wish to see the total abolition of a practice so repugnant to the feelings of humanity, I should consider the prohibition by law of a ceremony which is encouraged by the Shaster, as an infringement of that system of complete toleration in matters of religion, declared to be a fundamental principle of the British government in India, which might tend to shake the confidence at present reposed in it by all classes of its native subjects, and be eventually productive of dangerous consequences.[16]

Gardiner, like many others, was concerned about the potential 'dangerous consequences' of interfering with sati. His concern was not, however, based upon the threat of an immediate outcry, but on the idea that by violating the principle of religious toleration the British would undermine the legitimacy of their rule in the eyes of the Indian population, with adverse long-term effects. Similarly, J. Masters, the magistrate for Dacca, believed that

> ...the government has always stressed its policy of toleration and has tried to...impress upon their minds how decidedly such an interference was objected to. Here then would be a direct violation of such protestations, and the Hindoo would, with justice, continue distrustful of every future act of the legislature.[17]

While these statements do exhibit a clear concern for the stability of British India, they also demonstrate an appreciation that religious toleration was an ideological as well as a practical imperative.

Members of the 'civilian' population shared this sense of the importance of religious toleration as a matter of principle. The Baptist missionary organ *Friend of India*, for example, attacked the idea that religious toleration by the government was merely a political expediency, saying, 'It would be ungenerous to attribute the liberality of our system to the numerical difference between the governors and the governed, and not to reserve a portion of the credit due to...those noble and generous principles of religious freedom we imported with us from England.'[18] It is the omission of this interpretation of religious toleration as an ideal as well as an expediency that allows Lata Mani to portray the official debate on sati as lacking an ethical dimension. If we allow that the issue of religious toleration was a matter of principle as well as politics, however, we can see that rather than being a debate solely concerned with practicality, it also had a significant ideological component. This is even more apparent when we consider sati in the context of the contemporaneous debate in Britain about the nature of religious toleration that occurred in the run-up to Catholic Emancipation in 1829. As questions about religious toleration became increasingly salient in the metropole, the debate on sati became a forum in which the perimeters of religious freedom could be tested and debated. The question of the 'ethics' of tolerating sati was not confined to the issue of burning women, but came to represent the contest between two forms of freedom—the freedom from barbaric superstition and the freedom of religious observance. In this respect the sati debate was not only about the nature of colonial rule, but about the limits of state intervention in religion more generally, as it mirrored and magnified concerns that were particularly prevalent in Britain at the time.

Vague but Valuable Freedoms: Religious Toleration in Britain and India

Increased interest in the subject of sati in the early nineteenth century was to some extent symptomatic of a growing sense of Britain's 'duty' towards its ever-increasing constituency of foreign subjects. As Linda Colley points out, Britons were increasingly asking themselves how their new subjects should be treated: 'What responsibilities, if any, did the mother country have towards them? Did they have any claims on those vague but valuable freedoms that so many Britons considered to be peculiarly their own? Or could British subjects also be slaves as long as they were black and safely overseas?'[19] Deciding what 'freedoms' it should be the mission of the British race to bestow on their Indian subjects was far from unproblematic. That something was owed was increasingly widely accepted. As the East India Company chaplain, Thomas Thomason commented: '...we have annihilated the political importance of the natives, stripped them of their power and laid them prostrate, without giving them anything in return'.[20] For Thomason and others like him, the greatest gift that could be given was the Christian faith and with it a freedom from the barbarous superstitions and practices of Hinduism. For others, however, the imposition of this 'gift' was directly at odds with another great 'British' freedom, that of conscience. Of course, as we shall discuss later, the British constitution itself was far from entirely egalitarian in matters of religion, but this did not mean that the British did not pride themselves on their relative liberality in matters of religious toleration. It was with some satisfaction that the Government of India could announce that 'It is an invariable principle of the British Government to protect the whole of its subjects in the free exercise of their religion, and in the performance of their religious ceremonies.'[21] The hostility of the East India Company to missionary activity before 1813 is well known and, while it has been argued that this was primarily due to a fear that the missionaries would provoke a hostile response from the local population, there was a significant section of the British community who objected on moral as well as practical grounds. Charles James Fox, for example, claimed in 1793 that 'all systems of proselytisation are wrong in themselves',[22] while the Rev. Sydney Smith derided missionaries in the *Edinburgh Review* in 1808, claiming: 'The wise and rational part of the Christian ministry find they have enough to do at home.... But if a tinker is a devout man, he infallibly sets off for the East.'[23] Thus, while there was a general feeling that Britain had some degree of moral duty towards India, exactly what form that should take was open to debate, as a rising evangelical desire to spread Christianity and its values came into conflict with older ideals about religious toleration and cultural relativism. Of course, as subjects rather than citizens, Indians were not deemed to have inalienable rights in this respect, but the belief that to be legitimate the colonial rule had also to be just, raised the question of the extent to which Britain's own ideals could or should be exported to India.

The principle of religious toleration was one of the ideological cornerstones of Enlightenment thought. After the bonfires of the Reformation and Counter-Reformation, and the more recent persecution of dissenting groups such as the Huguenots, many of the philosophers and other influential thinkers of the time had moved away from organized religion, attacking its dogma and doctrinal intolerance. Though very few would have admitted themselves atheists, the rationalization of their conception of religion created a context in which various religious beliefs could be judged upon their own merit and their internal moral cohesion recognized, if not accepted. This is by no means to suggest that all religions were considered equal or accorded equal rights, but that there was a general trend, certainly by the nineteenth century, towards individual conscience rather than state control of religious belief. In Britain, while the Anglican Church retained its supremacy, numerous Protestant dissenting groups had emerged. Many of these, like the Baptists and Quakers, had their roots in the period before the Civil War, though others, like the Methodists, were of more recent origin. These groups were free to organize and worship as they wished, but from the late seventeenth century on they were also subject to certain forms of discrimination. The Tests and Corporation Acts of 1676 and 1661 respectively (passed in the wake of Cromwell's republicanism) prevented non-conformists from, among other things, holding office either in local or central government. Though many of the practical disabilities imposed by these acts had disappeared by the turn of the nineteenth century, their existence on the statute books remained symbolic of religious inequality in Britain. More practical in its effects was the discrimination directed at Roman Catholics, which had been legitimized in penal legislation passed in the wake of the Popish Plot (1678) and the Glorious Revolution (1689). Though the majority of these legislations had been repealed in 1791, Roman Catholics were, at the turn of the century, still debarred from holding public office, voting, and sitting in parliament.[24]

For many in Britain, even this muted form of religious intolerance was out of keeping with the ethos of the new century and the debate over the repeal of penal legislation raged throughout the 1810s and 1820s. Bills for Catholic emancipation were presented to parliament in 1812, 1819, 1821, and 1825 and in most cases were only defeated in the House of Lords by a narrow majority. As Llewellyn Woodward points out, '...a large and influential section of public opinion, including members of every administration since the Union, wanted to put an end to political disqualifications based on religious intolerance, whether in England or Ireland'.[25] The remaining disqualifications against dissenters were finally repealed in 1828, and the bill for Catholic emancipation was passed, in the face of a small but potent 'ultra-Tory' lobby, in April 1829—the same year that Bentinck passed his legislation against sati. Government measures are not always the best indicator of public opinion, but, as Linda Colley points out, on this occasion the relatively muted nature of the popular outcry against Catholic emancipation suggested that public opinion had in fact turned against religious chauvinism at home.[26] Under these circumstances it is possible to see the ongoing debate about sati as reflecting concerns not only about British governance in India, but also as contributing to a much wider debate about the nature and boundaries of religious freedom.

For many who opposed any government interference with sati on religious grounds, the principle of religious toleration was inviolable, regardless of their own personal distaste for the rites they were tolerating. As E.A. Kendall put it in an open letter to the *Asiatic Journal* in 1822:

...the conduct of the British nation in regard to the religion of India is of the same liberality, justice and wisdom as that of the Roman's towards the religion of the Roman provinces;[27] and it is solely because the burning of widows has its foundation, whether erroneously or not, in the religion of the country, that the British laws do not and ought not to interfere...the burning of widows is a spiritual and religious act (however detestable), and therefore only out of the reach of that code of criminal law that the British nation has permitted itself to impose on India.[28]

For Kendall then, religious toleration was an absolute that should not be conditional on British approval of the rites they were tolerating. Kendall's letter, which went on for several pages in a similar vein, provoked a heated response from readers of the *Asiatic Journal*, three of whose replies were printed in subsequent issues. Their responses, however, concentrated not on undermining the principle of religious toleration in general, but rather on discrepancies in Kendall's argument, on the notion that sati was not in fact sanctioned by religion, and on the fact that other religious rites had already been interfered with (of which more later). Indeed, it is rare in writing on sati for this period to find any suggestion that the toleration of Indian religious practices was wrong in principle. Rather, those who attack the toleration of sati as a 'disgrace to Britain', do so on the grounds that such toleration should not extend to the destruction of human life. As a correspondent to the *Bengal Hukuru* put it:

Tolerance has its limits, and those limits are clearly defined. The practices of superstition ought to be as free as the speculative tenets and opinions on which they are founded, providing they do not outrage the public decency, or break through the fundamental laws of what we may call natural morality: but no religion that demands power over the life of man, and insists on human sacrifices in order to satisfy religious pride or propitiate priestly avarice, can or ought to be endured by a government anxious for the welfare of its subjects.[29]

It is not the principle of religious freedom, then, but the definition of its limits that is open to interpretation. For the humanitarian John Poynder, the perimeters of toleration were defined by the very wording of the government's own declaration, which promised toleration only when it was 'consistent with the principles of morality, reason and humanity'.[30] Sati, he argued, was clearly not compatible with these principles. He then went on to draw on John Locke to provide a definition of religious toleration, saying that while Locke advocated the free expression of religious views, this should be allowed only in so far as it did not impinge on civil liberties. He quotes Locke as saying:

…if some have a mind to sacrifice infants, or practice any other such heinous enormities, is the magistrate obliged to tolerate them because they are committed in a religious assembly? I answer, No. They are not lawful in the ordinary course of life, nor in any private house, and, therefore, neither are they in the worship of God.[31]

For Poynder, '…at the moment a purely religious rite infringes upon the laws of society, its character is changed, and it becomes a civil crime'.[32] The precise religious status of sati is irrelevant, for even if '…the pundits had been more decided in their opinion, and had held the practice to constitute an integral part of their religion…',[33] the rite could still have been abolished without infringing the principle of religious toleration because it impinged on civil liberties.

Interestingly, many missionaries, of whom one might expect scant support for Hinduism, took a similar line when confronting the issue of religious toleration. The *Friend of India,* for example, commented:

That the principles of religious liberty are better understood in Britain and America than any other country, or that those principles are more clearly comprehended in the present than in any other former age, will not admit of a doubt. In more ancient times, the boundaries of religious freedom were contracted or enlarged by the caprice or clemency of the predominant party in the state. At present they are fixed both in our own land and in America upon the immutable foundation of sound and enlightened reason. And the superior civilisation of our day is marked by no token more unequivocal, than by the noble sentiments on the subject of religious liberty.[34]

The author then goes on at some length to decry Britain's own history of religious persecution and commend the contemporary predilection for tolerance and religious liberty. He comments:

In this country we have a gratifying instance of the happiness conferred on a remote dependency by these peaceful principles. Though the religion of the conquerors and the conquered may be considered almost as forming the two extremes of wisdom and folly, the natives are living in a state of perfect freedom from all anxiety. There is no instance recorded in history of any country which has enjoyed such happiness under masters of a different religion: we will even venture to affirm that under no Hindu monarch did India ever enjoy such freedom from vexation on religious grounds as under the sway of Britain. Though the native worship deities which we as Christians consider as insulting to the sovereignty of God, and a libel on the human understanding, we have granted them the fullest toleration....[35]

Religious toleration was thus seen as an indicator of just and enlightened rule, even if it was not synonymous with mutual respect. Of course, the fulsome praise of the missionaries for British tolerance of Hinduism is somewhat less surprising when we consider that a significant number of missionaries themselves came from non-conformist sects: Baptists, Methodists, and Lutherans. Under these circumstances it seems natural that they should defend to the hilt the principles of religious liberty that had allowed them their own freedom of worship, especially at a time when this very principle was being invoked at home to remove the last remnants of discrimination against them. Thus, we find the missionaries in a slightly anomalous position of defending the freedom of worship of a religion that in all other circumstances it was in their interests to deplore; a Gordian knot that they untied, as evidenced from the above passage, by making the toleration of even so degraded a religion a witness to the depth of British benevolence.

Despite their support for the principle of religious toleration, for many missionaries, and others who opposed the continued toleration of sati, some practices, supposedly enjoined by Hinduism, pushed the limits of religious toleration too far. A series of influential articles in the *Friend of India* put forward a variety of reasons, both general and specific, why religious tolerance should not be extended to sati. On a general level they declared that, 'There can be no greater abuse of those sacred principles than thus to hold them up as sanctioning murder...' and accused the Government of India of losing sight of '...the sacred boundaries of moral obligation, and confound[ing] virtue with vice, and the most barbarous crimes with the heavenly spirit of religious liberty'.[36] In so doing, they pre-empted Poynder's arguments about the nature of religious tolerance. The Hindu reformer Raja Rammohan Roy also placed a limit on the extent to which religious toleration should influence government policy, claiming that it should not extend to observances that were 'a nuisance and outrage to public feeling' and 'a reproach to civilised government'.[37]

Those who attempted to justify the continuation of sati on the grounds that religious toleration should not be applied selectively, faced criticism not only on a theoretical level but also in terms of the government's own previous actions. Those who wished to see sati abolished pointed out that the Government of India had, in fact, set a precedence for interference in religion with its policies on other issues. Fanny Parks, for example, commented derisively:

How very absurd all this is.... The Government interferes with native superstition where rupees are in question—witness the tax they levy on pilgrims at the junction of the Ganges and the Jumna. Every man, even the veriest beggar, is obliged to give one rupee for liberty to bathe at the holy spot; and if you consider that one rupee is sufficient to keep a man in comfort for a month, the tax is severe.[38]

It was common to find anti-sati campaigners pointing to areas in which religion had been set aside for various reasons. The most frequently cited among these instances of interference in religious matters were the law that made it possible to inflict capital punishment on Brahmins and the measures that had been taken to prevent female infanticide and the exposure of children at Saugor. Judge E. Watson, for example complained in 1816 that

We really think that there is as little justification for a woman burning herself with the remains of her deceased husband, as for a rajkoomor to destroy his daughters at their birth; burying alive for leprosy, where the party is desirous to die; human sacrifices at Saugor, putting sorcerers to death, or killing a human creature by any other means, without justification or excuse—all of which are expressly made capital offences by the Regulations. The killing in all these instances…has quite as much in its favour, on the score of erroneous prejudice and superstition, and perhaps of religion, as the practice of suttee; but we do not find that the punishment of death, denounced against these crimes, has at all been considered by the people an infringement of that complete toleration in matters of religion….[39]

Those who opposed the abolition of sati argued that practices such as female infanticide and the exposure of infants did not have the sanction of the Hindu religion. The Nizamat Adalat in 1817, for example, argued that infanticide and other abuses were never sanctioned by Hindu or Muslim law '…whereas the burning of a Hindoo widow, with the body of her deceased husband, has the express sanction of the authorities, which are held sacred by the women who devote themselves, as well as by the Brahmins and others who assist them in their voluntary sacrifice'.[40] The distinction was somewhat ambiguous, however, for, as William Ewer points out, while the act did not have direct textual sanction, '… the exposure of infants is in consequence of vows made by the mother, for the purpose of obtaining some favour from the gods; and that fulfilment of such is meritorious in the highest degree'.[41]

If the religious merit of infanticide was the cause of debate, few would argue that capital punishment for Brahmins manifestly violated the very strict and specific rules against Brahminicide and this was frequently referred to as having set a precedent for interference in religious matters. Even this was not as clear an example as it might seem, however. As Radhika Singha points out, although the expediencies of law and order meant that the British could not officially sanction the exemption of Brahmins from capital punishment, they continued for some time to be tentative in applying it, preferring instead to use the weapon of social stigma or transportation 'over the waters' as a deterrent.[42] In discussing which religious practices might be abolished and which must be tolerated, those who involved themselves in the debate on sati were playing a part in a wider theoretical discussion about the limits of religious toleration more generally. It is worth noting that Catholic Emancipation itself has been marginally defeated on more than one occasion because of a failure to agree on the relative degrees of papal prerogative and state control over priestly power.

Influence, Inheritance, and Ignominy: Non-religious Interpretations of Sati

If the toleration of a religiously sanctioned sati was controversial, some anti-sati campaigners sought to undermine any argument for allowing it by rejecting its religious status altogether. Divorcing sati from Hindu religion was made particularly difficult by the fact that eighteenth-century interpretations of the rite had placed it squarely within that arena, but throughout the two-and-a-half decades before 1829, those opposed to tolerating sati attempted to do exactly this. Their methods were not confined to scriptural analysis, although this was important, especially after 1818 when Raja Rammohan Roy's first pamphlet on sati was published. Instead, the process relied to a great extent on challenging some eighteenth-century assumptions about the nature and practice of sati as it existed at a popular level and resurrecting some of the early modern arguments about the rite's sociological components that had been all but subsumed in the rhetoric of religion. It also led to an increased emphasis on certain issues that had not previously received much attention, such as the financial motivations for sati. These issues were not newly discovered, of course, but the political importance of emphasizing issues other than religion gave them new prominence. In this way the specific circumstances of the early nineteenth century and the debate on sati itself played a significant role in shaping the popular image of the rite.

The impetus to divorce sati from religion by stressing other aspects of it was, of course, tied to the perceived need to circumvent the government's sensibilities about religious toleration in the campaign for abolition. For some, such as the missionaries and those supporting their activity, however, the need to separate sati from its religious context presented a significant paradox. Without this alienation the government's arguments about religious toleration were all the more valid, yet if they were too successful, and sati was proved not to be related to religion, the missionaries would lose one of their key weapons against Hinduism and one of their main tools in gathering moral and financial support for their cause. The main way in which the missionaries resolved this contradiction was by addressing different audiences in different terms. Missionary accounts that were directed to the home audience for the purpose of gathering funds (William Ward's *Farewell Letters*, the London Missionary Society's *Missionary Notices*, etc.) still concentrated on invoking moral outrage at sati as an indicator of the degrading influence of Hinduism in India. Publications aimed at an audience in India, with the purpose of pressing the issue of abolition (such as the *Friend of India*), on the other hand, emphasized the dubious nature of sati's religious sanction, its social roots, and its consequences.[43] The contradictory positions apparent in the missionary discourse with regard to sati's religious status were the result not of inconsistency on the issue, but rather of conflicting imperatives that required a different interpretation of sati in different circumstances.

Although very few would attempt to suggest, as William Ewer did, that sati had 'little or no connection with their [Hindu] religion',[44] those who opposed its toleration went to some length to illustrate that the sacrifice was primarily conducted for secular rather than religious reasons. The *Christian Observer*, for example, commented that

The poor creatures are forced to submit to this cruel death by the dread of the slow torment of a wretched life, prolonged only to feel insult, and to be pursued by reproach and obloquy, to which every woman is subjected who refuses to resign herself to this barbarous superstition. In most cases they are compelled to devote themselves to death to avoid the scorn and resentment of even their nearest relatives.[45]

In doing so the *Christian Observer* resurrected early modern ideas about the stigma of widowhood and fear of the future as the root causes of sati. The emphasis in this new version was significantly different to the early modern interpretation of the widow's action, however. While early observers maintained that the hardships of widowhood meant that many women 'chose' to become sati, by the nineteenth century these considerations are presented as having the power to 'force' or 'compel' her to this end. The re-emerging interest in the earlier sociological interpretations of the rite was not accompanied by the resurrection of the widow as a central agent in sati. Instead, rather than being seen simply as a passive victim of religion—a construction that would never entirely disappear—she was also now portrayed as the passive victim of societal and familial forces. Despite the fact that there are numerous examples of widows defying their families to become satis, the general assessment was that the widow had little or no intellectual input into the decision and many would have agreed with the *Friend of India* that '...with the victims themselves it [the decision] can scarcely be said to originate....'[46]

If sati was not caused by religion, or by the will of widow herself, the questions arose, with whom and why did it originate? Increasingly, anti-sati campaigners found the answer to this question in the supposed action of two groups, the widow's affinial kin and the Brahmin priests, both of whom were increasingly portrayed as acting from temporal rather than spiritual motives. Among these, from the family's point of view, were the social prestige attached to sati and the fear of dishonour arising from the widow's potential 'misbehaviour', both of which had been seen as significant factors in the early modern period. Most important, however, were the financial imperatives that were increasingly thought to underpin both the priests' promotion of and the family's connivance at sati.

Concern with the mercurial motivations for encouraging sati—conspicuously absent from earlier interpretations—emerged with force in the early nineteenth century and was tied both to the need to discredit the spiritual aspects of the rite and to the popular racial stereotype of Indians as rapacious and self-serving. Financial issues entered the debate in a number of ways. The most common was the assumption, made by the *Friend of India*, among others, that sati was supported due to the family's 'wish to get rid of a burden'—a factor exacerbated by the fact that among higher castes a widow could not marry again and so remained a relatively unproductive member of the household for the rest of her life. In addition to this, under the *dayabhaga* inheritance system common in Bengal, the widow could claim a portion of her husband's estate.[47] For the anti-sati campaigners this was more than enough to explain the affinial family's desire to see her out of the way. William Ewer, for example, saw one of the key factors in the emergence of sati as being the self-interest that '...began to whisper to the husband's relations, that the widow had a right to exclude them from his property during her life, but that she might be persuaded to accompany him...'.[48] Indeed, concern that widows were being sacrificed for their property led the Nizamat Adalat to propose the following in the draft regulation of 1817:

With a view to prevent the operation of any interested motive in promoting the illegal and criminal destruction of the lives of women, by burning or burying them alive...it is hereby declared that if in any case it can be established by judicial inquiry, that a woman has been burnt or buried alive after the promulgation of this Regulation, contrary to the rules therein prescribed, any property which may have devolved to the widow on the death of her husband, or which would have devolved to her had she not been so burnt or buried alive, shall be at the disposal of the government.[49]

The clause was later dropped on the basis that it might be subject to misinterpretation, but its original inclusion suggests a growing concern with the pecuniary causes for sati.

The statistics for sati in Bengal do not support the contention that its prevalence there was primarily caused by the local predominance of the dayabhaga system of law. As Anand Yang points out, the dayabhaga system was common to all Bengal, while high incidences of sati occurred only in certain areas, suggesting that, in some cases at least, sati was motivated by other considerations. Of course, the motivation for sati could be as varied as the myriad circumstances in which Hindu women lived and died. The majority of British observers believed that sati was a uniquely high-caste phenomenon, but in fact the demographic spread of the custom was more diverse than that. Ashis Nandy tells us that fifty-five per cent of satis in Bengal during this period occurred among high castes—a group that made up only eleven per cent of the population.[50] Despite the disproportionate number of satis among these castes, this still left forty-five per cent of cases occurring among the lower castes. Ashis Nandy has explained this by claiming that the majority of these lower-caste satis occurred in 'upwardly mobile, Sanskritising sectors of the lower castes'.[51] He claims 'The rite was becoming popular not among the rural poor or the small peasantry, but among the urban nouveaux riches who had lost part of their allegiance to older norms and had no alternative commitments with which to fill the void'.[52] He attributes both this upward mobility and the increase in sati primarily to the fractures in traditional society caused by the impact of colonialism. He quotes Joshua Marshman as commenting that 'the increasing luxury of the high and middling classes…and their expensive imitation of European habits' made them loath to incur the cost of maintaining widows.[53] Even if we accept Nandy's argument that the majority of 'lower'-caste satis actually arose out of the social aspirations of upwardly mobile groups, there does appear to be evidence that, in many cases, far from being murdered because of a surfeit of property, some widows at least were acting out of poverty. Some of the scarce testimony that can be gleaned from the widows themselves, suggests that fear for their future sustenance could be a key concern.[54] Joshua Marshman, for example, tells of a widow who, when asked why she was to commit sati, '…replied that she had no relative, no friend who would support her and no means of supporting herself; what could she therefore do?'[55] This construction of the widow acting out of worldly want is backed up by the fact that in not a few cases widows sacrificed themselves several years after the deaths of their husbands, a circumstance that prompted Magistrate William Bird to propose a rule that disbarred widows from sacrificing themselves after their husbands had been burned, unless they had good reason for not performing the rite at the time, in order to 'put an end to a practice, not at all unusual, of becoming suttee many years subsequent to the husband's death, in a fit of caprice or worldly disappointment...'.[56]

Despite the fact that there was ample evidence that reduced circumstances were an important factor, and George Forbes'[57] assertion that

...the practice is prevalent among the most ignorant and deluded of the people, while the numerous instances of the widows of the higher classes, continuing to live in affluence and respectability, afford the most satisfactory evidence that there is no imperious call to submit to, no dire disgrace attending the rejection of the dread alternative.[58]

The majority of British observers continued to stress inheritance as the major factor.[59] In some cases this may indeed have been the case. Anand Yang points out that in 1823, forty-one per cent of satis in Bengal were from Brahmin families.[60] While the geographical spread of sati suggests that its practice was confined to certain lineages, it is possible that within these lineages sati was indeed supported in part to help curb the alienation of property. That the widow's inheritance was sometimes a factor is illustrated by the tale, recounted in the *Asiatic Journal* in 1826, of a young widow whose immolation was prevented by her husband's guru, despite the family's desire that she burn. The dispute between the guru and the family seems to have revolved around the fact that the young widow, still a minor, was to inherit a considerable estate from her husband, which both the family and the guru wanted to secure, thus creating the unusual situation of the priest preventing sati because it was in his financial interests to keep the widow alive.[61]

So influential was the image of the sati being propelled to her death to further the financial interests of her family that it became common practice to assume, in cases where the widow was in possession of a fortune, that she was murdered for her money even when she apparently acted entirely from choice. Another account carried by the *Asiatic Journal* in 1826, for example, told of an immolation in which the apparently lucid widow set light to the pyre herself, mounted it once it was ablaze, and 'was consumed to ashes without a groan'.[62] Despite this apparent volition on the part of the widow,[63] the author still goes on to say that

By Hindu law she became the sole inheritor of his property, consisting of talooks, &c. to the value of 5000 or 6000 rupees per annum. The next heir is the only and *affectionate* brother of the deceased, who by thus *legally* murdering his sister, has possessed himself of his brother's fortune.[64]

The assertion that widows were murdered for their property may have had some basis in truth, though it is impossible to prove in the majority of cases. The tendency of the British to assume it, even in cases where there was only circumstantial evidence, suggests that the concentration on this aspect of the sacrifice may have had more to do with undermining the religious motivations for sati than with producing an accurate image of the sociological causes of the rite. Indeed, the suggestion that sati was forced upon the widow for financial reasons helped to position the rite firmly within the criminal sphere. A correspondent to the *Asiatic Journal*, for example, argued in 1826 that

A man who is the accessory to the murder of a woman, for the sake of a few paltry jewels, forfeits his life for the crime; but a brother who in the face of day is accessory to the cruel death of his sister by instigating her to become a suttee, that he may possess himself of thousands, is countenanced and protected. The former is called 'murder' and the man is hanged, that others may be deterred from the perpetrations of similar crimes; the latter is called a 'religious ceremony' and the man is countenanced that others may go and do likewise.[65]

The British stress on the role of property in motivating sati thus had some basis in fact, but their overemphasis on it at this particular juncture, where previously it had been ignored, can also be understood as a reflection of underlying domestic concerns. It is worth mentioning that growing British concern with the economic causes of sati coincided with a reworking of the laws relating to widows' inheritance in England. English law stated that for legal purposes a woman's being was subsumed in that of her husband, and any property that she might have brought with her into the union passed immediately to him. Indeed, Fanny Parks actually compared the status of married women to the sati, saying:

The laws of England relative to married women, and the state of slavery to which those laws degrade them, render the lives of some few in the higher, and thousands in the lower ranks of life, one perpetual sati, or burning of the heart, from which they have no refuge but the grave, or the cap of liberty—i.e., the widow's, either of which is a sad consolation.[66]

The only way that a woman could regain any economic independence was in widowhood, but even this was under threat in the early nineteenth century. The Dower Act of 1833 enabled wills to override a widow's traditional right to dower (the portion, usually one-third, of the husband's estate that the widow inherited for life). Ostensibly, dower rights, which related only to real property, were adjusted in order to reflect changing economic conditions. As Susan Staves points out, 'New commodities like stock and bank annuities replace land as major ingredients of wealth, and the law of dower changes to reflect this, limiting widows' rights to land but giving them equivalents in newer forms of wealth'.[67] Ultimately, however, it proved to favour men's property rights as widows were now only entitled to an 'equitable jointure' settled on them by their husbands during life, leaving valuable real estate to be left to male heirs. Staves notes the new law '...allowed legal intellectuals to feel that they had corrected an error but preserved for individual women no socially enforced rights; an individual woman got nothing except what her own husband privately elected to bestow.'[68] In the context of these metropolitan developments, the increased British concern with the nature of Hindu women's inheritance as a cause of sati takes on added significance, reflecting as it does contemporary domestic tensions between widows' rights and concerns about the alienation of property. It is hardly surprising that sati should be increasingly represented as the ultimate solution to the problem of widows' property rights by a British society that was in the throes of renegotiating its own inheritance laws.

The financial motivations for sati, both for the widow and for her family, are overshadowed by the emphasis placed on the cupidity of the Brahmin officiate. The role of the Brahmin as the instigator of sati had been recognized since the early modern period; the image of the devilish Brahmin superintending the rite had emerged with force in the seventeenth-century writings of Francois Bernier and had continued to be influential throughout the eighteenth century. Indeed, when one considers the way in which interpretations of sati generally changed over the preceding three centuries, the representation of the Brahmin priest's role in the rite remained remarkably consistent. This is all the more striking when we consider that outside the context of sati, the image of the Brahmin had been subject to considerable mutations, from the heroic scholar and mild-mannered gentleman of the Philosophes and Orientalists to the craven bully and corrupt religious despot of missionary and Anglicist accounts.

The consistency with which the Brahmin's role in sati was represented when other aspects of the rite had changed so significantly, raises a number of interesting questions about the way in which ideas about sati were constructed. If European reactions to the rite were based upon their interpretation of Hinduism, or their attitudes towards India in general, surely the image of the Brahmin would have undergone the same mutations as that of the widow. Yet, while the widow is in turn rational, irrational, heroic, faithful, indoctrinated, active, passive, and oppressed; the portrayal of the Brahmin as the wielder of abused authority remains constant. I would argue that this discrepancy between the shifting representation of the widow and the static image of the Brahmin suggests that images of sati were shaped by preconceived ideas that related not to the actors' joint identity as Hindus, but rather to their individual and racially non-specific identities as woman and priest. Thus, a changing European construction of womanhood and femininity meant that the values and ideas relating to sati had a different impact and different meanings at different times. The European construction of priesthood, on the other hand, though it was equally subject to regional and chronological shifts, was such that the same image of the devilish Brahmin could serve a variety of purposes for different people at different times. For the European priesthood, the unfeeling cupidity and cunning of the Brahmin officiate of sati was reflective of his role as the representative of a lesser and more barbaric faith. For others, such as the Philosophes, he was representative of the corruption of priesthood and dogmatic religion more generally, while for the Protestants and Nonconformists Protestants he could be seen as the reflection of that other great bogeyman, the Catholic padre. Thus, while the reasons for depicting the Brahmin priest in a negative light varied, no one had a reason for portraying his role in sati positively.

As we enter the nineteenth century, the reasons for highlighting the negative aspects of the priest's role in sati increase, and accordingly we find him painted in ever-darker hues. The missionaries in particular were keen to undermine the late eighteenth-century construction of the Brahmin as a scholar and a gentleman, or as the guardian of religious truth, and depicted him instead as a rapacious and self-serving con man. The *Friend of India* complained:

These Brahmuns receive even from the most indigent families something on the widow's actually devoting herself to the flames; and from some wealthy families, as much as 200 rupees on these occasions. While then it is the obvious interest of these Brahmuns that the wife should be induced to destroy herself when the husband dies, they have access to every family and are acquainted with the age and circumstances of the various inhabitants, especially those who are wealthy, that they should constantly recommend this dreadful practice, and prepare the female mind for the perpetration of the deed, particularly in the cases where the husband is aged or sickly, is the natural effect of their caring for their own support. But these Brahmuns, as they are in some cases the family priests, are in the habits of familiar acquaintance with the husband's relatives, and have much to expect from them. In what dreadful circumstances then must a helpless female stand, who has for her spiritual adviser on the subject of her living or dying, a man who has every kindness to expect from those who are the presumptive heirs to the property of her infant son, or who may merely dread her depending on them as a burden to the end of life.[69]

As in preceding centuries, the Brahmins were widely seen as the instigators of sati. However, as befitted a period in which assumptions about authentic religious motivations for sati were being contested, they were now usually seen as acting out of avarice rather than spirituality. On the odd occasion when it was admitted that the Brahmins had not been responsible for stirring up the impulse of 'sutteeism' in their victim, this was viewed as an exception that proved the rule. Magistrate J. Harrington, for example, commented in 1814 that of the widows burned in his district of Backergunge, most were between fifty and seventy years of age, and, 'It is therefore to be supposed that the persuasive means generally possessed by the Brahmins, in bringing their abstruse of religion in aid to their bigotry, to influence the weak minds of the innocent victims to a ready compliance of becoming a suttee, have not been practiced.'[70]

Not only were the Brahmins seen as the chief instigators of sati, but it was from them that the chief danger was perceived, should the rite be abolished. Magistrate H. Oakley, for example, asserted that

...a law for its abolition would only be objected to by the heirs, who derive worldly profit from the custom, by Brahmins, who partly exist by it, and by those whose depraved nature leads them to look upon so horrid a sacrifice as a highly agreeable and entertaining show; at any rate the sanction of government should be withdrawn, without delay.[71]

Some of the officers approached by Bentinck for their opinions, prior to the prohibition of sati, gave an even more sinister interpretation of possible events. Lt Col Paul warned that while he did not foresee any immediate problems, the issue of sati might:

...ere long be seized upon by the priesthood and be by them converted into a desire on our part of upsetting their religious customs and usages, and which they would take every opportunity of instilling into the mind of the sepoys on meeting them at their homes on furlough who I fear, blind to the justice and humanity of our motives, would be but too proud to listen to, and be guided by, a class who in all other matters so arbitrarily lead them....[72]

This concern that the abolition of sati might put a weapon in the hands of a hostile priesthood is interesting for the way in which it foreshadows later ideas about the causes of the Uprising of 1857. The imperialist interpretation of the uprising saw it as primarily motivated by religious grievances and the abolition of sati was deemed to be one of the core causes of the unrest. Perhaps more significantly, it reflected deep-rooted British concerns about the location of authority in India, for while the British were by this point firmly entrenched in their civil authority, religious and social authority continued to reside with the Brahmin. British perceptions of Indian society as static and caste ridden meant that they were prone to over-emphasize the influence of the brahmin castes on the other strata of society. The result was that while the British were to some extent reliant on the Brahmins for information and knowledge about the society they were governing, they also regarded them as their main rivals for authority within it. This paradox is well illustrated by the tensions that existed between British reliance on Brahmin pandits for the interpretation of sati's scriptural status that formed the basis of British policy, and their tendency to vilify them as the rite's key supporters and beneficiaries.

Moreover, the emphasis on the Brahmin's role in any present or future
trouble over sati allowed those who opposed its abolition to stress the
danger of interfering with the rite, without undermining the loyalty
of the army or the general population. For those who wished to see
sati abolished, a concentration on the role of the priests allowed them
to localize opposition into one small, if influential, section of the
community and to disassociate their spurious religious claims from
the thoughts, ideas, and feelings of the mass of the population.

Little Read and Less Understood Shastras: Brahminic Texts and Popular Hinduism

If a desire to undermine sati's religious status lead to the emergence,
or re-emergence, of alternative interpretations of the rite in the popular debate, within the 'official' discourse the assumption that the rite
had some religious authenticity continued to predominate. The precise nature of this authenticity and how it was to be quantified, was
the subject of some consideration and was far more complex than just
the negotiation and renegotiation of the rite's scriptural validity. Of
course, the question of the textual status of sati was extremely important, both in the official and unofficial debate on sati, as many British
officials believed that that they could not abolish sati '...until we are
armed with law opinions that the practice of suttee is not conformable
to the Hindoo law'.[73] Having officially accepted sati as a religious rite
in 1812, many believed that consistency required them to find a pretext
for changing their stance on the issue. For some, this was found in a
reinterpretation of Hindu law, inspired by Raja Rammohan Roy's
writings on sati, which stressed the lack rather than the strength of
scriptural sanction for the rite. Roy's use of scriptural arguments to
discountenance sati were seized on by the missionary press and the
anti-sati lobby even before the publication of the first *Parliamentary
Papers* on sati in 1821[74], and formed the basis of most non-official
arguments against sati's religious status. Government officials, anti-
sati campaigners, and Indian reformers alike stressed the fact that sati
was not demanded by the Hindu scriptures; that Manu, who was
increasingly being hailed as the most authentic source of Hindu tradition, did not mention it; and that theoretically a life of piety and
devotion was spiritually preferable.[75] These assertions were coun-
tered by those on the orthodox side of the debate, including Hindu
defenders of sati, who claimed that the rite did in fact have religious

sanction. The debate about sati did not concentrate exclusively on the issue of scriptural authenticity to the extent that some have suggested, however. Assumptions about local usage and popular belief also played a very significant role in informing the treatment of sati, particularly at a practical level. Indeed, I would argue that, while the textual status of the rite was often central in determining the government's policy in theory, in practice its application was riddled with inconsistency and often undermined by a realization on the part of officials that theological opinion and popular belief differed vastly.

Despite the widespread acceptance of terms such as 'legal' and 'authorized' when referring to sati, the actual legal position of widow-immolation remained confused and contentious. As Radhika Singha points out, there was never any government resolution or statute that specifically exempted sati from Section 3, Regulation 8 of 1799. Rather, toleration of sati was based on a construction of that section[76] as not extending to religiously sanctioned acts such as sati or the suicide of lepers.[77] This interpretation was given practical, though not official, implementation by the instructions to magistrates circulated in 1813. These instructions have been referred to as a regulation, but, in fact, although the Nizamat Adalat drafted them in this form, the governor general shied away from issuing such a formal statement on the status of sati for fear that it would be seen as sanctioning the rite. Because of this, while sati was generally understood to be permissible under certain circumstances, the legal status even of 'voluntary' sati remained ambiguous, and some contested the legality of permitting sati at all under the existing regulations. Judge E. Watson, for example, believed that no change in the law would be necessary to discontinue sati on the basis that Section 3, Regulation 8 of 1799 already prohibited it.[78] Watson's position was supported by the fact that British law saw no difference between murder and assisting suicide, a fact that made the toleration of sati without an official enactment even more tenuous. Magistrate C. Brown drew attention to this anomaly in advocating punishment for those assisting sati, saying, 'as they have usually been dealt with, these murders are converted into suicides. We do not question a suicide as to his willingness to die, we would if possible prevent the crime, or else must become accomplices in the murder'.[79] He was not alone in agreeing with Watson that '...no necessity whatever exists why those who assist in killing women in this way should not be treated as murderers...'.[80] For the most part, however, it was agreed that the discontinuance of sati would need a specific enactment and, while the debate about future action continued to rage, the immediate position was largely understood in terms of definitions of 'legal' and 'illegal' sati that corresponded roughly to 'sanctioned by the shastras' and 'not sanctioned by the shastras'. Even this construction of the difference between sati and murder was riddled with difficulties and ambiguities, both in terms of defining legality and enforcing it.

The definition of what constituted a 'legal' sati was neither clearcut nor static. Rather, it depended on a process of interpretation and reinterpretation of both religious texts and customary usage. From the outset, the Nizamat Adalat lacked a clear idea about the parameters of legal sati, and the definition of what was acceptable was in a constant state of flux. Indeed, as the government admitted in 1817 (five years after the first set of instructions on sati were issued), '...the information possessed by the government regarding the rules of Hindoo law, and the local usages prevailing in different parts of the country, as applicable to the ceremony of suttee, has hitherto been extremely imperfect'.[81] Thus while certain principles were recognized from the outset (the widow's volition, her age, her sobriety, non-pregnancy, etc.), other facets of sati had to be renegotiated as time went on. In 1814, for example, the Nizamat Adalat was forced to enquire of the pandits whether the burying alive of *jogi* widows was permitted and whether Brahmin widows might burn on separate piles to their husbands. The response was that 'the former practice was declared by the pundits to be legal, the latter illegal'.[82] Later still, there were controversies over whether any widow could burn on a separate pile from her husband and whether a mother of infant children could burn. All these renegotiations of what constituted a legal sati were based upon pandits' readings of the scriptures. Because of this Lata Mani has argued that the legal position on sati became dominated by a brahminic interpretation of Hinduism that did not allow for regional variations or customary practice. She tells us, 'the official discourse on sati was grounded in three interrelated assumptions about Indian society: the hegemony of brahminic scriptures, unreflective indigenous obedience to these texts, and the religious nature of sati',[83] and that 'the arguments of officials in favour of abolition were thus developed within the ambit of Brahminic scriptures. The pros and cons of sati were systematically debated as doctrinal considerations.'[84] While this may well have been true of the 'letter of the law' in Bengal, I would contest Mani's position as a general interpretation on two counts: that regional variations were recognized both in the practice of sati and in government policy, and that there was a significant divergence between the theoretical 'official' position on sati as based on the scriptures and the assumptions that informed the treatment of it at ground level.

Because Mani only focuses on official discourse on sati in Bengal, her account does not recognize the regional variations in both policy and practice that existed between the three presidencies. When we add the official discourses of Bombay and Madras to the picture, however, we see that they were quite prepared to adjust policy to take account of local circumstances and customary usage. The Bombay government in 1819, for example, chose to ignore the Supreme Government directive not to require prior permission for a sati on the basis that local custom under the Marathas had been to acquire it and that this action was therefore correct in its local context.[85] Even more striking, however, was the governor of Bombay's reluctance to adopt Bentinck's regulation abolishing sati in his presidency, on the basis that he had himself instigated a course of collaboration with leading Indians to the same effect, which he felt would be more suited to the conditions in Bombay. He told the members of the Bombay Presidency Council which supported and advised the governor, 'I shall not enter upon the reasons which induce me to prefer this course, many of which have particular reference to this presidency, and may not apply to Bengal.'[86] When taken together, the abolition of sati in the three presidencies, far from being the result of an incontrovertible reading of a homogenous scriptural tradition, was rather influenced by regional circumstances, such as the prevalence of sati and the stability of the region.[87]

Even within Bengal it was acknowledged that special customs, in deviation from the general rules and practice, existed in Bengal and Benares, and that 'the ceremonies practically observed differ as to the various tribes and districts, leading the government to conclude that it was not possible to require a strict adherence to any uniform process of carrying out a sati.[88] The recognition of regional variations in both the extent and mode of sati led some to conclude that it was 'the effect of local immorality, instead of general religious prejudice'.[89] Magistrate H. Oakley, for example, commented in 1818 that

The worship of the principal Hindoo deities is tolerably equal, wherever the religion extends. In one quarter one may prevail, and another in another; the forms of worship appropriated to each, and the pilgrimages and penances by which they are to be propitiated, are the same throughout India; and if suttee were really an act enjoined by religion, it would be universally meritorious, and equally observed, wherever that religion is followed; but as it is not, we must look for its prevalence among the Hindoos in the neighbourhood of Calcutta; not to their superior strictness in observing religious and moral duties in general, but to some peculiar circumstance affecting their moral character...it is notorious that the natives of Calcutta and its vicinity exceed all others in profligacy and immorality of conduct, and (barbarous as at best it is) we find the Hindoo superstition, in its most degraded and darkest state...we may fairly conclude that the vicious propensities of the Hindoos in the vicinity of Calcutta, are a cause of the comparative prevalence of the custom.[90]

For Oakley, then, the disparity in the practice of sati undermines its claim to be an authentic religious rite. Oakley's interpretation rests on an eighteenth-century construction of Hinduism that saw it as a coherent and unified religious system, in which 'legitimate' rites and practices would be universal. For the most part, however, as mentioned above, the British appear to be aware of the heterogeneity of popular Hinduism. Judge W. Leycester, for example, argued that sati could be safely abolished in those areas where it was little practiced, '...on the principle that it was not consistent with the general local usage of those parts, and that there were many doubts as to whether the best construction of Hindu law would authorize the practice. On a great many points the Hindoo law is merely a local practice. It is not one general law, but is one thing here, and diametrically opposed in other parts.'[91] The suggestion was rejected, however, on the basis that this 'partial abolition' would fail of success and incite a 'spirit of fanaticism'. Lata Mani notes this widespread recognition of regional variety, although she sees it as a relatively minor aspect of the discourse. She contends that

The insistence on textual hegemony is challenged by the enormous regional variation in the mode of committing sati.... Colonial officials acknowledged these differences and instructed magistrates to allow natives 'to follow the established authority and usage of the province in which they reside'. However, such diversity was regarded as 'peripheral' to the 'central' principle of textual hegemony.[92]

While this may be true of the theoretical legal position, and while the official emphasis placed on scriptural hegemony may have been a lasting legacy of the sati debate, in practice at the time and at the grass roots level, regional variation and popular conviction consistently took precedence over textual hegemony, as technically 'illegal' satis were repeatedly mitigated or overlooked on the grounds of local belief.

The inconstancy between the theoretical legal position on sati and its practical implementation was exacerbated by a British understanding of the influence of Hindu religion that confused and complicated issues such as motive and intent. As Radhika Singha has pointed out, there was considerable consternation among the British as to the extent to which they could expect to understand the Indian motivation behind certain 'criminal' acts. As one judge in the Nizamat Adalat put it: 'With regards to Hindoos, no example can be of any avail; their motives are above human control....'[93] The assumption of the predominance of religion in ordering Hindu life, if carried to its logical conclusion, could be seen as robbing the Hindu protagonist of any agency whatsoever. If the 'criminal' could be demonstrated to be acting out of religious belief, however misguided, it became difficult, in keeping with their perception of the nature of Hinduism, to find him guilty of a premeditated crime. In the case of a sati which took place in Furruckabad in 1819, for example, the relations of a seventeen-year-old Brahmin widow persisted in aiding her immolation, despite the fact that they had repeatedly been warned by police that it was illegal for her to burn on a separate pyre. Theoretically, as the local magistrate pointed out, those who assisted her should be considered murderers, but the Nizamat Adalat decided to take no further notice of the matter, 'In consideration of the degree of influence from superstition and almost absence of free agency under which the parties who assisted appear to have acted'.[94] Thus while the intention to implement and abide by a codified legality on the subject of sati existed, in practice the alien nature of Hindu motivations undermined the due processes of law—the Hindu could not be tried according to Western principles of jurisprudence because to do so would undermine the Western construction of him as irrational and subject to superstition, on which the discourse of European supremacy was based.

The divergence between theory and practice in terms of implementing the rules on sati was exacerbated by the fact that there was considerable slippage between what the Nizamat Adalat had determined to be 'legal' and what was understood to be acceptable by the local population. This was even more the case with an issue like sati, in which the difference between religious act and criminal act was a matter of interpretation. Thus the British determination to 'allow the practice in those cases in which it is countenanced by their religion; and to prevent it in others in which it is by the same authority prohibited',[95] was complicated by a myriad of differing local interpretations, a situation exacerbated by the nature of the British policy on the rite, which was said to have '...thrown the ideas of the Hindoos upon the subject into a complete state of confusion. They know not what is allowed and what is interdicted...'.[96] In contradiction to Lata Mani's assertion that government officials assumed the primacy of scriptural authority in everyday Hinduism and 'unreflective indigenous obedience to these texts',[97] the practical implementation of the sati legislation suggests that they recognized a significant divergence between popular belief and textual authority, and that this gap allowed numerous violations of the official rules on sati to pass either unnoticed or unpunished. Despite the British assertion that 'the burning of a women...in direct opposition to what is enjoined in the Shaster...[is]...manifestly an act of illegal violence',[98] the perpetrators of such actions could often escape on a plea of ignorance—a plea made all the more convincing by the British belief that the vast majority of Hindus lacked even a basic knowledge of their 'little read and less understood Shastra'.[99]

Even when the death of the sati was 'manifestly an act of illegal violence', the perpetrators were rarely punished to the full extent of the law. In May 1821 a fourteen-year-old widow of Brahmin caste was burnt without the body her husband. The widow, Homalia, apparently mounted the funeral pyre of her own accord, but when the flames reached her she found the pain too much and leapt from the pyre. She was quickly seized by her uncles Sheolal and Bichok Tawari and thrown back on the pile. Escaping again, she ran to a nearby river, where Sheolal approached her and told her to sit on a sheet which he spread on the ground for the purpose. Terrified for her life, the report informs us, she replied, 'No! She would not do this, he would again carry her to the fire, and she could not submit to this; she would quit the family and live by beggary; anything if they would have mercy upon her'.[100] At this point her uncle is said to have sworn on the Ganges that if she sat on the sheet they would use it to carry her home, but when she acquiesced he bound her up in it and threw her back on the fire. Escaping for a third time, her struggle for life was finally ended when '...at the instigation of the rest, the moosulman Buraichee, approached near enough to reach her with his sword, and cutting her through the head, she fell back and was released from further trial by death'.[101]

Homalia's death was illegal on a number of counts. At fourteen, she was two years below the age of discretion required for even a voluntary sati. Moreover, as a Brahmin, technically she should not have been permitted to burn on a separate pile from her husband. Most shocking, however, was the very clear demonstration of her lack of volition in the sacrifice, as this young woman three times fought her way free of the fire. It would seem that this was a flagrant abuse of the regulations regarding sati and there should have been little doubt that in this instance the widow had been murdered and that the perpetrators should therefore suffer the full consequence of the law. Indeed, two of the judges adjudicating in the matter felt that the penalty should be death. Chief Judge W. Leycester felt that Sheolal and the Muslim Bhuraji should suffer death, adding, 'I do not see how we could be justified in passing any other sentence',[102] while R. Rattray, the fourth judge of the Banaras Circuit Court, exclaimed,

I verily believe that I echo the wishes of nineteen twentieths of even the Hindoos in this community, when I urge death as a requital for this atrocity. In justice all the prisoners should be equally condemned to this atonement, but the example may be deemed sufficient if it is extended only to the first three mentioned.... There never was and never can be a more crying occasion for example, and never can be subjects entitled less to sympathy than these convicted monsters. I leave them to the disposal of the court without the power or desire of interposing one plea in mitigation of that punishment which it would be false and erring feeling to wish to shield them from.[103]

The second judge, however, confessed himself to differ entirely in his opinion, to the point that he would not even pass a custodial sentence. He argued that

I think the uncle Sheolal, who could have had no malice towards his niece, and who seems to have acted under the impression of the indelible disgrace that would accrue to his family if the suttee, once begun, should not be completed, is an object of pity rather than punishment. The suttee was irregular in as much as the police officer was not there, and as the widow (a brahminee) burnt without the corpse of her husband; but frequent irregularities occur in this detestable practice, yet no one has ever been hanged for it, or even punished, as I can recollect, by temporary imprisonment for a misdemeanour.[104]

Despite the fact that the Nizamat Adalat had found that there was no textual basis for the supposed stigma involved in retracting an intention to perform sati, either for the family or the widow, here a local belief in the shamefulness of such a retraction was put forward in mitigation of this most brutal murder. The final verdict of the Nizamat Adalat in this case was that, although the rite was manifestly illegal on a number of counts, '…making allowances for the superstitious prejudices of the Hindoos concerned and ignorance of the Mahomedans, the court do not discern in any of them the guilt of murder'. It sentenced Bhuraji to five years with labour, 'Roosa Moosulman' (for being present and abetting) to three years with labour, and the rest, including Sheolal and Bichok, to two years without labour. Not only did the Hindu perpetrators of this violence against a fourteen-year-old girl escape punishment for murder, they even received lighter sentences than the Muslims present, despite the fact that the Muslims were acting at their instigation. This differentiation in punishments is rationalized on the basis that the Muslims, though acting in ignorance, did not have the excuse of religious superstition to explain their actions. The Hindu perpetrators of this crime are thus exculpated as their motive has been discovered to be religious belief, despite the fact that the form that this belief took was directly contrary to British understanding of the textual position on sati.

The case of Homalia is a graphic example of the British understanding of Hindu religion in action, for while the case violated a myriad of prescriptions for a legal sati, the Hindus involved were practically acquitted on the grounds that they were acting out of religious conviction. Thus, while the technical authority for sati could be found in the shastras, the implementation of it at ground level was far more dependent on local religious practice and belief. Indeed, the government actually made allowances for this. In a regulation drafted (though never published), the Nizamat Adalat proclaimed that its toleration of religious practices extended to '…a just regard of established customs and usages, even in matters not directly connected with religious worship and duties'.[105] Even as early as 1817, the rationale for the toleration of sati was not just that it was prescribed by the Hindu texts, but that it retained local religious significance. In 1821 Judge S. Goad objected to a proposal for the abolition of sati on the basis of religious toleration and 'because the rite of suttee has existed for ages'.[106] The Hindu texts might be the official source of authority on the custom's legality or illegality, but at ground level it was subject to an understanding of popular Hinduism that, if not legitimizing sati, certainly mitigated the guilt of those performing it.

Sati and the 'Rule of Colonial Difference'

The British finally abolished sati in 1829, after nearly twenty-five years of prevarication on the subject. Although this regulation stressed that that sati was not enjoined by the Hindu religion 'as an imperative duty', it did not in fact rely on any new scriptural evidence for, as we have seen, this was fundamentally the same position as Colebrooke had taken in 1794. Rather, it sought to stress the abuses in the actual performance of sati as the main reason for prohibition. The preamble to the regulation states:

...by a vast majority of that people throughout India the practice is not kept up, nor observed: in some districts it does not exist; in those in which it has been most frequent it is notorious that in many instances acts of atrocity have been perpetrated which have been shocking to the Hindus themselves, and in their eyes unlawful and wicked. The measures hitherto adopted to discourage and prevent such acts have failed of success, and the Governor General in Council is deeply impressed with the conviction that the abuses in question cannot effectually be put an end to without abolishing the custom altogether.[107]

The fact that the regulation did not attempt to deny religious status to sati is significant for it suggests that the final prohibition of the rite was based more on practical considerations that on textual authority. Of course, it is well known that Bentinck made an extensive survey of the opinions of officers and magistrates prior to abolition, in order to ascertain their opinions on the safety of interfering in the rite, and his minute on sati talks mainly about practical issues, indicating that the British chose to act at this time primarily because it was safe to do so. Despite the rhetoric of a proclamation that attempts to justify interference with sati in terms of defending the purity of Hinduism, the British decision to abolish sati was based on a non-scriptural assessment of the rite's popular status—the degree of public attachment to it—rather than a reinterpretation of the texts. Even those who argued against abolition on the basis that sati's religious status made interference dangerous, did so on the basis of popular belief rather than scriptural authenticity. Lt Col Playfaire, for example, in warning that interference with sati might cause commotion in the ranks of the Indian army, commented that:

It has been said that the practice is not enjoined by the shrastra. This may be a fact, but if so, the knowledge, or belief of it, is confined to a few; I think

I may affirm that nine-tenths of the Hindus, from the caste of Gwallas upwards, think otherwise. They regard the rite as sacred, and a certain passport to endless felicity hereafter.[108]

Similarly, A.J. Trotter commented: 'The practice too is of a very old date, and whatever other sanction it may have, it has come down to the present time with the authority of custom, which is supposed with the Hindoos to be as binding as law itself.'[109] In the final analysis, then, although the lack of direct textual authority was a useful justification for interference, in practical terms the scriptural status of sati was of very little importance in its abolition. The majority of officers understood that whatever the British might declare about the custom's authenticity, it was and probably always would be considered a religious rite by the Hindu community.

If the British understanding of the religious status of sati did not alter fundamentally prior to abolition, we are left with the question: on what basis did the British overcome their previous principle of religious toleration and prohibit the rite? It has been argued that the abolition of sati was reflective of a more general shift in attitudes about India from Orientalist admiration to Anglicist contempt, which meant that Hinduism was no longer seen as worthy of toleration. While this may well have played a part, there is enough evidence to suggest that the Government of India had not yet reached the stage where it was prepared to openly 'attack' local religion or abandon its policy of religious toleration. Bentinck repeatedly stressed the government's continued commitment to this policy, and it was widely recognized that the government did not wish the abolition of sati to be viewed as a religious issue. Indeed, the London Missionary Society went as far as to warn its publications not to print any letters thanking Bentinck for the abolition of sati, on the basis that, 'Lord Bentinck, I should suppose, would not feel obliged to any person for leading the public to imagine that in any one measure he was for a moment guided by representations of Missionaries.'[110]

Far from being the result of an acknowledged shift in policy, the British decision to abolish sati even in the face of their policy of religious toleration can be seen instead as an early instance of what Partha Chatterjee has dubbed the 'rule of colonial difference'. For Chatterjee, the moral justification of the imperial project rested on the dissemination of the structures and institutions of the modern 'civilized' state, yet he points out:

The colonial state, we must remember, was not just the agency that bought the modular forms of the modern state to the colonies; it was also an agency that was never destined to fulfil the normalizing mission of the modern state because the premise of its power was a rule of colonial difference, namely the preservation of the alienness of the ruling group.[111]

While the moral rationale behind the imperial project was the introduction of such values as impartial justice, free speech, meritocracy, and religious toleration, these values could never be impartially applied without undermining the basis of imperial power. There is no 'new' discovery in terms of the scriptural status of sati, yet the terms of the debate have changed significantly and sati's religious sanction can no longer be seen as sufficient to protect it. Thus, at the same time as Britain's Catholics and Nonconformists are being brought into the fold at home, in India Britain's Hindu subjects are being redefined as unequal and unworthy of unconditional toleration. This idea can also be seen at work in the way in which sati cases were tried and convicted, for, while part of the justification for the colonial project was the dissemination of impartial justice, the British understanding of the Hindu character created a situation in which the objective and impersonal workings of jurisprudence was confused by subjective questions of belief and superstition, characteristics deemed to be specific to the Hindu character. Thus, while customs such as sati were understood through processes that emphasized the location of similarities as well as differences among the colonized, the real politic of colonial rule meant that in pragmatic terms the maintenance of empire increasingly required the assertion of a British 'otherness', equating to supremacy. Bentinck makes this point of view abundantly clear in the very first paragraph of his famous minute on sati, when he states that the only justifiable reason for tolerating sati was if abolishing it would 'put to hazard...the very safety of the British Empire in India, and to extinguish at once all hopes of those great improvements...which can only be expected through the continuance of our supremacy'.[112] Justification of empire eventually required an assumption of Indian 'difference', which stressed their incapacity for self-government or self-improvement: the greatest disaster that could befall the Subcontinent was not the continuation of sati-immolations but the removal of Britain's guiding hand. Under these circumstances, the abolition of sati can be seen as indicative of a colonial government that in the consolidation of its power is also consolidating its strategies of rule and securing its position as the dominant 'other'. The assumption of Hindu 'difference' was thus used in this instance to justify the differential application of 'universal' ideals. In arguing this, however, it is not my objective to simply echo the very Saidian paradigm that it has been the intention of much of this book to challenge. Rather, it is to show that rather than being the normative trope as has so often been assumed, ideas of 'otherness', while serving particular political imperatives at particular times, could exist within a broader, more complex framework in which the conscious and subconscious recognition of similarity played as significant a part as the assertion of difference.

Notes

1. *Asiatic Mirror*, 1811, cited in Johns, *Some Facts and Opinions*, p. 35.
2. Mani, *Contentious Traditions*, p. 26.
3. Ewer argued that by tolerating satis, the British were not '…showing a proper forbearance towards the religious customs or long established prejudices of the Hindoos' but were virtually sanctioning the murder of widows by their relations, a practice which he claimed was nowhere enjoined by the shastras, and which 'in our own country would carry the penalty of death'. William Ewer, Lower Provinces, to Government of India, 18 November 1818, *PP*, 18, p. 229.
4. Minute of W. Leycester, 25 May 1821, *PP*, 17, Paper 466, 1823, p. 63.
5. Regulation XVII of 1829 of the Bengal Code, 4 December 1829.
6. Colebrooke had seen sati as the preferred action of the widow, and ascetic widowhood as the lesser alternative, while the regulation reversed this order. Colebrooke, 'On the Duties'.
7. By Dipesh Charkrabarty, in an endorsement on the back cover of Mani's book.
8. The interconnectedness of the various discourses is particularly well illustrated by John Poynder, the philanthropist, abolitionist, and anti-sati campaigner, in his speech made in 1827, to the Proprietors of East India Stock. In it Poynder uses the material in the *Parliamentary Papers* (the same material that forms the source of Mani's study of the official discourse) to raise and address the issues of the wider contemporary debate on the matter and push for prohibition (Poynder, *Human Sacrifices in India*). The volume of *Parliamentary Papers* that Poynder used, complete with annotations in the margin in his own hand, is available for study in the British Library and is a striking example of the interaction between 'popular' and 'official' discourses.
9. Mani, *Contentious Traditions*, p. 15.

10. Government of India to the Nizamat Adalat, 5 February 1805, *PP*, 18, p. 24.
11. Government of Madras to the Magistrate of Combeconum, 31 August 1813, *PP*, 18, p. 269.
12. Mani, *Contentious Traditions*, p. 20.
13. Minute of G.L. Prendergast, Bombay, 5 November 1817, *PP*, 18, p. 245.
14. Governor Madras to the Court of Directors, 4 January 1822, *PP*, 17, p. 69.
15. Nizamat Adalat, to Government of India, 5 June 1805, *PP*, 18, p. 27.
16. R.B. Gardiner, Behar, to W. Ewer, Lower Provinces, 30 December 1818, *PP*, 18, p. 240.
17. J. Masters, Dacca, to W. Ewer, Lower Provinces, 12 December 1818, *PP*, 18, p. 240.
18. *Friend of India*, vol. 6:14, pp. 450–1.
19. Linda Colley, *Britons: Forging the Nation, 1707–1857* (London: Yale University Press, 1992), p. 323.
20. Andrew Porter, 'Religion, Missionary Enthusiasm and Empire', in William Roger Lewis (ed.), *The Oxford History of the British Empire*, vol. 3, (Oxford: Oxford University Press, 1999), p. 230
21. Nizamat Adalat, 25 June 1817, Draft Regulation, *PP*, 18, p. 126.
22. Andrew Porter, 'Religion, Missionary Enthusiasm and Empire', p. 230
23. Ibid.
24. Irish Roman Catholics had been permitted to vote and to sit in the Irish Parliament since 1793. When the Act of Union dissolved the Irish Parliament in 1800, these rights were transferred to the UK Parliament.
25. L. Woodward, *The Age of Reform* (Oxford: Clarendon Press, 1962), p. 339.
26. Colley, *Britons*.
27. I hope it will not harm my argument too much here if I remark that some of the more notorious Roman emperors were known to have a predilection for making human torches out of Christians, and their much vaunted toleration did not extend to those who would not swear allegiance to the emperor.
28. *Asiatic Journal*, vol. 13, 1822, p. 447.
29. Cited in *Asiatic Journal*, vol. 20, 1825, p. 389.
30. Poynder, *Human Sacrifices*, p. 13.
31. Ibid., p. 14.
32. Ibid., p. 15.
33. Ibid., p. 17.
34. *Friend of India*, vol. 6:14, pp. 450–1.
35. Ibid., pp. 453–4.
36. Ibid., p. 455.
37. Cited in Singha, *A Despotism of Law*, p. 118.

38. Parks, *Wanderings Of A Pilgrim*, p. 162.
39. E. Watson, Nizamat Adalat, 16 April 1816, *PP*, 18, p. 99.
40. Proceedings of the Nizamat Adalat, 25 June 1817, *PP*, 18, p. 109.
41. William Ewer, Lower Provinces, to Government of India, 18 November 1818, *PP*, 18, p. 229.
42. Singha, *A Despotism of Law*, p. 102.
43. Mani, *Contentious Traditions*, pp. 51–7.
44. W. Ewer, Lower Provinces, to Government India, 18 November 1818, *PP*, 18, p. 228.
45. The *Christian Observer*, cited in Johns, *Some Facts and Opinions*, p. 100.
46. Extract from the *Friend of India*, in the Nicolls Collection OIO, Eur. Mss.
47. In fact, in the absence of a son, son's son, or son's son's son, the widow could succeed to her husband's property under both the dayabhaga and mitakshara schools. In both cases, she held the property only for her lifetime, after which it reverted to her husband's nearest living heir. The key difference was that mitakshara only allowed this if her husband held a separate estate, whereas dayabhaga also allowed it when he was part of an undivided coparcenary. Thus the widow's right to inheritance had a far greater impact on relations in a joint estate under the dayabhaga system than under the mitakshara one. See J. Nair, *Women and the Law in Colonial India* (New Delhi: Kali for Women, 1996), p. 64.
48. W. Ewer, Lower Provinces, to Government of India, 11 January 1819, *PP*, 18, p. 231.
49. Proceedings of the Nizamat Adalat, Draft Regulation, 25 June 1817, *PP*, 18, p. 131.
50. Ashis Nandy, *At the Edge of Psychology: Essays in Politics and Culture* (New Delhi: Oxford University Press, 1980), p. 5.
51. Ibid.
52. Ibid.
53. Ibid.
54. It is impossible to generalize about the widow's motivation on the basis of what little testimony we have. Some did indeed refer to worldly want as a cause for their sacrifice, while others, when offered subsistence if they did not perform the sacrifice, rejected it out of hand.
55. Cited in Johns, *Some Facts and Opinions*, p. 21.
56. W.W. Bird, Benares to the Court of Circuit of Benares, 23 July 1816, *PP*, 18, p. 133.
57. Forbes was Judge of the First Calcutta Court of Circuit at the time.
58. He goes on to comment that '...there are fifty-seven civil suits, involving property amounting to four lacks of rupees, now pending in this court, in which Hindoo widow ladies are parties', suggesting that some widows, at least, lived to contest their inheritance. G. Forbes, Calcutta

Court of Circuit, to Nizamat Adalat, 5 August 1819, *PP*, 18, p. 243. Forbes was unusual among British observers of the time in attributing sati to the lower rather than higher castes; the vast majority of British observers considered it a peculiarly Brahmin custom.

59. The image of the widow murdered for her money gained considerable currency during the early nineteenth century, but closer inspection shows that the British understanding of the economic motives for sati was somewhat inconsistent. On the one hand the widow was often portrayed as being forced into sati because she feared a future with no certain means of support and her family could not afford to maintain her. On the other, it was her very access to her husband's property that made her a threat that the family might wish to remove. This contradiction is more understandable when we consider that the depiction of sati in the campaign against its toleration was designed to provoke public hostility to the rite rather than provide an accurate sociological representation of its causes. As a result, the worst potential features of sati were often combined to form a generic image of the rite, even though they may actually have been contradictory.

60. Anand Yang, 'Whose Sati? Widow Burning in Early 19th Century India, in *Journal of Women's History*, vol. 1:2, p. 23.

61. *Asiatic Journal*, vol. 22, 1826, p. 442.

62. Ibid.

63. Obviously we will never know what forces were at work in motivating this sati, and my intention here is not to preclude the possibility that she was coerced, but rather to highlight the degree to which the British assumed foul play, even in the absence of evidence.

64. *Asiatic Journal*, vol. 22, 1826, p. 442.

65. Ibid.

66. Parks, *Wanderings Of A Pilgrim*, vol. 2, p. 420.

67. Susan Staves, *Married Women's Separate Property in England, 1660–1833* (London: Harvard University Press, 1990), p. 32.

68. Ibid., p. 49.

69. Extract from the *Friend of India*, reproduced in the Nicolls Collection OIO Eur. Mss.

70. J. Harrington, Backergunge, to W. Ewer, Lower Provinces, 14 December 1818, *PP*, 18, pp. 34–5.

71. H. Oakley, Hooghly, to W. Ewer, Lower Provinces, 19 December 1818, *PP*, 18, p. 237.

72. Lt Col Paul to Captain Benson, 29 November 1828, in 'Documents Omitted From The Correspondence Of Lord William Cavendish Bentinck' OIO Eur. Mss.

73. Minute of W. Leycester, 25 May 1821, *PP*, 18, p. 63.

74. Roy's first pamphlet on sati was published in 1818.

75. There was a more sinister aspect to this argument, however, as the rejection of sati's scriptural status was necessarily accompanied by the glorification of ascetic widowhood as the preferred alternative. Although emphasis placed on the scriptural merit of enforced widowhood by Rammohan Roy and others was useful in the context of the sati debate, it did nothing to improve the lot of those widows who survived, and may even have hardened attitudes against widow remarriage.
76. This regulation stated that '...it shall not justify a person convicted of wilful homicide that he, or she, was desired by the party slain to put him or her to death...'. Singha, *A Despotism of Law*, p. 82.
77. Ibid.
78. E. Watson, Nizamat Adalat, 16 April 1816, *PP*, 18, p. 99.
79. Board's Collection (Oriental and India Office), BC vol. 1506, Col. 59097, Judicial letter from Government Bombay to Court of Directors, 12 February 1830, C.P. Brown, Trichinopoly, 3 June 1829.
80. E. Watson, Nizamat Adalat, 18 April 1817, *PP*, 18, p. 99.
81. Government of India to the Nizamat Adalat, *PP*, 18, p. 142, in response to a letter of 9 September 1817.
82. Nizamat Adalat to Gen. Sir George Nugent, vice president in Council, Fort William, 4 October 1814, *PP*, 18, p. 34.
83. Mani, *Contentious Traditions*, p. 29.
84. Ibid.
85. Bombay judicial consultations, 1 November 1819, *PP*, 18, p. 254.
86. BC, vol. 1525, Col. 60268, minute by the governor, 12 January 1830.
87. This regional diversity between the presidencies was even more apparent during the debate on the abolition of sati in the Princely States after 1830, when the governments of Bengal and Bombay displayed quite different attitudes to intervention on the matter.
88. Proceedings of the Nizamat Adalat, 25 June 1817, *PP*, 18, p. 106.
89. H. Oakley, Hooghly, to W. Ewer, Lower Provinces, 19 December 1818, *PP*, 18, p. 237.
90. Ibid.
91. Minute of W. Leycester, 25 May 1821, *PP*, 17, p. 63.
92. Mani, *Contentious Traditions*, p. 30.
93. Criminal cases adjudged by Nizamat Adalat in 1810, *PP*, 18, p. 26.
94. Proceedings of the Nizamat Adalat, 21 May 1819, *PP*, 18, p. 226.
95. Government of India to Nizamat Adalat, 5 December 1812, *PP*, 18, p. 31.
96. Proceedings of the Nizamat Adalat, 7 August 1821, *PP*, 17, p. 67.
97. Mani, *Contentious Traditions*, p. 29.
98. Draft of instructions, 17 April 1813, *PP*, 18, pp. 32–4.
99. R. Morrieson to William Ewer, 18 December 1818, *PP*, 18, p. 238.
100. Proceedings of the Nizamat Adalat, 7 August 1821, *PP*, 17, p. 67.
101. Ibid.

102. Ibid.
103. Ibid.
104. Ibid.
105. Draft Regulation, 25 June 1817, *PP*, 18, p. 126.
106. Minute of S.T. Goad, 25 May 1821, *PP*, 17, p. 63.
107. Regulation XVII, 1829 of the Bengal Code, 4 December 1829.
108. Lt Col Playfaire to Captain R. Benson, Sitapur, 24 November 1828, in C.H. Philips (ed.) *The Correspondence of Sir William Cavendish Bentinck: Governor General of India 1828–35* (Oxford: Oxford University Press, 1977).
109. A.J. Trotter to Captain Benson, Gya, 16 May 1829, Documents Omitted From The Correspondance Of Lord William Cavendish Bentinck OIO, Eur. Mss.
110. J. Pearson to H. Townley, L.M.S, Chinsurah, 7 April 1831 (LMSP).
111. Partha Chatterjee, *The Nation and its Fragments* (Princeton: Princeton University Press, 1993), p. 10.
112. W. Bentinck, 'Minute on Sati', in *Speeches and Documents on Indian Policy 1750–1921*, vol. 1 (London: Oxford University Press, 1922).

7

CONCLUSION

CR80

On 4 December 1929 *The Times* proudly announced that exactly a hundred years had passed since the 'British Governor General of India struck a decisive blow against one of the cruellest rites ever practiced by superstitious men'.[1] In a series of articles and editorials marking this centenary the newspaper lauded Lord William Bentinck, whose actions were looked back on as one of the most significant of the so-called Era of Reform—a graphic symbol of the beneficence of British colonial rule for the backward society of India. For *The Times*, the rectitude of Bentinck's action was in no doubt. Sati, it claimed, was 'only a euphemism for murder'[2] and the action of the British in preventing it was the logical reaction of a civilized nation when encountering such barbarity. Any delay that had occurred was due solely to the fear that interference with this religious rite would provoke a violent response amongst a bigoted Hindu population. The British are thus portrayed as moral arbiters and the catalysts for beneficial social change in India. As the author of the article in *The Times* put it:

It is possible that Hinduism might have repudiated a custom...condemned by enlightened Hindus.... But without any disparagement to their efforts, it must be admitted that the long resistance to such social reforms as the abolition of child marriage suggests that generations might have passed before the prevention of suttee was carried out by the Hindu reformers alone...is it unfair then to ask how the social progress of India would have fared without contact with Europe and without the religious and social ideas of the West?[3]

Such examples of the civilizing mission in action would have been particularly loaded in 1929, as Mahatma Gandhi and the Indian National Congress prepared their second major campaign for *swaraj* (self-rule). Increasingly vocal calls for Indian self-determination were being buttressed by the exercise of autonomy in the social sphere, as Indian-led reforms such as the 1929 Sarda Bill outlawing child marriage were being used to suggest that Indians were capable of putting their own house in order without British help. Indeed, Indian nationalist journals such as the Calcutta-based *Modern Review* reacted angrily to British treatment of the sati issue, claiming that eulogies to Bentinck were obscuring the importance of the contribution of Indian reformers like Raja Rammohan Roy and Dwarkanath Tagore and thus creating a false image of India's internal capacity for reform.[4] The British representation of their role as the saviours of Indian women, so conspicuous in the articles on the centenary, was thus highly politically charged. It was also highly misleading, relying on an oversimplified construction of the British encounter with sati that saw British opposition to the rite as a moral constant—something that was very far from being the case. Rather, the European response to sati was characterized by mutability and ambivalence, in which revulsion was juxtaposed against admiration, and in which the 'otherness' of the rite was mitigated by the recognition of underlying resonances with European culture.

The passing of Bentinck's regulation in 1829 had the effect of enshrining certain British attitudes both in the statutes of British India and in history, with the effect that these attitudes and ideas have since been regarded as static and absolute, rather than as just one particular manifestation of ideas in a shifting process of understanding. The attitudes expressed in the early nineteenth century that have become so influential in forming current ideas about sati were not reflective of an instinctive moral reaction of a 'civilized West' to barbaric oriental customs, but were instead the result of a confluence of ideas and forces that produced a particular reaction to sati at that specific historical juncture. Far from unconditional horror being the normative moral reaction to sati, the near totality of the British vilification of the rite in the early nineteenth century was in fact unusual. European encounters with sati both before and after the period of abolition, were characterized instead by a mixture of disapproval and admiration. J. Ramsey MacDonald, for example, could write in 1910 that:

This practice has been much talked about and has helped to prejudice us a great deal against India and her social customs. Yet it had a beautiful side—a very romantic side. The idea that after the husband is dead the wife has no interest in life, and that she would serve him and her own desires best if she followed him into the other world. This is a beautiful idea, but where the sacrifice is involuntary, or demanded of a child widow it turns into a cruel horrible thing.[5]

She here conforms to the early nineteenth-century construction of 'good' and 'bad' sati based on the volition of the widow, but in her recognition of the meritorious aspects of voluntary sati she also echoes the attitudes of many early modern and eighteenth century observers, which were for the most part suppressed in the early nineteenth century and which have not generally been understood as characteristic of the Western response to the rite, despite their continued importance.

The existence of positive facets in the European construction of sati, as well as the manner in which the components of the popular image of the rite changed over time, suggest a process of understanding that was based as much on analogy and the location of affinities as it was on the assumption of diametric opposition between the races, although this was not always recognized. Writing in 1929 about a sati that had taken place in Barh in 1927, former policeman R.J. Hurst commented that:

Sati must be one of those things that look quite different from different view points. If we cannot see it from the orthodox Hindu's side, we cannot know what aspect it shows to him. Nor can we expect to persuade him that our view of it is clearer or truer than his.[6]

Although Hurst is here trying to make the relatively liberal point that attitudes to sati depend on the cultural viewpoint of the observer, his statement makes two interrelated assumptions that this study has attempted to undermine: that there is a unified and consistent Western viewpoint with regard to sati, and that this viewpoint is diametrically opposed to that of the orthodox Hindu.

In reality, as we have seen, the European image of sati was fluid and changeable and incorporated a multitude of different facets, the relative importance of which changed over time and from person to person. The Western discourse on sati was far from monolithic; it was crosscut by counter-hegemonic voices, contradictions, and changing assumptions. It was also deeply affected by the circumstances in which it was produced. The political and ideological circumstances of the time affected the way in which sati was perceived and portrayed, and the factors that contributed to the shaping of the West's image of sati could be as general as changing attitudes to women or as specific as a particular moral or political campaign. In the second half of the nineteenth century, for example, it became common practice for campaigners against the ban on widow remarriage to rehabilitate the image of sati as the lesser of the two evils. For these reformers, the few minutes of agony suffered by the widow in the flames was preferable to the lifetime of 'cold sati' suffered by the widow.[7] Of course, these comments were not aimed at revivifying sati, but were rather used to emphasize the horrors of ascetic widowhood, which was the contemporary *cause celebre*. They nevertheless reflect the extent to which the image of sati that was promoted by the West was contingent on the ideological climate in which it was produced rather than on a consistent moral stance with regard to it.

The idea that European views on sati were diametrically opposed to orthodox Hindu ideas was also fallacious, for as we have seen, European understanding of the rite often concentrated on aspects of sati that resonated with their own ideas and culture. The interpretation of the rite was closely dependent on patriarchal assumptions about the nature of woman, the importance of chastity and fidelity, and the idea that woman's existence should be subsumed in that of her husband. These ideas were common to both cultures, and sati, as the ultimate expression of these values, could be understood by European observers in familiar terms. Their reaction to these aspects of the rite was thus often not so very dissimilar to Hindu responses. Images used to depict sati were as varied as the witch, the martyr, the suicide, the faithful wife, and the madwoman; but all were icons that were commonplace within Western culture and could be used to explain sati in familiar terms. Hurst's assumption of two distinctly different racial understandings of sati is thus, far too rigid. The gap between the European and the Hindu conceptions of sati, while apparent, was cross-cut by areas of agreement and the existence of universal or non-racially specific factors in the interpretation of the rite.

Not only was sati understood as much in terms of similarity as of difference, but the European fascination with it suggests that it appealed to the European consciousness on a more meaningful level than as a representation of Hindu 'otherness'. There were numerous other

Hindu rites and customs that attracted Western attention and that could be used to denigrate Indian society and justify both missionary and colonial enterprise, yet none of these other Hindu 'atrocities' received the same degree of obsessive attention as sati. It has been the intention of this study to show that sati intrigued Europeans because it reflected and embodied their own preoccupations and ideas. The precise nature of these preoccupations changed over time; in the early modern period, for example, sati could be incorporated in the debate about the nature of women, while in the eighteenth century it became more significant as an example in a debate about the nature of religious superstition. By the nineteenth century it had gained significance on several levels, incorporating as it did issues relating to religious toleration, suicide, madness, and the treatment of the human body. I would argue that it was its salience to these wider debates, as much as its connotations for Britain's relationship with India, that made it such a widely debated subject in the early nineteenth century. Rather than being about burning Indian women, sati was an arena in which the British could play out some of their own concerns about the nature of their society and their identity.[8]

Sati was thus of far more importance than merely an issue of social reform or a vehicle through which the British could demonstrate the benevolence of their rule. As an issue that impacted on ideas in Britain and on the formation of British identity, it is reflective of the dialogical nature of colonialism. European understanding of sati was not unidirectional, something that they created and imposed upon the colonial society, as Edward Said might have us believe. Rather, it was part of a multidirectional process through which India had a significant impact on Europe and its ideas. This is true both in a general sense, as demonstrated by the way in which the issue of sati became incorporated in wider debates in the metropole, and in the specific way in which the rite itself was perceived. Rather than Europe independently creating its own construction of sati, its image of sati was constantly adjusted and renegotiated in response to its experiences in India and its exposure to Indian ideas on the subject. The dialogue that took place between the British and the Indian princes in the years prior to its abolition in princely India, and the concomitant reassessment of certain British ideas about the rite are prime examples. Thus, while the colonial power was just that, the formation of colonial knowledge on sati was not something imposed on India, but something which India took a large part in creating.

Finally, returning once again to the exchange in the *Guardian*, we must ask: if European objection to sati was not a moral constant, how then should we understand our attitude to the rite in the present? Indeed, we should ask ourselves whether our treatment of certain iconic images of other societies—the burka, forced marriage, stoning for adultery, and so on—do not tell us as much about our own concerns and preoccupations as they do about the societies that practice them.

Notes

1. *The Times*, 4 December 1929.
2. Ibid., 10 December 1929.
3. Ibid., 4 December 1929.
4. *Modern Review*, vol. 44:6, December 1927, p. 744. This particular article was complaining about Edward Thompson's 1827 book on sati, of which it said, 'As for the apportioning of credit for the eradication of this custom, every educated Indian is expected to have at least so much historical knowledge and regard for accuracy as to supply the omission of the name of Raja Ram Mohan Roy.'
5. *Modern Review*, vol. 3:2, August 1910.
6. R.J. Hurst, *The Police Journal*, vol. 2, 1929, in Indian Police Collection, vol. 171 (OIO, Eur. Mss.).
7. See for example J. Ramsey MacDonald's comments in the *Modern Review*, vol. 3:2, August 1910.
8. In this respect I am echoing the argument of Javed Majeed in *Ungoverned Imaginings: James Mill's The History of British India and Colonialism* (Oxford: Clarendon, 1992).

BIBLIOGRAPHY

ᏟᏒᏖᏙ

Primary Sources: Unpublished

The Oriental and India Office Collection

European Manuscripts

Letter from Abraham Caldecott to Miss Pettet 14 September 1783.
Indian Police Collection: 1765–1961,vol. 170, Suttee, Papers on its History and Practice.
Letters and Papers of Major-General John Ludlow, 1819–54.
Memoirs of Maria Sykes 1781–1865, Wife of Captain John Sykes, Bengal Army, 1799–1815.
Nicolls Collection, 1838–43.
Documents Omitted from *The Correspondence Of Lord William Cavendish Bentinck.*

East India Company: Board's Collections

Collections relating to sati, 1832–57

East India Company: Dispatches from the Board of Directors

Letters relating to sati, 1832–57

Baptist Missionary Society Archives, Angus Library, Regent's Park College, Oxford

Baptist Missionary Society Correspondence
William Ward's Missionary Journal, transcribed by E. Daniel Potts

The Council for World Mission Archive, SOAS, London

London Missionary Society Papers

West Bengal State Archives, Kolkata

Judicial Proceedings

National Archives of India, New Delhi

Home Department Proceedings
Foreign Department Proceedings
Rajputana States Agency Records

Primary Sources: Published

Hansard Parliamentary Debates

Vol. 5, 1821 1217–1222; vol. 9, 1017–1021, 1923; Burning of Hindu Widows
Vol. 13, 1043–1047, 1825, Hindu Widows: Female Immolation
Vol. 24, 1355–1356, 1830, Abolition of Suttees
Vol. 2, 60–62, 1830, Hindu Superstitions
Vol. 4, 576–8, 1831, Suttees

Parliamentary Papers: On Hindu Widows

Vol. 18, Paper 749, 1821
Vol. 17, Paper 466, 1823
Vol. 23, Paper 443, 1824
Vol. 24, Papers 508 and 518, 1825
Vol. 20, Paper 354, 1826–7
Vol. 23, Paper 547, 1828
Vol. 27, Papers 178 and 550, 1830

Newspapers and Periodicals

Asiatic Annual Register
Asiatic Journal
Asiatic Quarterly Review
Asiatick Researches
Bengal Past and Present
Bombay Gazette
Calcutta Gazette
Calcutta Journal
Circular Letters of the Baptist Missionary Society

234 *Pious Flames*

Edinburgh Review
Friend of India
Guardian
Journal of the Asiatic Society of Bengal
Journal of the Asiatic Society Bombay
Missionary Notices of the Wesleyan Missionary Society
Modern Review
Oriental Herald
Oriental Observer
Palmer's Index to The Times
*Periodical Accounts of the Baptist Missionary Society (British News paper Library,
 Colin date)*
Quarterly Oriental Magazine
The Police Journal
The Times

Books and Tracts

Aitcheson, C., *A Collection of Treaties, Engagements and Sanads Relating to India and Neighbouring Countries* (Calcutta: Government of India Central Publications Branch, 1932).

Anon., *Deplorable Effects of Heathen Superstitions, as Manifested by the Natives of Hindustan* (Dunfermline: John Miller Cheap Tracts, 1828).

———, *On Suicide,* Religious Tracts, No. 154, (London: Religious Tracts Society, 1799).

———, *The Suttee: A Poem With Notes* (London: Seely, Burnside And Seely, 1842).

———, *Thoughts On Suicide: In A Letter To A Friend* (London: Payne And Foss, 1819).

Ayescough, F., *A Discourse Against Self-Murder* (London: 1755).

Barbosa, Duarte, *A Description of the Coasts of East Africa and Malabar in the Beginning of the Sixteenth Century,* trans. Henry E.J. Stanley (New York: Johnston, 1970).

Bentinck, W., 'Minute on Sati', in *Speeches and Documents on Indian Policy 1750–1921,* vol. 1 (London: Oxford University Press, 1922), pp. 208–26.

Bernier, Francois, *Histoire de la dernier revolution des etats du gran Mogol* (Amsterdam: Paul Marrat, 1699).

———, *Travels In The Mogul Empire,* AD *1656–1668* (Delhi: S. Chand and Co., 1969).

Binsley, A.H., *Rajputs* (New Delhi: Asia Educational Services, 1986).

Biswas, H.C., 'Job Charnock's Hindu Wife: A Rescued Sati', in *Hindustan Review,* vol. 22: 133 September 1910, pp. 298–301.

Bushby, H.J., *Widow Burning: A Narrative* (London: Longman and Co., 1855).

Campbell, Donald, *A Journey Overland To India* (Philadelphia: T. Dobson, 1797).

Carre, Abbe, *Travels of Abbe Carre in India and the Near East 1672–74*, ed. C. Fawcett (New Delhi: Asian Education Services, 1990).

Catrou, F.F., *The General History of the Mogol Empire: Extracted from the Memoirs of N. Manouchi, A Venetian and Chief Physician to Orangzebe for Above 40 Years* (London: Jonah Bowyer, 1709).

Chaplin, William, 'The Suicide Of Hindu Widows By Burning Themselves with The Bodies of Their Deceased Husbands is A Practice Revolting To Natural Feeling And Inconsistent with Moral Duty', *Primitive Orientals* (Calcutta: 1803–4).

Chevalier, T., 'Remarks On Suicide', *The Pamphleteer*, vol. xxiii, 1824.

Cockburn, Rev. John, *A Discourse on Self Murder* (London: 1716).

Colebrooke, Henry T., 'On the Duties of a Faithful Hindu Widow', in *Asiatick Researches,* vol. 4, 1793–4, pp. 205–15.

Cope, C., *A New History of the East Indies* (London: Cooper, Reeve, and Sympson, 1754).

Cope, Harriet, *Suicide: A Poem In Four Parts* (London: H. Bryer, 1815).

Coverte, Robert, *A True and almost Incredible Report of an Englishman* (1612, reprint New York: Da Capo Press, 1971).

———, 'The Voyage and Travels of Captain Robert Coverte', in T. Osbourne (ed.), *A Collection of Voyages And Travels* (London: Thomas Osborne of Grays Inn, 1745).

Craufurd, Quentin, *Sketches Relating to the History, Religion, Learning and Manners of the Hindoos* (London: T. Cadell, 1792).

Della Valle, Sig. Pietro, *The Travels Of Sig. Pietro Della Valle: A Noble Roman, Into East India And Arabia Deserta In Which The Several Countries, Together With The Customs, Manners, Traffique, And Rites Both Religious And Civil, Of Those Oriental Princes And Nations Are Faithfully Described In Familiar Letters To His Friend Sig. Mario Schipano* (London: J. Mattock For John Place, 1665).

———, *The Travels of Pietro Della Valle in India*, E. Grey and G. Havers (eds) (New Delhi: Asian Educational Services, 1991).

Dellon, Charles, *A Voyage to the East Indies* (London: D. Browne, A Roper, T. Leigh, 1698).

Dow, Alexander, 'The History of Indostan', in P.J. Marshall, *The British Discovery of Hinduism* (Cambridge: Cambridge University Press, 1970), pp. 107–39.

Dubois, Abbe J.A., *Hindu Manners, Customs And Ceremonies* (New Delhi: Book Faith India, 1999).

Essays by the Students of Fort William, vol. 1 (Calcutta: 1802).

Fay Eliza, 'Original Letters From India', Letter XX, 5 September 1781, in P. Thankappan Nair (ed.), *Calcutta In The Eighteenth Century* (Calcutta: Firmakum, 1984), pp. 200–5.

Federici, C., *The Voyage and Travaile into the East India* (1588, reprint 1971).

Flemming, C., *A Dissertation On The Unnatural Crime Of Self-Murder* (London: Edward and Charles Dilly, 1773).

Frederick, Caesar, 'Extracts of Master Caesar Frederike of Venice, his eighteen year's Indian Observations', in Samuel Purchas, *Purchas his Pilgrimes, the second part* (London: William Stansby For Henrie Fetherstone, 1625), pp. 83–143.

Fryer, John, *A New Account of the East Indies, Being Nine Years Travels 1672–1981*, ed. W. Crooke (New Delhi: Asian Educational Services, 1992).

Grandpre, L. de, *A Voyage in the Indian Ocean to Bengal, Undertaken in the Years 1789 and 1790* (London: C.J. Robinson, 1803).

Grant, Charles, *Observations on the State of Society Among the Asiatic Subjects of Great Britain* (London: House of Commons, 1813).

Grose, John Henry, *A Voyage to the East Indies with Observations On The Several Parts There* (London: Hooper and Morley, 1757).

Guyon, Abbe de, *A New History of the East Indies, Ancient and Modern* (London: R. and J. Dodsley, 1757).

Halhed, Nathaniel Brassey, *A Code of Gentoo Laws, or Ordinations of the Pundits* (London: 1776).

Hawkins, William, 'Hawkins' Voyages', in William Foster (ed.), *Early Travels In India, 1583–1619* (London: Oxford University Press, 1921), pp 60–121.

Herber, R., *Narrative of a Journey Through the Upper Provinces of India, 1824–25* (London: Murray, 1828).

Hey, R., *Three Dissertations On The Pernicious Effects Of Gaming, On Duelling And On Suicide* (Cambridge: J. Smith, 1812, 1st edn 1783).

Hodges, William, *Travels in India During the Years 1780, 1781, 1782 and 1783* (New Delhi: Munishram Manoharlal, 1999).

Holwell, John Zephaniah, *Interesting Historical Events Relative to the Province of Bengal* (London: Becket and de Hondt, 1767).

———, 'The Religious Tenets of the Gentoos', in P.J. Marshall, *The British Discovery of Hinduism in the Eighteenth Century* (Cambridge: Cambridge University Press, 1970), pp. 45–106.

Hough, Rev J., 'Immolation Of Hindoo Widows', in W. Ellis, (ed.), *The Missionary; Or Christian's New Year Gift* (London: Seely And Sons, 1833), pp. 13–21.

Johns, William, *A collection of facts and opinions relative to the burning of widows with the dead bodies of their Husbands: and to other destructive customs prevalent in British India: respectfully submitted to the consideration of government, as soliciting a further extension of their humane interference* (London: 1816).

Jones, William, *Institutes of Hindu Law* (Calcutta: 1794).

Kircher, A., *China Illustrata*, trans. and ed. C.D. van Tuyl (Oklahoma: Indiana University Press, 1987; Latin edn 1677).

van Linschoten, John Huygen, *Voyage of John Huygen Van Linschoten to the*

East Indies, ed. A. Coke Burnell (New Delhi: Asian Educational Services, 1988).

Lockman, J. (ed.), *Travels of the Jesuits* (London: T. Piety, 1743).

Lord, Henry, *A Discovery Of Two Foreign Sects In The East Indies, Viz. The Sect Of Banians, The Ancient Inhabitants Of India And The Sect of Parsees, The Ancient Inhabitants Of Persia, Together with the Religion and Manners Of Each Sect* (London: S. n., 1630).

MacDonald John, *Memoirs Of An Eighteenth Century Footman, Travels 1745-1779* (London: Routledge, 1927).

Mandelslo, J.A., 'The Voyages And Travels Of J. Albert De Mandelslo Into The East Indies 1638–40', in Adam Olearius (ed.), *Voyages And Travels Of The Ambassadors* (London: John Starkey and Thomas Basset, 1669).

Mandeville, John, *The Travels and Voyages of Sir John Mandeville* (London: J. Osborne, 1700).

Manucci, Niccolao, *Storio Do Mogor or Mogul India, 1653–1708*, ed. W. Irvine (Calcutta: Indian Edition, 1966).

Methold, William, 'Relations of the Kingdom of Golchonda', in Samuel Purchas, *Purchas His Pilgrimage Or Relations Of The World And The Religions Observed In All Ages And Places Discovered From The Creation Unto This Present* (London: William Stansby For Henrie Fetherstone, 4th edn 1626).

da Pordenone, Odorico, 'The Journal of Friar Odoric', in A.W. Pollard (ed.), *The Travels of Sir John Mandeville* (London: Macmillan, 1900), pp. 326–26.

Olearius, A., *Travels of the Ambassadors,* trans. John Davies (London: Starkey and Bassett, 1669).

Ovington, John, *A Voyage to Surat in the Year 1689,* ed. H.G. Rowlinson (New Delhi: Asian Educational Services, 1994).

Parks, Fanny, *Wanderings Of A Pilgrim In Search Of The Picturesque* (Karachi: Oxford University Press, 1975).

Pegg, Rev. James, *The Suttees' Cry To Britain: Showing From Essays Published In India And Official Documents That The Custom Of Burning Hindoo Widows Is Not An Integral Part Of Hindooism And May Be Abolished With Ease And Safety* (London: Seely And Son, 1827).

———, *India's Cries to British Humanity* (London: Seely and Son, 1830).

Pelsaert, Francisco, *Jehangir's India: The Remonstrantie of Francisco Pelsaert,* trans. W.H. Moreland (Cambridge: Heffer and Sons, 1925).

Phelps, *The Suttee* (Oxford: H. Bradford, 1831).

Picart, Bernard, *The Ceremonies And Religious Customs Of The Idolatrous Nations* (London: W. Jackson: 1733).

Piggott, Rev. Samuel, *Antidote To The Follies, Vices And Crimes Of Youth, To Gambling, Melancholy And Suicide In A Series Of Anecdotes And Actual Narratives* (London: J. Robins, 1831).

Polo, Marco, *The Travels of Marco Polo,* ed. Col. H. Yule, vol. 2 (London: John Murray, 1875).

Poynder, John, *Human Sacrifices in India: A Speech to The Court of Proprietors of East India Company Stock* (London: J. Hatchard and Son, 1827).

Primitiae Orientalis (Calcutta: 1803–4).

Purchas, S., *Purchas His Pilgrimes, The Second Part* (London: William Stansby for Henrie Fetherstone, 1625).

———, *Purchas His Pilgrimage Or Relations Of The World And The Religions Observed In All Ages And Places Discovered From The Creation Unto This Present* (London: William Stansby For Henrie Fetherstone, 4th edn 1626).

Roe, T., *The Embassy of Sir Thomas Roe to India,* ed. W. Foster (New Delhi: Munishram Manoharlal, 1990).

Roger, Abraham, *Le Theatre del' Idolatrie, ou La Porte* Ouverte, (Amsterdam: J. Schipper, 1670).

Scrafton, Luke, *Reflections on the Government of Indostan* (London: W. Richardson and S. Clark, 1763).

Sleeman, W.H., *Rambles and Recollections of An Indian Official* (London: Hatchard, 1844).

Sonnerat, Pierre, *A Voyage To The East Indies And China Between The Years 1774 And 1781,* trans. Francis Magnus (Calcutta: Stuart And Cooper, 1788).

Starke, Marianne, *The Widow of Malabar* (London: William Lane, 1791).

Statham, J., *Indian Recollections* (London: Samuel Bagster, 1832).

Sutton, Amos (ed.), *A Narrative Of The Mission To Orissa: The Site Of The Temple Of Jugurnath* (Boston: David Marks for the Free Will Baptist Connexion, 1833).

Sym, Rev. John, *Life's Preservative Against Self Killing* (1637; reprint London: 1988).

Tavernier, Jean Baptiste, *Tavernier's Travels In India,* 1676 trans. John Phillips (London: reprint 1677 Calcutta: Bangabasi, 1905).

Terry, E., 'A Voyage To East India', in William Foster (ed.), *Early Travels In India, 1583–1619* (London: Oxford University Press, 1921), pp. 288–322.

Tennant, Rev. William, *Indian Recreations: Consisting chiefly of strictures on the domestic and rural economy of the Mahometans and Hindoos* (London: C. Stewart, 1802).

Tod, Col. J., *Annals and Antiquities of Rajasthan* (New Delhi: Rupa, 1997).

Twining, Thomas, 'The Hindoo Widow', in H.K. Kaul (ed.), *Traveler's India* (New Delhi: Oxford University Press, 1979), pp 92–6.

de Varthema, Ludovico, 'The Itinerary Of Ludovico de Varthema', in J. Winter Jones (ed.), *Travellers in Disguise* (Cambridge, Mass.: Harvard University Press, 1963), pp. 173–239.

———, *The Travels of Ludovico De Varthema,* trans. J.W. Jones (New York: Burt Franklin, 1963).

Ward, Rev. William, *Farewell Letters to a Few Friends in Britain and America on Returning to Bengal in 1821* (London: Black, Kingsburg, Parbury and Allan, 1821).

Williams, Leighton and Mornay (eds), *Serampore Letters: Being The Unpublished Correspondance Of William Carey And Others With John Williams, 1800-1816* (London: The Knickerbocker Press, 1892).

Wilson, H.H., 'On the Supposed Vedic Authority for the Burning of Hindu Widows', in *Journal of the Royal Asiatic Society*, vol. 16, 1856, pp. 201–14.

Witherington, Nicolas, 'A Brief Discovery Of Some Things Best Worth Noting in the Travel's of Nicholas Witherington', in W. Foster (ed.) *Early Travels in India 1583–1619* (New Delhi: Oriental Reprint, 1985), pp. 188–233.

Secondary Sources

Adams, P.G., *Travellers and Travel Liars, 1600–1800* (Berkeley: University of California Press, 1962).

Ahmed, A.F.S., *Social Ideas and Social Change in Bengal, 1818–35* (Leiden: Brill, 1965).

Ahuja, D.R., *Folklore of Rajasthan* (New Delhi: National Books Trust, 1980).

Altekar, A.S., *The Position of Women in Hindu Civilization: From Prehistoric Times to the Present-day* (Delhi: Motilal Banarsidass, 3rd edn,1959).

Anand, M., *Sati: A Writeup of Raja Ram Mohan Roy About Burning of Widows Alive* (Delhi: B.R. Publishing, 1989).

Bannerjee, A.C., *The Rajput States and British Paramountcy* (New Delhi: Rajesh Publications, 1980).

Bannerjee, Poompa, *Burning Women: Widows and Early Modern European Travellers in India* (New York: Palgrave, 2003).

Barker, F. *et al., Europe and its Others* (Colchester: University of Essex, 1985).

Bassnett, Susan, 'Constructing Cultures: The Politics of Travellers' Tales' in Susan Bassnett (ed.), *Comparative Literature: A Critical Introduction* (Oxford: Blackwell, 1993), pp. 92–114.

Basu, M., *Hindu Women and Marriage Law: From Sacrament to Contract* (New Delhi: Oxford University Press, 2001).

Bayly, Christopher, 'From Ritual to Ceremony: Death Ritual in Hindu North India', in J. Whaley (ed.), *Mirrors of Mortality: Studies in the Social History of Death* (New York: St Martin's Press, 1981), pp. 154–86.

———, *Imperial Meridian: The British Empire and the World, 1780–1830* (London: Longman, 1989).

———, *The Raj, India and the British 1600–1947* (London: National Portrait Gallery, 1990).

———, *Empire and Information: Intelligence Gathering and Social Communication in India* (Cambridge: Cambridge University Press, 1999).

Bhargava, H.B., *Royalty, Feudalism and Gender: As Portrayed By Foreign Travellers* (Delhi: Rawat, 2000).

Bishnoi, B.L., 'Sati Suppression in Rajput States', in G.L. Devra (ed.), *Socio-Economic Study of Rajasthan* (Jodhpur: Gahlot Research Institute, 1980), pp. 79–89.

Bose, M. (ed.), *Faces of the Feminine in Ancient, Medieval and Modern India* (New Delhi: Oxford University Press, 2000).

Boxer, M.J. and J.M. Quataert (eds), *Connecting Spheres: Women in the Western World 1500 to the Present* (Oxford: Oxford University Press, 1987).

Breckenridge, C.A. and P. van der Veer, *Orientalism and the Post Colonial Predicament* (Philadelphia: University of Pennsylvania Press, 1993).

Browne, A., *The 18th Century Feminist Mind* (Brighton: Harvester, 1987).

Bulbeck, Chilla, *Reorienting Western Feminisms: Women's Diversity in a Post Colonial World* (Cambridge: Cambridge University Press, 1998).

Caine, Barbara, *English Feminism, 1780–1980* (New York: Oxford University Press, 1997).

Campbell, M.B., *The Witness and the Other World: Exotic European Travel Writing 400–1600 A.D.* (Ithaca: Cornell University Press, 1988).

Cannadine, David, *Ornamentalism: How the British Saw Their Empire* (New York: Oxford University Press, 2001).

Chatterjee, A., *Representations of India, 1740–1840: Creation of India in the Colonial Imagination* (London: Macmillan, 1998).

Chatterjee, Partha, *The Nation and its Fragments: Colonial and Postcolonial Histories* (Princeton: Princeton University Press, 1993).

Chaudhury, S., 'A Note on Sati in Mediaeval India', in *Indian Historical Congress Proceedings*, Part 2, Section 2, 1967, pp. 75–83.

———, 'Sati as a Social Institution and the Mughals', in *Proceedings of Indian History Congress,* 37th session, Calicut. pp. 218–23.

———, 'Medieval India, Society, State and Social Custom: Sati as a Case Study', in *Calcutta Historical Journal,* 7:1–2, 1983–4, pp. 38–60

Chen, M.A., *Perpetual Mourning: Widowhood in Rural India* (New Delhi: Oxford University Press, 2000).

Chowdhury, Indira, *The Frail Hero and the Virile History: Gender and the Politics of Culture in Colonial Bengal* (New Delhi: Oxford University Press, 2001).

Clarke, J.J., *Oriental Enlightenment: The Encounter Between Asian and Western Thought* (London and New York: Routledge, 1997).

Cohn, Bernard, *The Colonial State and its Forms of Knowledge: The British in India* (Oxford: Oxford University Press, 1996).

Colley, Linda, *Britons: Forging the Nation, 1707–1857* (London: Yale University Press, 1992).

Copland, I., *The British Raj and the Indian Princes: Paramountcy in Western India, 1857–1930* (London: Curzon Press 1982).

Courtright, P.B. *From the Margins of Hindu Marriage* (Oxford: Oxford Univeristy Press, 1995).

Crawford, C. 'Ram Mohan Roy on Sati and Sexism', in *Indian Journal of Social Work,* vol. 41:1, 1980, pp. 74–91.

Crocker, L.G., 'The Discussion of Suicide in the 18th Century', in *Journal of the History of Ideas,* vol. 13, 1952, pp. 47–72.

Dalmia-Luderitz, Vasudha, 'Sati as a Religious Rite, Parliamentary Papers on Widow Immolation, 1821–1830', in *Economic and Political Weekly*, vol. 27: 4, 26 April 1986, PE 58–PE 64.

Daly, M., *Gyn/Ecology: The Metaphysics of Radical Feminism* (London: Women's Press, 1979).

Datta, V.N. *Sati: A Historical, Social and Philosophical Enquiry into the Hindu Right of Widow Burning* (New Delhi: Manohar, 1987).

Davidoff, L. and C. Hall, *Family Fortunes: Men and Women of English Middle Class*, 1780–1850, (London: Hutchison, 1987).

Devra, G.L. (ed.), *Social-Economic Study of Rajasthan* (Jodhpur: Gahlot Research Institute, 1980).

Donaldson, L. *Decolonizing Feminisms: Race, Gender and Empire-Building* (Chapel Hill: University of North Carolina Press, 1992).

Drew, John, *India and the Romantic Imagination* (New Delhi: Oxford University Press, 1987).

Dyson, K.K., *A Various Universe: A Study of the Journals and Memoirs of British Men and Women in the Indian Subcontinent, 1765–1856* (New Delhi: Oxford University Press, 1978).

Figueira, Dorothy, 'Die Flambierte Frau: Sati in European Culture', in John Stratton Hawley, *Sati: The Blessing and the Curse* (New York: Oxford University Press, 1994), pp. 55–78.

Fisher, M., 'The Resident in Court Ritual, 1764–1858', in *Modern Asian Studies*, vol. 24:3, 1990, pp. 419–58.

———, *Indirect Rule in India: Residents and the Residency System* (New Delhi: Oxford University Press, 1991).

Foster, William, (ed.), *Early Travels In India, 1583–1619* (London: Oxford University Press, 1921).

Foucault, M., *Discipline and Punish: The Birth of the Prison* (New York: Vintage, 1979).

Fox-Genovese, Elizabeth, 'Women and the Enlightenment', in R. Bridenthal, C. Koonz, and S. Stuard (eds), *Becoming Visible: Women in European History* (Boston: Houghton Mifflin, 1987), pp. 251–75.

Fraser, Antonia, *The Weaker Vessel: Women's Lot in Seventeenth Century England* (London: Weidenfeld and Nicholson, 1984; reprint London: Octopus, 1989).

Gadol, J.K., 'Did Women Have a Renaissance?', in R. Bridenthal, C. Koonz, and S. Stuard (eds), *Becoming Visible: Women in European History* (Boston: Houghton Mifflin, 1987), pp. 137–64.

Gaskill M., *Crime and Mentalities in Early Modern England* (Cambridge: Cambridge University Press, 2000).

Gates, B., *Victorian Suicide: Mad Crimes and Sad Histories* (Princeton: University of Princeton Press, 1988).

Gaur, M., *Sati and Social Reform in India* (Jaipur: Publication Scheme, 1989).

Ganguly, K., *Cultural History of Rajasthan* (Delhi: Sundeep Prakashan, 1983).

Ghose, I., *Memsahibs Abroad: Writings by Women Travellers in Nineteenth Century India* (New Delhi: Oxford University Press, 1998).

———, *Women Travellers in Colonial India: The Power of Female Gaze* (New Delhi: Oxford University Press, 1998).

Groneman, Carol, 'Nymphomania: The Historical Construction of Female Sexuality', *Signs*, vol. 19:2, 1993–4, pp. 337–47.

Gupta, S. and R. Gombrich, 'Another View of Widow Burning and Womanliness in Indian Public Culture', in *Journal of Commonwealth and Comparative Politics,* vol. 22, 1984, pp. 262–74.

Hall, C., 'Private Persons vs Public Someones', in *British Feminist Thought: A Reader,* ed. T. Lovell (Oxford: Blackwell, 1990), pp. 51–67.

Hampson, N., *The Enlightenment* (London: Penguin, 1968).

Hardgrove, A., 'Sati Worship and Marwari Public Identity in India', in *Journal of Asian Studies*, vol. 58:3, August 1999, pp. 732–52.

Harlan, L., *Religion and Rajput Women: The Ethic of Protection in Contemporary Narratives* (Berkeley: University of California Press, 1992).

Hartog, F., *The Mirror of Herodotus: The Representation of the Other in the Writing of History* (Berkeley: University of California Press, 1988).

Hawley, J.S., *Sati: The Blessing and the Curse* (New York: Oxford University Press, 1994).

Hitchcock, T., *English Sexualities, 1700–1800: Social History in Perspective* (Basingstoke: Macmillan, 1997).

Hodgen, M.T., *Early Anthropology in the Sixteenth and Seventeenth Centuries* (Philadelphia: University of Philadelphia Press, 1964).

Hughes-Hallet, Lucy, *Cleopatra: Histories, Dreams, Distortions* (London: Pimlico, 1990).

Inden, R., 'Orientalist Constructions of India', in *Modern Asian Studies,* July 1986. pp. 401–46.

———, *Imagining India* (Oxford: Blackwell, 1990).

Jacobson, D., 'The Chaste Wife: Cultural Norm and Individual Experience', in S. Vatuk (ed.), *American Studies in the Anthropology of India,* (New Delhi: Manohar, 1987), pp. 94–138.

Jacobson, D., and S. Wadley, *Women in India: Two Perspectives* (New Delhi: Manohar, 1977).

James, L., *Raj: The Making and Unmaking of British India* (London: Softback Preview, 1997).

Joshi, V., *Polygamy and Purdah, Women and Society among Rajputs* (New Delhi: Rawat, 1995).

Kabbani, R., *Imperial Fictions: Europe's Myths of the Orient* (London: Pandora, 1994).

Kane, P.V., *A History of Dharmasastra*, vol. 2 (Poona: Bhandarkar Oriental Research Institute, 1974).

Kavita Shobha, Kanchan Shobita, and Sharada 'Rural Women Speak', in *Seminar*, vol. 342, 1988, pp. 40–4.

Kaul, I., 'The Origin of Sati', in *Illustrated Weekly of India,* 18 January 1981.

Kaul, H.K., *Travellers' India: An Anthology* (New Delhi: Oxford University Press, 1979).

Keay, J., *A History of India* (Delhi· HarperCollins, 2000).

Kejariwal, O.P., *The Asiatic Society of Bengal and the Discovery of India's Past* (New Delhi: Oxford University Press, 1988).

Kopf, David, *Orientalism and the Bengal Renaissance: The Dynamics of Indian Modernization, 1773–1835* (Berkeley: University of California Press, 1969).

Korte, B., *English Travel Writing,* trans. C. Matthias (Basingstoke: Macmillan, 2000).

Krishnamurty, J. (ed.), *Women in Colonial India* (New Delhi: Oxford University Press, 1989).

Krishnaraj, M. and A. Thorner, *Ideals, Images and Real Lives: Women in Literature and History* (Bombay: Orient Longman, 2000).

Kulke, H. and Dietmar Rothermund, *A History of India* (London: Routledge, 1990).

Kumar, N. (ed.), *Women as Subjects: South Asian Histories* (Delhi: Stree, 1994).

Kumar, R., *The History of Doing: An Illustrated Account of the Movement for Women's Rights and Feminism in India* (New Delhi: Kali for Women, 1993).

Lach, D.F., *India in the Eyes of Europe in the 16th Century* (Chicago: University of Chicago Press, 1968).

Laird, M. (ed.), *Bishop Heber in Northern India: Selections from Heber's Journal* (Cambridge: Cambridge University Press, 1971).

Leask, N., *British Romantic Writers and the East: Anxieties of Empire* (Cambridge: Cambridge University Press, 1992).

Leslie, J., *The Perfect Wife: The Orthodox Hindu Woman According to the Stridharmapaddhati of Tryambakayajvan* (New Delhi: Oxford University Press, 1989).

————,(ed.), *Roles and Rituals for Hindu Women* (Delhi: Motilal Banarsidass, 1992).

Liddle, J. and R. Joshi, 'Gender and Imperialism in British India', in *South Asia Research,* vol. 5:2, 1985, pp. 147–63.

————, *Daughters of Independence: Gender, Caste and Class in India* (New Delhi: Kali for Women, 1986).

Loomba, A., *Gender, Race, Renaissance Drama* (Manchester: Manchester University Press, 1989).

Lowe, Lisa, *Critical Terrains: French and British Orientalisms* (Ithaca: Cornell University Press, 1991).

MacClintock, A., *Imperial Leather* (London: Routledge 1995).

MacDonald, Michael, 'The Secularization of Suicide in England 1660–1800', in *Past and Present,* vol. 3:2, May 1986, pp. 50–100.

MacDonald, Michael, and T.R. Murphy, *Sleepless Souls: Suicide In Early Modern England* (Oxford: Clarendon, 1990).

MacFie, A.L., *Orientalism: A Reader* (Edinburgh: Edinburgh University Press, 2000).

McGowan, R., 'The Body and Punishment in 18th Century England', in *Journal of Modern History*, vol. 59, 1989, pp. 651–79.

MacKenzie, John, *Orientalism: History, Theory and the Arts* (Manchester: Manchester University Press, 1995).

Majeed, Javed, *Ungoverned Imaginings: James Mill's*, The History of British India *and Orientalism* (Oxford: Clarendon, 1992).

Mallison, F., 'A Note on the Holiness Allowed to Women; Pativrata and Sati', in *Ludwick Sternbach Felicitation Volume* (Lucknow: Akhil Bharatiya Sanskrit Parisad, 1979).

Mani, Lata, 'Production of an Official Discourse on Sati in Early 19th Century Bengal', in *Economic and Political Weekly*, vol. 21:17, 1986, pp. 32–40.

————, *Europe and its Others: Proceedings of the Essex Conference on the Sociology of Literature, July 1984* (Colchester: University of Essex, 1995).

————, *Contentious Traditions: The Debate on Sati in Colonial India, 1780–1833* (Berkeley: University of California Press, 1998).

Marshall, P.J., *The British Discovery of Hinduism in the 18th Century* (Cambridge: Cambridge University Press, 1970).

————, 'The Moral Swing to the East: British Humanitarianism, India and the West Indies', in K. Ballhatchet and J. Harrison (eds), *East India Company Studies: Papers Presented to Prof. Sir Cyril Phillips* (Hong Kong: Asian Research Service, 1986), pp. 69–93.

Marshall, P.J. and Glyndwr Williams, *The Great Map of Mankind: British Perceptions of the World in the Age of Enlightenment* (London: Dent, 1982).

Matus, Jill, *Unstable Bodies: Victorian Representation of Sexuality and Maternity* (Manchester: Manchester University Press, 1995).

Mazumdar, V., 'Comment on Sati', in *Signs*, vol. 4, 1978, pp. 269–73.

Mehta, Uday Singh, *Liberalism and Empire: India in British Liberal Thought* (New Delhi: Oxford University Press, 1999).

Metcalfe, Thomas, *Ideologies of the Raj* (Cambridge: Cambridge University Press, 1998).

Mezciems, Jenny, ''Tis Not To Divert The Reader: Moral and Literary Determinants in Some Early Travel Narratives', in P. Dodds (ed.), *The Art of Travel* (London: Frank Cass, 1982), pp. 1–19.

Mills, S., *Discourses of Difference: An Analysis of Women's Travel Writing and Colonialism* (London: Routledge, 1991).

Mitter, P., *Much Maligned Monsters: History of European Reactions to Indian Art* (Clarendon Press, 1977).

Mittra, K., 'Suppression of Suttee in the Province of Cuttack', in *Bengal Past and Present*, vol. 76, 1957, pp. 125–131.

Mohanty, C.T., 'Under Western Eyes: Feminist Scholarship and Colonial Discourses', in *Feminist Review*, 1988, pp. 61–88.

Monter, W., 'Protestant Wives, Catholic Saints and the Devil's Handmaid: Women in the Age of Reformations', in R. Bridenthal, C. Koonz, and S.

Stuard (eds), *Becoming Visible: Women in European History* (Boston: Houghton Mifflin, 1987), pp. 201–19.

Moore-Gilbert, Bart, (ed.), *Writing India 1757–1990: British Representations of India* (Manchester: Manchester University Press, 1996).

———, *Post-Colonial Theory: Contexts, Practices, Politics* (London: Verso, 1997).

Moorehouse, G. *India Britannica*, (London: Harvill, 1983).

Nair, J., *Women and the Law in Colonial India: A Social History* (New Delhi: Kali for Women, 1996).

Nandy, Ashis, *At the Edge of Psychology: Essays in Politics and Culture* (New Delhi: Oxford University Press, 1980).

———, *The Intimate Enemy: Loss and Recovery of Self Under Colonialism* (New Delhi: Oxford University Press, 1983).

Narasimhan, S., *Sati: Widow Burning in India* (New Delhi: Harper Collins, 1998).

Narayan, U., *Dislocating Cultures: Identities, Traditions and Third World Feminism* (New York: Routledge, 1997).

Neogy, A.K., *The Paramount Power and the Princely States of India, 1858–1881* (Calcutta: K.P. Bagchi, 1979).

Oddie, G.A., *Popular Religion, Elites and Reform: Hook Swinging and its Prohibition in Colonial India, 1800–1894* (New Delhi: Manohar, 1995).

Pawar, K., *Women in Indian History: Social, Economic and Cultural Perspectives* (New Delhi: Vision and Venture, 1996).

Penrose, B., *Travel and Discovery in the Renaissance, 1420–1620* (Cambridge, Mass.: Harvard University Press, 1952).

Phillips, C.H., (ed.), *The Correspondence of Lord William Cavendish Bentinck* (Oxford: Oxford University Press, 1977).

Porter, Andrew, 'Religion, Missionary Enthusiasm and Empire', in William Roger Lewis (ed.), *The Oxford History of the British Empire*, vol. 3 (Oxford: Oxford University Press, 1999), pp. 222–45.

Porter, Dennis, 'Orientalism and its Problems', in Patrick Williams, and Laura Chrisman, *Colonial Discourse and Post Colonial Theory* (Hemel Hempstead: Harvester Wheatsheaf, 1994), pp. 150–161.

Prasad, R.C., *Early English Travellers in India: A Study in the Travel Literature of the Elizabethan and Jacobean Periods with Particular Reference to India* (Delhi: Motilal Banarsidass, 1965).

Pratt, M.L., *Imperial Eyes: Travel Writing and Transculturation* (New York: Routledge, 1992).

Rajan, B., *Under Western Eyes: India from Milton to Macaulay* (New Delhi: Oxford University Press, 1999).

Rajan, R.S., 'The Subject of Sati: Pain and Death in the Contemporary Discourse on Sati', in *Yale Journal of Criticism*, vol. 3:2, 1990, pp. 1–27.

———, *Real and Imagined Women: Gender, Culture and Postcolonialism* (London: Routledge, 1993).

Ray, A.K., *Widows are not for Burning* (New Delhi: ABC Publishing House, 1985).

Robertson, B.C. (ed.), *The Essential Writings of Raja Rammohan Ray* (New Delhi: Oxford University Press, 1999).

Rocher, Rosalind, 'British Orientalism and the Eighteenth Century: The Dialectics of Knowledge and Government', in C.A. Breckenridge and P. van der Veer, *Orientalism and the Post Colonial Predicament* (Philadelphia: University of Pennsylvania Press, 1993), pp. 215–45.

Rosselli, J., *Lord William Bentinck: The Making of a Liberal Imperialist, 1774–1839* (Brighton: Sussex University Press, 1974).

Rousseau, G.S. and R. Potter (eds), *Exoticism in the Enlightenment* (Manchester: Manchester University Press, 1990).

Roy, B.B., *Socioeconomic Impact of Sati in Bengal and the Role of Raja Rammohan Roy* (Calcutta: Naya Prokash, 1987).

Said, Edward, *Orientalism* (London: Penguin, 1995).

Sangari, K. and S. Vaid, *Recasting Women: Essays in Colonial History* (New Delhi: Kali for Women, 1989).

———, 'Institutions, Beliefs, Ideologies: Widow Immolation in Contemporary Rajasthan', in *Economic and Political Weekly,* vol. 26:17, 27 April 1991, pp. WS 2–WS 18.

———, 'Sati in Modern India: A Report', in *Economic and Political Weekly,* vol. 16:31, pp. 1285–88.

Saxsena, R.K., *Social Reform: Infanticide and Sati* (Delhi: Trimurti, 1975).

Schwab, Raymond, *The Oriental Renaissance: Europe's Rediscovery of India and the East* (New York: Columbia University Press, 1984).

Seed, G., 'The Abolition of Suttee in Bengal', in *History,* October 1955, pp. 286–99.

Sen, S. (ed.), *Social and Religious Reform Movements in 19th and 20th Century* (Calcutta: Institute of Historical Studies, 1979).

Sharma, Arvind, *Sati: Historical and Phenomenological Essays* (Delhi: Motilal Banarsidass, 1988).

Sharpe, J., *Allegories of Empire: The Figure of Woman in the Colonial Text* (Minneapolis: University of Minnesota Press, 1993).

Schromer, K. (ed.), *The Idea of Rajasthan* (New Delhi: Manohar, 1994).

Shekhewat, P.S., 'The Culture of Sati in Rajasthan', in *Manushi,* vol. 30:4, 1987, pp. 30–4.

Showalter, Elaine, *The Female Malady: Women, Madness and English Culture, 1830–1930* (London: Penguin, 1987).

Schwab, R., *The Oriental Renaissance: Europe's Rediscovery of India and the East* (New York: Columbia University Press, 1984).

Singh, J.G., *Colonial Narratives, Cultural Dialogues: Discoveries of India in the Language of Colonialism* (London: Routledge, 1996).

Singha, Radhika, *A Despotism of Law: Crime and Justice in Early Colonial India* (New Delhi: Oxford University Press, 2000).

Singhi, N.K. and R. Joshi, *Religion, Ritual and Royalty* (Jaipur: Rowat, 1999).

Sinha, M., *Colonial Masculinity: The 'Manly' Englishman and the 'Effeminate' Bengali* (Manchester: Manchester University Press, 1995).

Sinha, S., *Women and Violence* (Delhi: Vikas, 1989).

Spivak, Gayatria, 'Can the Subaltern Speak? Speculations on Widow Sacrifice', in *Colonial Discourse and Post Colonial Theory* (Hemel Hemstead: Harvester Wheatsheaf, 1994), pp. 66–118.

Sprott, S.E., *The English Debate on Suicide from Donne to Hulme* (La Salle: Open Court Publishing, 1961).

Staves, Susan, *Married Women's Separate Property in England, 1660–1833* (London: Harvard University Press, 1990).

Stein, D., 'Women to Burn: Suttee as a Normative Institution', *Signs,* vol. 4:2, 1978, pp. 253–68.

———, 'Burning Widows, Burning Brides: The Perils of Daughterhood in India', in *Pacific Affairs* vol. 61, 1988, pp. 465–85.

Stern, R., *The Cat and the Lion: Jaipur State and the British Raj* (Lieden: Brill, 1988).

Stokes, E., *The English Utilitarians and India* (Oxford: Oxford University Press, 1959).

Stone, L., *The Family, Sex and Marriage in England, 1500–1800* (New York: Harper and Row, 1979).

Stutchbury, E., 'Blood, Fire and Meditation: Human Sacrifice and Widow Burning in 19th Century India', in N. Allen and S.N. Mukherjee (eds), *Women in India and Nepal* (Canberra: Australian National Monographs on South Asia, No. 8), pp. 21–74.

Suleri, S., *The Rhetoric of English India* (Chicago: University of Chicago Press, 1992).

Sutherland, S.J., 'Sita and Draupadi', in *Journal of the American Oriental Society,* vol. 109:1, 1989, pp. 63–79.

———, 'Suttee, Sati and Sahagamana: An Epic Misunderstanding?', in *Economic and Political Weekly,* vol. 29:26, 25th June 1994.

Teltscher, K., *India Inscribed: European and British Writing on India, 1600–1800* (New Delhi: Oxford University Press, 1995).

Thapar, R., 'In History', in *Seminar,* vol. 342, 1988, pp. 14–19.

Thomas, K., *Religion and the Decline of Magic: Studies in Popular Beliefs in Sixteenth and Seventeenth Century England* (London: Penguin, 1991).

Todd, Barbara J., 'The Remarrying Widow: A Stereotype Reconsidered', in M. Prior (ed.), *Women in English Society, 1500–1800* (London: Methuen, 1985), pp. 54–92.

Upreti, H.C. and N.Upreti *The Myth of Sati: Some Dimensions of Widow Burning* (Bombay: Himalaya Publishing House, 1991).

Vaid, Thapar, *et al.,* 'Symposium on Sati', *Seminar,* Special Issue, vol. 342, 1988.

Vashishtha, V.K., *Rajputana Agency 1832–1858* (Jaipur: Alekh, 1978).

Vidal, D., *Violence and Truth: A Rajasthani Kingdom Confronts Colonial Authority* (New Delhi: Oxford University Press, 1997).

Vyas, R.P., 'Social and Religious Reform Movements in the 19th and 20th Century in Western Rajasthan', in S. Sen (ed.), *Social and Religious Reform*

Movements in 19th and 20th Century (Calcutta: Institute of Historical Studies, 1979), pp. 177–96.

————, 'Social Change in Rajasthan from the Middle of the 20th Century', in G.L. Devra (ed.), *Social Economic Study of Rajasthan* (Jodhpur: Gahlot Research Institute, 1980) pp. 130–48.

Williams, P. and L. Chrisman, *Colonial Discourse and Post Colonial Theory: A Reader* (Hemel Hemstead: Harvester Wheatsheaf, 1994).

Winks, R. and J. Rush (eds), *Asia in Western Fiction* (Manchester: 1990).

Wittenberger-Thomas, C., *Ashes of Immortality: Widow Burning in India* (New Delhi: Oxford University Press, 2000).

Wolpert, S., *A New History of India* (Oxford: Oxford University Press, 1993).

Woodward L., *The Age of Reform* (Oxford: Clarendon Press, 1962).

Yang, Anand, 'Whose Sati? Widow Burning in Early 19th Century India', in *Journal of Women's History,* vol. 1:2, pp. 8–26.

————, *Crime and Criminality in British India* (Tuscon: University of Arizona Press, 1985).

INDEX

CRCS

voluntary sati 42, 97, 146–7, 161,
    168, 228

Ward, William 124, 155, 174, 178
Warner, E. Lee 161–2, 196, 209
Wellesley, Lord Marquis 114–15,
    117
West, Western 13, 106, 108, 171,
    173, 227, 228–30
  femininity 80
  ideas and attitudes 9
  depiction of women 8
  discourse on sati 4–6, 10–11, 17,
    176
  interaction with India 18
  jurisprudence system 213
  morality 3–5
  political and technological domi-
    nance 6–9 understanding of
    East 6
  women 10, 44, 178–9
Westernization 112
wet-nursing 156
widow(s), widow's, 32, 38, 76, 90,
    93, 97–100, 111, 131, 132, 134,
    147, 150–6, 161, 165–70, 175,
    180n^5, 185, 200–1, 204, 205–6,
    228
  agency 45–8, 54, 58, 59, 97, 146–
    7, 161, 173 convulsion and
    agonies 122
  conduct 51–2
  helplessness 22
  iconography 91
  maternal instinct 154
  punitive nature of treatment 47
  remarriage, issue 40–1, 53, 229
  sexuality 38, 80, 113

state of mind 161–2, 165, 167
status 30, 47
widowhood 40, 48–51, 78, 111,
    199, 229
Wilberforce, Sir William 112
Wilkins, Charles 110
willingness 39, 58, 92, 158, 168,
    170, 209
Wilson, Horace Hayman 87
witch burning 36
  and sati, widow burning 37, 38–
    9
witch-craze, witchcraft 34, 39, 42,
    66–7n^{63}, 133, 144n^{36}
  in Europe and popularity of sati
    in India, correlations 38
Witherington, Nicholas 30, 41
Wollstonecraft, Mary 154
womanhood 150, 205
woman, women, women's
  see also sati, widow
  Hindu and European, compari-
    son 83
  of honour, agency and coercion
    in sati 45–8
  nature 148–52
  preconceived ideas 31
  rights 3
  sinfulness 62
  disinclination to suicide 168
  status 31
Woodward, Llewellyn 192

Yang, Anand 201–2

Zoffany, John 91